THE STONE TRUMPET

SUNY Series, Democracy and Education
George H. Wood, Editor

The Stone Trumpet

A Story of Practical School Reform 1960–1990

RICHARD A. GIBBONEY

STATE UNIVERSITY OF NEW YORK PRESS

Published by
State University of New York Press, Albany

© 1994 State University of New York

For information, address State University of New York
Press, State University Plaza, Albany, N.Y., 12246

Production by E. Moore
Marketing by Fran Keneston

Library of Congress Cataloging-in-Publication Data

Gibboney, Richard A., 1927–
    The stone trumpet : a story of practical school reform, 1960–1990
/ Richard A. Gibboney.
        p.   cm. — (SUNY series, democracy and education)
    Includes bibliographical references (p.) and index.
    ISBN 0-7914-2009-4 (alk. paper). — ISBN 0-7914-2010-8 (pbk. :
alk. paper)
    1. Educational change—United States.   2. Education—United
States—Evaluation.   3. Educational planning—United States.
4. Educational innovations—United States.   5. School management and
organization—United States.   I. Title.   II. Series.
LA210.G49   1994
370'.973'09045—dc20   93-42681
                                                                  CIP

10 9 8 7 6 5 4 3 2 1

To
Scott Street and Roy Robinson
the teachers at the
Andrew Jackson Elementary School
Ferndale, Michigan

and

Patricia Carini
The Prospect School
North Bennington, Vermont

who made progressive education work for children
and for me

. . . and there you were . . . sitting at the base of that pedestal wherefrom a brave stone soldier, frowning, blows the silence of a stone bugle searching into the North . . .
—*James Agee* Let Us Now Praise Famous Men

*The most notable distinction between living and
inanimate things
is that the former maintain themselves by renewal.*
—*John Dewey* Democracy and Education, 1916

CONTENTS

LIST OF PHOTOGRAPHS AND PHOTOGRAPHIC ESSAYS

Foreword

This is a book about school reform. Fundamental school reform: reforms that cultivate intelligence and predispose us to the democratic virtues. As one who struggles daily with a clashing array of interest groups, I remind myself of the most radical and fundamental reform of all: the creation almost 150 years ago of our free and universal system of public education to serve the people and the common good. Revisionist critics and too many of us who practice education have forgotten that the nation's public schools have responded well over our short history to depressions, advancements in civil rights, the fresh waters of immigration, the need for vocational education decades ago, and yes, wars and even local hysterias of one kind or another. Today we are being asked to reduce accidents among young drivers, eliminate teenage pregnancy, keep students in school, blunt the effect of dysfunctional families, eliminate substance abuse, establish community schools, and reduce crime. There is nothing new in these demands of society on its public schools. What is new is that until recently the public (correctly or not) had faith that its public schools could carry the social responsibilities placed on it.

Whatever the influence on our schools of acute social problems, on the one hand, or the sleepy attitude of too many school officials that denies the rigidities and blandness in public schools, on the other, Richard Gibboney's account lays out the practical and conceptual terrain we must negotiate if reform is ever to strengthen public education.

Anyone who reads *The Stone Trumpet* should no longer believe (as do too many of us who practice education in "real life") that the unexamined ideas and values we hold about what is good in education are benign. Gibboney gives us a comprehensive analysis of over thirty reforms since 1960 that not only reveals how ideas influence practice, but how bad most of the reforms were that those in foundations, governments, and universities created for public schools. We have much to learn about *fundamental* reform and one thing this book teaches us is that most reforms are hurtful to teachers and to children, that hurtful reforms are most likely to be adopted by schools, and that good reforms are massively ignored by the university and public school establishment, or are so corrupted in practice that they, too, become hurtful.

DONALD M. CARROLL, JR.
Secretary of Education
Commonwealth of
Pennsylvania

ACKNOWLEDGMENTS

Writing is an obsessive and lonely art. In this too-small-space I am honored to thank colleagues who did so much to widen and smooth my path.

For reading drafts of the manuscript, I thank: Roland Barth, Morton Botel, Terrance Furin, Ellen Griffis, Peter Hlebowitsch, Kenneth Kastle, Ralph Page, William Schubert, Bruce Smith, and Clark Webb.

Debra Oltman gave patient advice on the photographs and jacket design.

Deborah Stewart made primary source materials available on Individually Guided Education from the Center for Education Research, University of Wisconsin, that give my account of this reform a more life-like quality.

Harris Sokoloff, Louis King, James Comey, Marvin Lazerson, Charles Dwyer, Bruce Wilshire, and John Puckett offered help at critical junctures.

Ida Kerns did yeoman work in typing the manuscript times beyond count and Ruth Ebert, both on our divisional staff, kept one eye on the manuscript and other on the Chicago manual of style.

My debt is great to William Van Til who introduced me to the people and ideas that energized progressive education, and to John Goodlad on whose work I draw and for suggesting that I develop more fully ideas in a *Kappan* article that led to this book.

The Birchrunville School in Pennsylvania was built in 1863 as a one-room school, grades 1 to 8. A second floor was added in the 1890s for grades 9 and 10. Reforms such as a school-within-a-school are efforts to recapture the personal warmth and the student's sense of responsibility that marked our early small schools at their best. The seventh- and eighth-grade boys in Birchrunville shoveled coal, took out the cinders, and carried water from a spring. "Community service" was then part of a way of life. "We didn't have to argue about teaching values," says former teacher Pauline L. Keller. "They just learned them. The older kids watched out for the little ones on the playground because no teacher could watch them all. On Friday afternoons we swept and dusted the room." Information given by Pauline L. Keller who taught in the Birchrunville School from 1939 to 1942. Photograph by Richard A. Gibboney.

Students of the Birchrunville School ca. 1940, grades 1 to 8. The boy on the right in the leather jacket was killed in World War II. Notice the arm-in-arm stance with a friend. Photograph and information courtesy of Pauline L. Keller.

CHAPTER 1

Taking Reform
Seriously: The Anger
and the Tears

Armies of education governors roam the land. Legislators for-
age in the ravines of their mindscapes and offer restrictive mandates
and high-stakes testing to make schools better. A self-proclaimed
education president and his governor allies offer six stirring goals,
but they seem not to understand that hunger, crime, and poverty
teach lessons better than any school. Overstuffed panels of the socially elite rain reform reports on a public distracted by sports and
television. Teachers, who must till the fields of reform, still being
trained rather than educated, are told to march boldly forward with
oxen and wooden ploughs. Too many administrators efficiently
manage a system strangled by problems and cannot muster the vision and moral courage that leadership requires. This was the spirit
of educational reform in the 1980s. Politicians and many in the
press corps marched happily in this parade. They sang loudly of
their concern and often proclaimed success, confusing paper intentions with concrete results. Many citizens were indifferent, and

those closest to the children in our schools—teachers and principals—were not applauding and they surely were not singing. They were not doing much reforming either.

Any credible or practical discussion of education reform—or any reform proposal—must take into account the larger social environment in which public school educators live and do their work. This environment is too often overlooked by reformers themselves or by academics who write about reform. Most often the working environment of educators is not only hostile but punishing. Practitioners know that this environment and some of its anti-reform characteristics must be acknowledged if my discussion of reform is to be not only realistic but fair. Few corporations or universities function in a social environment so consistently hostile to their mission as that which surrounds public schools. Little wonder educators are often indifferent to the blandishments of reformers.

THE ANTI-REFORM SOCIAL ENVIRONMENT

To be a public school teacher or administrator today is to live in a society that cares too little about what is good for its children. One-third of preschool children are likely to fail in school because of poverty, sickness, and the lack of adult protection and support. Fifteen million children are being reared by single, divorced mothers who earn about $11,500 a year—close to the poverty line.[1] We probably spend much more money buying and maintaining our cars than it would cost to give every needy child food, a place to live, and medical care. Let us recall, too, other less lethal but mind-sapping influences in our culture that educators do not create but which influence the work they do. School must compete with football, rock videos, cult movies, and a culture exploding with things to buy, from pump sneakers to the calculated commercial style in popular music. Youth learn things today in the soothing visual images of television and advertising caught between a sip of Coke and a telephone conversation with a friend.

The power relations in our society that tolerate poverty and inadequate health care for children cannot be ignored. Neither can the cultural message, implicit in commercial television and other mass media, that "buying things" is a virtue itself (it keeps the economic machinery humming). The cultural apparatus defines knowledge, as John Dewey and other critics have repeatedly said. Michael Apple reminds us how the culturally taken-for-granted educates. "Televi-

Relatives and community members meet to mourn the death of 37 teen-agers slain on the streets of West Philadelphia (July 1, 1993). Two other similar memorials in the city bear the names of 76 youth. The painting de-picts children running through a meadow toward an inviting horizon. Pho-tograph by Bonnie Weller, The Philadelphia Inquirer.

sion and mass media, . . . billboards, films," Apple writes, make im-portant contributions to how we construct social meaning. When these media influences are coupled to the social meanings embed-ded in the school's curriculum, the conditions exist for the contin-uation of an "unequal social order."[2] Democracy demands that educators know the culturally implicit and "natural" ways schools deny social and economic benefits to the poor while extending so-cial goods to those who are suffering less.

Educators and school board members did not create a society that seems indifferent to poverty and the relative neglect of its youth. We need fresh thinking—among both liberals and conserva-tives—on ways to make a more just and caring community that supports family life. One statistic suggests the radical and chilling changes that have taken place in American families since the 1950s. Four decades ago, 81 percent of white children lived with both par-ents until the age of 17; of white children born in the early 1980s, only 30 percent will live with both parents until the age of 17. "The corresponding rate for black children has fallen from 52 percent in the 1950s to only 6 percent today," writes William Galston in a review of the literature on the family titled "Home Alone."[3] These numbers reflect changes of earthquake proportions in family life. Children are coming to school from unstable families. Children get too little nurturing at home. Miss Jones who teaches fourth grade is part of a better America, but many education critics forget that Miss Jones is not all of America.

While educators try to stay afloat in a culture in which students are increasingly disengaged from their family, community, and learning, and while educators work in a culture that has not recently recognized the gashes that poverty inflicts on the young, some reform goes on in other parts of the society. It is salutary to look at the reforms proposed in American business corporations—institutions which, like the schools, are believed to have a "quality problem,"—and to contrast the temper of these reforms with those proposed by the establishment for schools. The fortuitous appearance of two articles on reform, one on education and the other on business, in the same issue of *USA Today* makes an ironic and unintended juxtaposition of power and conflicting values.

The education story is headlined "Student skills 'not good enough.' " This story reports the latest test results from the National Assessment of Educational Progress, a federal project that periodically tests a national sample of students. The public is told yet one more time that fewer than 20 percent of our fourth-, eighth-, and twelfth-grade students are proficient in mathematics. But there might be better news, too. Students did as well in mathematics, science, and reading as their parents did twenty years ago. The U.S. Secretary of Education and some governors say that this is not good enough (and it is not). "For the first time we are saying how good is good enough," said Colorado governor Roy Romer. The learning gap between whites and students of color narrowed. And last, as if to hint at the complexity of this reform business, the test data show a direct link between the parents' education and a child's mathematics knowledge. A teachers' union president denounces the finding as technically indefensible and misleading.[4]

The animating ideas behind this article are that proficiency in learning can be objectively measured, that federal initiatives can develop an assessment process through which student learning can be compared within a group of states, and that testing students and publicizing the results are good ways to reform education.

I turn to the business section of *USA Today.* The topic is achieving quality in American business. The month of October is being given over to a national series of symposia and conferences on ways to improve quality. Public television will show an IBM-funded documentary on ways to improve the quality of American products. The events planned for this month include a half-day forum sponsored by the American Society for Quality Control, sparked by the chief executive of IBM. The forum will examine quality issues in Germany, Japan, and the United States, and will be seen via satellite by one hundred thousand people in seventeen countries.

The lead story is about an executive who was called in five years ago to rescue Buick's LeSabre plant from decline. The LeSabre ranked close to the bottom in every quality survey. Reduced literally to tears of desperation, the executive studied other plants that seemed to have surmounted the quality-of-product problem. The same words kept coming up in these visits—"teamwork, communication, worker empowerment." The LeSabre man realized, the story reports, that the secret to improving quality is not issuing orders or in installing gee-whiz technology. Quality hinges on giving the people closest to the making of the car encouragement to share their ideas and to act on them. Buick is now run by two hundred teams of fifteen to twenty workers who use Toyota's six-step plan to eliminate defects. The results have been good. For the last four years, Buick has been the number one domestic car in customer-satisfaction surveys.[5]

The story recounts some of the things that American companies have learned in their by-no-means-always-successful efforts in reformation. I learned, for example, that in 1980 the average American car had 250 percent more defects than a Japanese car. By 1990 that quality gap had shrunk to 50 percent. Although the majority of American consumers regard American-made products as high in quality, fewer than 25 percent of Germans and Japanese hold the same opinion (might Americans be culturally constituted—the frontier, the lack of a guild tradition, egalitarianism and all of that— to be just a bit sloppy when it comes to the refinements that quality demands?). Many companies, perhaps in imitation of their education brethren, look for the quick fix and are "mouthing the right words but are continuing to do everything cosmetically." Three ideas from this article stand out. Direct conversations must be held among those designing, making, and selling the product as well as straight talk between upper management and those on the front lines. Second, quality cannot be defined too narrowly. People's attitudes must change, based on Buick's experience. Quality cannot be defined statistically to find only where the defects are. A totally new approach might be better than trying to perfect an "old and bureaucratic process." And third, the intangible "look and feel" of the car is important as a driver sees it. A former executive at Ford tried to broaden the definition of quality by describing how a customer should feel: in "perfect harmony with the vehicle, its features, and its overall design."[6]

The only common element in how America's important institutions—its schools and its businesses—approach reform is the tears of frustration shed by the Buick executive. His tears match those shed by many teachers and, I am sure, some exhausted principals and superintendents who, having tried for the good in the face of strong opposition, say, The hell with it. I feel the anger rising in myself as I compare the *quality* of the responses to reform in the two stories. I shall offer only a short comparison. Business reform wisdom says that there must be direct conversations up and down the management line and between those designing, making, and selling the product. Education reform wisdom says that the governors and an education president know best. Teachers, principals, and others who are "close to the student" are defined out of the conversation. Business reform wisdom says that peoples' attitudes must change if reform is to be firmly grasped and that quality control cannot be based on statistical analysis alone. Education reform wisdom says that the use of tests and statistics will not only reform public education, but in the scary words of one governor, tests and the statistical analysis of test scores can tell how "good is good enough"[7]— a task that in times past would have been seen as a problem that should stand before wisdom rather than before a machine analysis of mere numbers. Business reform wisdom says that such intangible and elusive factors as whether or not the driver "feels in harmony with the car and its overall design" are critically important. Education reform wisdom says that to be concerned with teachers' and students' feelings about being in harmony with the overall design of what they learn and how they learn it in school is to sink into the swamp of "soft pedagogy," which sucks the necessary rigor out of learning and teaching. Besides, say the governors and the legislators and not a few others, "to be in harmony with something" surely cannot be measured and put on a wall chart for state comparisons; since this is their definition of reality, "to be in harmony with learning" does not exist. An implicit axiom arises: there is life only where there is number.

I do not begrudge business its humanistic pillars of reform. I am encouraged to see human considerations emerging as part of good business.[8] It *is* shameful, however, when the leaders of business reform and their political allies do not give the same humane consideration to America's children and her teachers.

The contrast between the values and the implicit theories that shape at least some business reforms and the values and implicit theories that have directed much of the state-initiated reforms through the eighties and into the early nineties adds yet another dimension to the practicing educator's working environment.[9] Humanistic theories are invoked to build better cars, while technological and depersonalized theories are invoked in hopes of better educating children. Surely this is life imitating the most satiric art.

THE ANTI-REFORM EDUCATIONAL ENVIRONMENT

But if society is often hostile to reforms based on intellectual and democratic values (discussed in chapter 2), the more immediate educational environment, which educators *themselves* create, is little better in some important respects. This environment, too, is part of the soil in which fundamental reform must grow. One of the themes about reform that I shall develop in this book is that the ideas and values educators carry in their minds and feelings is a critical factor in mounting and sustaining educationally worthy reforms.

Since truth sometimes comes in the small bursts of ordinary experience, I shall relate two anecdotes about the education of teachers and administrators. The teacher anecdote will be related first because it is consistent with the findings of a major research study on teacher education.

An activist senior high school principal who leads a school of ninety teachers and eighteen hundred students related this story to me. "Most of our interviews with teacher candidates put you to sleep," he says in a voice that reveals disbelief and frustration. "It's like someone is standing outside the door with a cookie cutter. Almost all of them are boringly similar." This principal and the teachers on the interview committee are looking for signs that the candidates know something, that they care about some things, that they "have professional verve," in the words of the principal. An unbelievable response came from a teacher who was interviewing for an art position. When he was asked what kind of projects he would like to see his students doing, there was a long pause and he replied, "That's a very good question. I'll have to think about it." A more amazing response came from all thirty-five candidates. When they were asked if they had read any of the reports on the high school, such as the books by John Goodlad, Theodore Sizer, or Ernest Boyer, not one teacher-to-be had read them! The principal later wrote a letter to the head of secondary teacher education in a regional university, many of whose recent graduates were interviewed, in which he related their responses. The university person dismissed the inquiry by writing that "we mentioned Goodlad's book in one course last semester."

The principal says he and his staff want to know if there "is any intelligence there, some spark." Often there is not. The teacher candidates were most interested in the textbooks used in the subjects they teach. The principal asked questions of this kind: "If we visited your class two months into the term, what might we see?" Thirty of the candidates had a hard time coming up with anything other than routine responses.

On the other hand, my students tell me that they have to be careful not to appear to be too thoughtful in job interviews for administrative positions with most school systems. To introduce ideas in their responses that may be interpreted to question standard practice, however humbly expressed, is to be kissed by failure. Rarely, the students say, are questions asked that probe issues of learning and teaching. Rarely is a hint given in these interviews that the school system is trying to do better beyond the adoption of packaged programs in inservice training or in curriculum (some of which I shall describe and critique in chapter 4). The message in these interviews is clear. We have things under control. Our way works. How will you fit in with what we are doing? Reform is not on the day-to-day agenda of board members, teachers, or administrators in the vast majority of our schools. Reform may ride the air waves and soak tons of paper with ink, but the "trickle down" theory of educational reform does not work any better than its cousin in economics works in giving more money to the bottom quartile of our citizens.

What are the chances for reform being initiated *within* the profession with candidates—and interviewers—who reflect the intellectual and professional attitudes of those in my anecdotes? I believe candidates with sleepy minds are more common than uncommon, but I will not try to make a case for this belief.

The anecdote about the teacher interviews could serve as a summary of the chapter titled "Becoming a Teacher" in John Goodlad's book, *Teachers for Our Nation's Schools.*[10] Goodlad and his colleagues studied twenty-nine representative colleges and universities that educate teachers. With very few exceptions Goodlad's story is a dreary one. Teacher education programs are incoherent, starkly anti-intellectual, and technique-bound. Teachers are being prepared for schools as they are, Goodlad writes, rather than graduating with the ideas, drive, or moral sense necessary to fuel a reform in education.

Consider what the study says, for example, on what it means to make the transition from the status of "student" to the office of "teacher." For most students this was an occupational rather than an intellectual change. Students shifted from being students to being teachers in a school, rather than becoming "inquirers into teaching, learning, and enculturation." Becoming a teacher meant being "able to do it" as the mentor teacher did it. Goodlad draws the following critical conclusion from these findings: "Neither of these orientations could be considered intellectual."[11] And that is really the end of the story, is it not? Without the active use of intelligence, one is hard put to even call it teaching. We might call it something like "automated humanoid instruction" perhaps, but it defiles a high art to call it teaching.

History and philosophy of education have passed away with the hornbook of the eighteenth century. I will admit that taking a survey course in the history of education or philosophy, taught by lecture from a four-pound textbook, probably did what many ill-taught academic courses do for students—made them hate it. But as long as it was there, there was hope. Goodlad says we typically have an introductory education course in its place (also taught by lecture) which deals with such intellectually engaging topics as program requirements, how to manage a class (removed from a sound educational theory and a concrete example, general prescriptions for "classroom management" inevitably slip into anti-intellectual how-to recipes), or how to pass a minimum competency test. Other topics included AIDS instruction or multicultural education, with one class period devoted to each.[12] The atomized chop-chop of the high school curriculum has filtered up to higher education. If we want professional teachers who are fired up about educational reform and whose techniques emerge from the pursuit of a demanding educational and social vision, do not expect most teacher education institutions to share the dream.

How can discipline be truly taught if the content and means employed to teach it are themselves professionally and intellectually undisciplined?

Gary Campbell sampled an array of ERIC studies as well as articles on in-school teacher education in the *Phi Delta Kappan*, *Educational Leadership*, and the *Harvard Educational Review* for the years 1978–89. Other publications, such as those from the National Staff Development Council, were also reviewed. He located 405 documents from all sources, of which 104 were narrative or descriptive studies. Most of the studies were research studies in the experimental-quantitative tradition. Campbell chose mostly journals read by principals and superintendents because he believed the articles published were a better index of what educators in practice were doing and concerned about than were articles published in research-oriented journals.

Over 90 percent of the narrative and descriptive accounts of inservice programs suggested that they were fragmented, were devoid of a conceptual framework, emphasized teaching skills, and were directed to very specific goals (such as increasing student scores on standardized achievement tests).

The quantitative studies revealed a similar pattern. Over 80 percent of the inservice programs were based on the findings of the research on effective teaching or the research on effective schools. These studies draw inferences about effective teaching or effective schools based on statistical correlations between specific teacher behaviors or school characteristics and student scores on standardized achievement tests. Because of the research methods used, variables that can be easily quantified are studied. Most of the inservice programs ignored the thinking processes teachers use to select and organize their actions while teaching. The theory behind the prescriptions, weak as it is, was not discussed.

Fewer than 10 percent of the inservice programs Campbell reviewed dealt either with such student outcomes as thinking or problem solving or with such important outcomes as how to encourage students to take an interest in learning, to exercise responsible initiative, and to feel better about their talents and abilities. None of the in-school programs required serious reading or discussion.[13] (The effective-teaching research as a reform is critically discussed in chapter 4. The effective-schools research is briefly described and critiqued in appendix C.)

Campbell's literature review is not exhaustive. His review is part of a practitioner's systematic account of a five-year reform effort to remake a secondary school. This reform effort was rooted in the idea of a dialogue among the school's staff which brought reading and ideas to bear on school practice.[14] Campbell made test borings through the soil and rock of the inservice literature and drew conclusions about the quality of its core based on one intellectual perspective. If the literature is selected on other grounds, to inform school improvement efforts, or on ways to build a professional environment for teachers, which Ann Lieberman has done so well, a different literature emerges.[15] This literature deals less with more routine inservice work.

Since the intellectual and professional environment educators create for themselves is a critical and overlooked condition for reform—and because it is something which educators directly influence—I want to give one last bit of evidence that suggests how impoverished this environment is in many school systems. When a story about the inservice education of teachers hits the front page of a major metropolitan newspaper, it is a sign that something very serious is amiss.

The Philadelphia Inquirer ran an article about one teacher in a suburban district who turned four videotape courses into an $8000-a-year raise. Teachers are turning to "nontraditional courses," which are often taught in one weekend in a classy motel and for which a semester's credit is given. Communications courses offered in Disney World and other esoterica are popular. One teacher took a 45-semester-hour course in "Keys to Motivation" in five days at a Ramada Inn (the course was offered by a college in the area). She put her finger on one problem from the teacher's side of reform when she defended this course by saying, "A lot of universities are teaching theory. What these courses teach are things teachers can use in the field."[16] Would that more colleges and universities taught theory! What this teacher means by "theory" is any course that is not perceived as how-to. A course in the "keys to motivation" removed from a more comprehensive view of education is practically and intellectually useless. To isolate "motivation" or "thinking" from the context of life in classrooms and schools is like a family therapist recommending a three-day course in "motivation for better family life" to a family that is in the process of falling apart.

I have sketched some of the factors in society and within education itself that condition our willingness to take on the moral and intellectual burdens of reform. There are many good reasons why we have not made significant progress in reforming our schools in intellectual and democratic ways since 1960. Our nation's tolerance of poverty, for example, since the political coalition that launched Lyndon Johnson's "war on poverty" dissolved in the early 1970s,[17] is not one of our country's great achievements, and it poses serious obstacles not only to reform but to what we might consider ordinary learning and teaching. One does not need to be a social policy analyst to know that children come to the school from families and to know that what strengthens the family strengthens the school. Poverty kills. It is as direct as that. I see once more in my mind's eye, as I think about the social disgrace that poverty is, the broken look in the eyes of the children and wives of white tenant farmers in Alabama as they stare at me from Walker Evans's masterful photographs, and I recall James Agee's words as he tore himself apart struggling with how to express in words the poverty he and Evans saw in 1936. In the early pages of *Let Us Now Praise Famous Men*, Agee says of his struggle,

> If I could do it, I'd do no writing at all here [in Alabama]. It would be photographs; the rest would be fragments of cloth, bits of cotton, lumps of earth, records of speech . . . phials of odors, plates of food and excrement. Booksellers would consider it quite a novelty; critics would murmur, yes, but is it art; and I would trust a majority of you to use it as you would a parlor game.
>
> A piece of body torn out by the roots might be more to the point.[18]

Until society sees a "piece of body torn out by the roots," educators, too, must live with poverty's dank smell.

Slick proposals from governors and presidents, visual images afloat on electromagnetic waves that invade our homes, egalitarianism and democracy in pursuit of quality in the manufacture of cars while meritocracy and authority drive the pursuit of better education for children—these things exist and influence educational reform. But they are beyond our direct control and pale before the damage we do by our inability to reconstruct the impoverished inschool teacher education programs we create for ourselves. If we cannot educate ourselves, on what do we rest our claim to educate others? Administrators must share the major responsibility for the poor quality of inservice programs because it is they who most often bring these skill-oriented "packages" to teachers.

If reform is to come alive, we must better attend to the intellectual and democratic quality of our own education. Surely the brief account I have given in this chapter, which delineates the anti-

.ntellectual nature of the education we give ourselves in colleges and universities and in inservice programs, should give anyone who believes in the democratic social mission of the public schools cause for concern—if not outrage. Reform begins when we question what we *know* as we also question what we *do*. Reform is not a separate goal or prize to be pursued apart from the texture and quality of our daily practice; it is not an add-on like a stereo system in an old car. *As we make our practice of education more intelligent, we shall see that reform is no more than a by-product of thoughtful practice.* Reform evolves slowly as practitioners become more critical and thoughtful in their daily work. Grand strategies, national goals, and restrictive state standards imposed on an unthoughtful enterprise will do no more than tell us to run while placing boulders in our path.

If school practice and reform are to become more thoughtful, we must learn to ask not only, How effective is this reform? but to ask first, What is the educational worth of this reform? I discuss in the next chapter two concepts that guide my analysis of a reform's worth. The question of a reform's educational worth was rarely asked in the decades I studied. Its worth was assumed, or its worth was masked by a narrow interest in the promised effectiveness of the reform in improving the achievement of children living in poverty, for example, or in ways of teaching that made claims to effectiveness by invoking the findings of research. Faced with a blizzard of reforms, from interactive computers to thinking skills to mastery learning to whole language, educators need a rational and informed basis on which to judge a reform's worth.

In a profession of averted eyes that too often is reluctant to speak to the good, and is embarrassed to say that something is bad, I am hopeful that my analysis of reform, whatever its imperfections may be, might serve as an example of what a principal and a school faculty could do for itself as they improve the quality of their own learning. At the very least I hope to offer an alternative to the present practice of making numbers, rather than ideas and values, the primary basis for judging the worth of a reform proposal.

We must abandon the grand highways of routine practice and our fear of constructive criticism, either by ourselves or others. These roads do not jostle or disturb. The ride is pleasant if unremarkable, but these highways are taking us at high speed to the possible dissolution of the American public school system. Country roads have their charm. In the following chapters I try to show how an informed critique of proposed reforms can help teachers, principals, and others separate worthy reforms from unworthy reforms. My analysis is one example of what educators can do for themselves in their own schools through open and informed conversation. It is the country road of mind and conversation that we must travel if American schools are to begin to capture the power of intellectual and democratic values for *all* her children. Country roads bring us to reality. Here we see the colors and catch the scent of the forest and the field. Here we cannot forget the children.

CHAPTER 2

Judging the Worth
of Reform: A
Deweyan-Progressive
Perspective[1]

Reforms abound. The large number of reforms available to educators is one characteristic of the 1960–1990 period. I once had a list of seventy-five reforms that had gained some attention or notoriety in these decades. The large number of reforms, coupled with the incessant chatter about reform in journals and newspapers, give one the impression that school reform is a big thing. But my own professional experience was more conflicted. It was as if the chattering classes were filling my "reading eye" with the symbols of reform while my other eye, the eye that looked at what was going on in schools and in schools of education, saw very few changes nor witnessed much interest in reform. This apparent contradiction led me to track the grand entrances and quiet exits of the reforms I had noted on my list.

The light of attention that falls on some reforms may be bright, but it is a flickering light that does not last long. How many educators today, for example, can recall the excitement created in the early 1970s by the federal government and its Office of Economic

Opportunity with "performance contracting," in which business corporations contracted with schools to raise test scores and were to be paid on the basis of score gains? The flickering light went out of this reform when studies showed that businesses were no more successful than schools in teaching poor kids to read (see appendix C). The business image today enters reform through talk of "market incentives" and "competition" among schools. Having been burned with direct intervention, business corporations are wisely content to let Adam Smith's "invisible hand" of the market do the hard work of reform. Consider another reform. In the 1960s Jerrold Zacharias, a physics professor at the Massachusetts Institute of Technology, and the National Science Foundation seemed to be on a rocket ride to reform with the new science and mathematics curriculums. Few educators today, not to mention education governors and presidents, could identify Zacharias or his reforms on a multiple-choice test. Let us go back even further. My first recollection of the reform fever that, in retrospect, burdened much of my professional life, was the Washington-like figure of James Bryant Conant, former president of Harvard and American ambassador to Germany, striding through the land and offering his lean recommendations in 1959 to reform the comprehensive high school and to improve the education of able students. Principals eagerly proclaimed in the press that they had "Conant schools" within a few months of the report's release. I remember wondering as a young employee of the Pennsylvania state education department about the miracle of this transformation. Somewhere in my nervous system a sedimentary layer of doubt was laid down that made me suspicious of reform and reformers. What is going on with this television-like change of image each historical minute? How can these fleeting images be captured better to understand our seeming obsession with reform?

To capture some meaning from the swirl of events that is and has been inherent in our reform efforts is an uncertain enterprise. But I feel impelled to try. If the future of public education is at stake, and I believe it is as this century flows into the next, we cannot afford these reform rides to nowhere. Educators at the very least have to become more intellectually awake and aware. In this chapter I shall introduce two critical perspectives through which I try to find meaning in thirty years of school reform.

One assumption of those who advocate or adopt a reform, is that the reform is more educationally *worthy* than practices it replaces. This is common sense. What rational person would assert that the adoption of unworthy reforms is sensible reform? Although it is common sense to say that only worthy reforms will advance

American education, it is a common sense that has escaped most of our practice. My description and critique of thirty-four representative reforms adopted by schools since 1960, for example, show that less than 20 percent of these reforms were educationally worthy (I shall present the two ideas that guided this analysis shortly). In the three chapters that follow I offer the supporting detail and argument that lead to this conclusion. If I may anticipate the discussion in these chapters, it is clear that public school educators are not alone in the choice of unworthy reforms: foundations, universities, the educational research establishment, and federally funded research and development centers, which created some of the reforms, were more than equal partners in developing and spreading educationally unworthy reforms.

If my analysis is reasonable, it raises the question: how is it that the vast majority of proposed reforms could be so bad? If most of the reforms proposed are unworthy, it could be argued that, knowing little else, to resist reform is a good thing. A second question arises. If some reforms are better than others, and these reforms are neglected, why is this so? I shall try to answer questions such as these in the chapters that follow. A rational and clear assessment of a reform's worth is essential if reform is to move beyond the zero-sum game it has been for the past thirty years.

In the next section I shall define two concepts that guide my analysis of reform: fundamental reform—reform that is worthy—is reform that embraces intellectual and democratic values; unworthy reform—reform that does not improve present practice—is reform rooted in the values of the technological mindset. These two concepts, each of which comes from a long and rich tradition, are comprehensive enough to assimilate many of the complexities of reform without trivializing it. They do not omit important dimensions ignored by a narrower or exclusively empirical framework of analysis. And they focus on learning and teaching, on curriculum and the classroom. The deeper meaning of these concepts (and their possible limitations) will become clear in context when they are used to assess particular reforms.

TWO BASIC CONCEPTS USED IN THIS ANALYSIS

I suggest below what I mean by fundamental reform.

The Intellectual and Democratic Criterion

Fundamental reform is reform that is intellectual and democratic. This is the shortest, minimally-adequate criterion of goodness that

I know. Its richer meaning, and the other salient dimensions related to it, can be directly explored in John Dewey's *Democracy and Education*, as well as some of his other books, and in histories such as Lawrence A. Cremin's *Transformation of the School* and William J. Reese's *Power and the Promise of School Reform*.[2] I suggest below some of the qualities that give substance to my shorthand criterion that fundamental reform must engage intellectual and democratic values in learning and teaching; these qualities also suggest *why* this criterion is useful if we are concerned with ways to improve learning and teaching.

Since the intellectual and democratic dimensions are interwoven in Dewey's comprehensive theory of education, along with many other elements such as discipline and the relationship of curriculum content to intellectual growth and to significant issues in society, I cannot give a simple, crisp definition of this criterion. The relationship between the intellectual and the democratic is suggested, however, when Dewey discusses the democratic conception in education and says that in a modern democratic society in which the area of shared concerns is widening (such as the concern today with education or global warming), it would be fatal to that society to permit social divisions along race or class lines; therefore society must ensure "that intellectual opportunities [not skills alone] are accessible to all on equable and easy terms."[3]

One important aspect of the intellectual dimension in this criterion is that a teacher cannot give an idea directly to a student. What the student gets is a fact dressed as an idea. This is so because we truly get an idea only by wrestling with it firsthand in a situation that has some purpose or meaning to us, that elicits some engagement of the imagination and emotions as well as of the mind. The student must "figure it out" with the help of the teacher and other students in a classroom *environment* that is rich in materials and things to do that give access to community and regional life and to organized knowledge. In these *shared activities* (notice how a democratic and supportive social medium relates to thinking) the teacher is also a learner and the student a teacher.[4] Ideas come alive when they are used (acted upon). Acting on an idea not only provides an empirical test of the idea, but it also provides the basis for further *observations* of the learning activity by the teacher and the student and offers an antidote to student passivity in school. This activist condition in thinking is similar to Jean Piaget's constructivist idea. Reciting correct answers removed from wrestling with an idea, with making meaning, is not educative and therefore is not intellectual.

⌐In a classroom that values mind and democratic values, the learner has opportunities to make choices about how a project or task might be completed, or about what units or projects could be studied within the broad requirements of the curriculum. The educational possibilities of various projects are explored among the students and teacher. Options and constraints are weighed. Individual and collective interests are expressed and debated. In all of this, the students are learning to use oral language, gaining confidence in expressing their views, and disciplining themselves to hear and respond to other views. Moreover, as the students shape an area of study with the teacher's guidance, they are developing an interest in it. They are now more active learners, talking and thinking about something that is important to them. ⌐

Good method, in the Deweyan-progressive sense, recognizes that a *pattern* of learning and teaching that depends on drill to impart facts drawn from science, for example, or which tries to teach writing or mathematics as a series of codes learned in isolation from thinking with subject matter, shuts out the true growth of intelligence. Good method recognizes that while results of this kind can be hurried and forced, the quality of the intellectual processes used in learning cannot be. If education is our aim rather than training, it is the quality of the mental processes that count.

Teaching has one primary goal: to cultivate thought. One cannot think without knowledge. One does not think without some purpose to think. One cannot think if the subject matter and the learning process make little sense—the situation that obtains when learning is severed from the student's present experience and contained within the moats of passive listening and doing routine exercises dictated by the teacher. A pattern of this kind of instruction (not teaching) over the years kills the mind as surely as the drought kills the plant. We have become a society dependent on electronic images not alone from the power of this medium, but because too many schools, in their passion to instruct, have led us to abhor books and to believe that ideas and conversation are boring. What an inversion of the true order of things! What is the social value of a citizen who can read, but who refuses to read? Of what social value is his passing reading score locked up in the high school or college archives?

One way to make school more sensible for students and teachers—to make school more intellectual—is to encourage projects that are sustained over several months at the very least. Could not, for example, an ordinary social studies class learn much from studying the use of land in its community? What are the effects on housing, parks, jobs, taxes, and the social composition of the community given present land use patterns? What are the predicted effects of alternative patterns? It is easy to see that projects such as this have the potential to integrate content from several subjects, to raise important civic issues, and to link the community to the school. Properly planned and carried out, sustained efforts on important and complex social issues offer students and teachers something intellectually solid to pursue. An education that in twelve years never explores significant social issues is deficient. An education that values intellectual and democratic ends would engage more students in such studies. Significant projects give students an opportunity to plan, to execute, and to take some responsibility for their actions. Students would then have an opportunity to do something complex that required foresight, having a purpose in mind. Students would not only think, they would act. Their actions would initiate consequences in a lifelike situation. Thinking and doing, the theoretical and the practical, would now be linked rather than separated; we would have created an educational unity from something that was separate and partial. This reasserts the Deweyan notion that mind is in experience, not outside experience. In a time of fragmented families and so-called communities lost in a Los Angeles–type sprawl, whose social arteries are the concrete pathways of highway networks, we should not neglect the deep human need for sharing, communication, and wholeness. We have a deep psychological need to see our work culminate in a form which is an organic completion of all the earlier stages in its development. This progressive completion of a process is all we mean by intellectual coherence. School conceived as a series of discrete lessons about fragments of subject matter, however elegantly tailored, satisfy neither the mind nor the feelings. The traditional school teaches pieces of subjects untied to either the mind or the community; the progressive school links mind and community in all that it teaches.

The acute need for schools to encourage "sharing, communication, and wholeness" cannot be overstressed when many students are bored in school with excessive teacher talk and routine drill exercises. Ira Shor, for example, writes eloquently about the need for "critical classrooms." In critical classrooms teachers talk *with* and not *at* students; in critical classrooms students engage life-relevant issues (generative themes) such as the way news is produced and distributed by the mass media. Shor uses his structured media theme in a way that builds on the students' present knowledge to be sure, but the whole "lesson" becomes a "participatory academic problem" that challenges the "students' intelligence and ingenuity." Critical classrooms integrate "structured knowledge into the students' speech and understandings. . . ." Democratic participation requires the give-and-take of discussion, "mutual discussion is the heart of the method," Shor writes.[5] This is one way to make schools more sensible for students and teachers alike. If school study is "sensible," the cultivation of intelligence cannot be far behind.

Essential content, in schools aware of their social function in a democratic society, is that content which is of the widest and most general social significance. Now this idea cannot be translated into a precise metric of a content's worth. Its power lies in its very abstractness. Courts, for example, try to achieve justice. That they sometimes fail in no way reduces the social importance of their quest. In the same spirit, teachers and principals need to be aware that knowledge is too often taught in a narrow, technical way. Specialized knowledge—science taught for scientists-to-be, for example, which ignores the impact of science on our lives—reflects an imbalance between science viewed as a technical study and science viewed as a body of content of great social significance. [The social import of science was neglected by the new science curriculums of the 1960s, which I discuss in chapter 3.]

The social significance of the content taught suggests also that the needs of present community and regional life are worthy subjects of study as discussed earlier. I need only add here that the hope of the school in teaching content of high social significance is that, by teaching such content, the quality of social and individual life might be improved by democratic means.

One idea will round out this sketch of what the intellectual and democratic criterion of educational worth means: *any human being who is within the broad normal range has a great capacity to learn.* One could build an excellent class or a fine school on this idea alone. To believe that any normal student has a great capacity to learn asserts the idea that what is taught, and how it is taught, should not be narrow and practical for the many while offering broad and more liberal studies for the few. Such a theory perpetuates class and ethnic differences because those groups with social power may dictate to others less powerful how and what to think.

Every time we *routinely* slot a child from the less economically privileged classes to a special education room, a remedial reading class, or a vocational program, we violate this progressive value. Is it not common knowledge in our profession that gifted children

are taught in ways that would greatly enhance the quality of learning for less socially privileged children? Where is the psychology
that says that only students whose aptitude for learning is presumed
to be high can profit from reading real books and discussing them,
while others are given only textbooks to read and workbook sheets
to fill in? Where is the psychology that says that giving students
with presumed academic aptitude many opportunities to talk and to
raise questions is good for them, but that it is harmful if less privileged children engage in the same activities? I believe that almost
all students above the trainable category need and can profit from
the same kind of considerate, challenging teaching simply because
they are human and all humans share certain needs. What student,
for example, does not want and need purpose and meaning in her
learning? What student would prefer a textbook to a real book?
What student needs a teacher who believes he cannot learn? [The
discussion of the federally funded Chapter 1 remedial programs in
chapter 4 is an example of a multi-billion-dollar reform that oper-
ates on a principle opposite to the one expressed here.]

A simple but warranted faith in our ability to learn, for students and teachers alike, would itself effect a revolution in education. We have let the system define most of the key players in
education as learning handicapped. Must not something be very
wrong when it is widely believed that many of the swimmers on the
swim team are not very good swimmers? The ability to learn is a
normal human capacity. This idea is so important that I want to let
a teacher speak to it. Maggie Cox teaches fifth and sixth graders in
Barbourville, Kentucky. She teaches students who are poor. Over 80
percent of her students receive free school lunches in some years.
Maggie Cox is a teacher in Foxfire's Eastern Kentucky Teachers Network. Most of her students tested so low in language arts that many
of them doubted their ability to "complete a [writing] project until
they were taught some basic writing skills, not by fill-in-the-blank
or multiple-choice exercises, but by putting words and thoughts on
paper," Ms. Cox writes. The first year the class wrote, submitted,
and received funding for a proposal to Foxfire, that was funded in
addition to completing a study of the county and its resources,
which led the students to interview local working people. In all this
work, the students planned, talked, and shared.

Ms. Cox recounts a complex story of this class over two years
that cannot be summarized in a way that retains its narrative
thread. Her story is a teacher's story of initial student apathy, flu
outbreaks, stolen computer discs that contained the final versions

of the students' stories, visiting folk artists, her struggles with the computer, extensive student writing and editing, improvement in the students' ability to write, awakening student interest, and finally a book of the children's stories titled *Fifth Grade Kid Tales*. The students made all of the important decisions related to the book: students wrote and chose the stories to be included, edited the stories, and decided on the title and cover design.

Another important story is the last tale Ms. Cox tells. The school year was over. Her class had published a book of stories written by each student, including mainstreamed special education students. One of these students saw Ms. Cox and her husband in a doctor's office the following summer and asked her if, next year, she was going to get

> "The good group or the slow group, you know. . . ." I don't think my husband and I, or the people in the doctor's office, will ever forget the honesty and sincerity of the child. This child had many personal problems and had developed a poor self-image [but her attitude had improved]. She really liked seeing her work in print. . . .
>
> That child's statement proved in public a point that I had been making for years: that students in my school label themselves before they ever reach the fifth grade. This project, *Fifth Grade Kid Tales*, allowed these students the opportunity to feel good about themselves. After all, they were the first to accomplish something no other class at our school had attempted to do. They published a book with everyone having an equal part.[6]

Maggie Cox's story reveals the human core in the abstraction "all children can learn and the social medium educates."

My elaboration of the intellectual and democratic criterion for fundamental reform provides ground on which we can stand to critique present practice, and, at the same time, it points to a worthy end that embraces solid intellectual, social, and moral content. If we accept this aim—to make our schools more intellectual and democratic—we can more easily do one important thing: be more rational in our choice of means that the aim suggests so that there is more conceptual and practical consistency between our aim and the means chosen to attain it. To the extent that we learn to be more rational and effective in linking means to important ends, we simultaneously do a second important thing: we provide the essential intellectual, social, and moral dimensions to the practice of education, which are too often neglected and which are the primary way to truly professionalize education because they link idea (theory) and practice. The theory and research side of education might also improve because ideas and good research would be in greater demand and enjoy more respect in practice than they do presently. Such a development might spur a much-needed improvement in the overall quality of the thinking and writing by university faculty whose work too often suffers from overspecialization and pedantry, according to some scholars.[7]

I turn now to a definition of the concept of the technological mindset—the dominant view of our time.

The Technological Criterion

The technological mindset is an attitude that poses problems and their solutions in terms such as technique removed from idea, numbers devoid of context, managerial efficiency removed from a consideration of worthy educational goals, and the pursuit of short-term objectives such as lining up a curriculum behind a standardized test,[8] without understanding that low-quality means lead to low-quality ends. The technological mindset ignores, in sum, the psychological and social contexts in which all learning and teaching are rooted. The technological attitude is captured in E. L. Thorndike's idea of intelligence. Thorndike rejected the view that "qualitative differences exist between the minds of lower animals and man" and held that one's intelligence is the *quantity* of the stimulus-response connections in the brain.[9] In one stroke the behaviorist view of learning ignores uniquely human qualities such as language and the social environment in favor of physiological connections in the brain, and stands in sharp opposition to the humanistic spirit of the Deweyan view. Behaviorist psychology is part of the unseen technological veil that makes reform more difficult. Behaviorism justifies an erroneously direct skill approach at the expense of contextual factors in learning such as the quality and amount of normal language use in the classroom and a democratic social environment—essential factors in a more humane and holistic view of intelligence and learning.

The technological mindset is too concerned with matters of measurement, prediction, control, and efficiency—and too dependent on specialized experts—to define and address human problems according to Robert V. Bullough and his colleagues.[10] This overconcern with such things as measurement and control is based on the false assumption that a narrow view of science can alone produce valid social knowledge.

Scientific rationalism fills the intellectual air and is the "dominant preoccupation of our epoch," according to Alfred North Whitehead.[11] When this preoccupation moves beyond the minds of the academics and into the minds and hands of practitioners and policymakers, one essential precondition for reform will have been created.

My concern with the influence of the scientific-technological tradition on the quality of human life, and on life in schools, is not a matter of speculation. This problem has long occupied serious educational practitioners and thinkers within the fields of science as well as those within the philosophy of science itself. For example, the philosopher William Barrett writes in *Death of the Soul: From Descartes to the Computer,* that science and technology are the driving forces in modern civilization and that the discrepancy between science and the human world becomes a central and disturbing theme in modern thought and continues into our time. Descartes separated the human mind from the physical world in order to understand Nature. He cast the knowledge gained in the universal language of mathematics, and, in doing so, invented the foundations of modern science. But there was a price exacted for science's brilliant accomplishments. Over time, this separation of the human mind from the natural and social world led us to devalue those things that do not lend themselves to the rigor and exactitude of scientific methods—such things as literature and history, life experience, feelings, and human creations such as communities. The texture, richness, and human detail of these studies and activities, and their inherent uncertainty, were given a lower status by those who extolled the power and rigor of scientific method and of the technology it spawned.[12] Studies and social concerns that fell beyond science and the efficiencies of technology were too often dismissed by mainstream social science and the educational establishment as hopelessly subjective.

Stephen Toulmin, a philosopher and physicist, might have been thinking about education and reform when, writing about the limitations of the mechanical view of the world offered by the old Newtonian science in today's world of cultural diversity and interdependence, said that, if we continue to impose on thought and action the rigor, exactitude, and system of an unreformed science, "we risk making our ideas and institutions not just stable but sclerotic. . ." and we also risk not being able to modify them in reasonable ways to meet the unseen demands of new situations.[13]

The differences in world views between the scientific and humanistic approaches are of practical importance to educators. Because the differing views of what constitutes valid knowledge—such as those in the physical sciences and those in the social sciences or education—are little discussed in either the theoretical or practical literature in education, I shall give one last example to point up the practical importance of these philosophical differences. The older Cartesian-Newtonian philosophy has dominated education research, for example, for most of this century, although the recent move toward more contextual and qualitative approaches, such as ethnography, has begun to modify the hold of the experimental-quantitative philosophy of knowledge. Alfred North Whitehead saw this problem in 1925 when he wrote in *Science and the Modern World* that educated people construct the "mentality of an epoch" from their world views, which vary over centuries. Science, art, ethics, and religion each suggest a way of looking at the world. He makes explicit what is implicit in twentieth-century thought with this statement: ". . . each age has its dominant preoccupation; and, [during the last three centuries], the [outlook] derived from science has been asserting itself at the expense of older points of view with their origins elsewhere." Scientific materialism expresses certain facts of brute matter "to perfection," Whitehead states. But if we want other meanings, or other kinds of intellectual coherence beyond the physical realm, "the [scientific] scheme breaks down. . . ."[14] The same general criticism could be made of inappropriate applications of technology to human-social problems, such as the use of standardized achievement tests—a modern technology—as the primary means to determine the "productivity" of schools (i.e., their educational quality).

Descartes' dream of creating an objective method to put knowledge about the physical world in mathematical language has been realized. Anyone living today knows the power of physical science to make verifiable statements about things as remote as the stars and as "close" as our genes. These discoveries are breathtakingly brilliant and they often have practical consequences which the nonscientific person can easily see. But when we seek the legitimate precision of the physical sciences in the hazy realm of human affairs we get into trouble. This idea was expressed by the French quantum physicist de Broglie, who believed our ideas about Reality are useful only when they are formulated in a slightly vague way. When too much precision is sought, our ideas "become ideal forms whose real content tends to vanish away." Using the example of the difficulty of defining an "Honest man," de Broglie concluded that, in the inexact sciences, the more strict the definition of something was—we could take "learning" as an example—the less useful it was in our ordinary lives.[15] And exactness is what the technological mindset seeks: an idealized precision that is not permitted by the complexity of the human subject matter being studied or the human activity it is trying to redirect or influence (such as learning and teaching). The complexity of human activity is ignored so that a method of research, teaching, or measurement can be imposed—the real content vanishes and we are left with the distorted artifacts of technique.

The near-fixation of modern culture with technique flows from our recognition of the undeniable power of the physical sciences to *know* things and to *do* things. The complex structure of our technology, from plastics to cars to computers to atomic energy, are applications of what science knows. We are awed by these ideas and technologies not only because they are creative and brilliant, but also because *we do not fully understand them.* How many of us can give one hypothesis about Reality from quantum physics, for example? How many of us can fix our car or television set? So modern man uneasily lives with the mysteries and with a rational and material magic whose secrets are known only to the few—the new medicine men of science and engineering. This condition is intimidating. This condition creates a new kind of dependence. When the electricity goes out in New York city, planes cannot land and people are stuck on a train or in a building until the electricity comes on again—while the pregnancy rate climbs! I suspect, in the deep workings of our cultural mind, that our dependence and fear and our admiration—our love-hate relationship with the technological world—creates some powerful psychological juices. One effect of this chemistry is that we rip out some of the techniques of the scientific method—we *can* understand that scientists measure things, use numbers, and proceed most of the time in a methodical manner—and with the zealous enthusiasm of the unknowing we apply these techniques to human affairs that cannot properly accept them. It is important to say, however, that while we take the techniques of science, we studiously avoid recognizing the power of its conceptual underpinnings. This is why the proper method and techniques of the physical sciences and technology intrude into the world of education, where technique defines our *operational* theory of mind, knowledge, and teaching. This is why many philosophers, such as Whitehead and Barrett, have said that the cultural power of science has pushed aside other ways of knowing that are more appropriate to human affairs—literature, art, ordinary life experience, history, philosophy—and why feelings and moral issues are shunted aside as "merely subjective" and, therefore, presumably lacking in power to affect our lives in practical ways. Is it not common sense to say that the methods and techniques used to unlock the secrets of inert matter and forces in the physical universe—things without a directive intelligence or feelings of their own—cannot routinely be applied to other "objects" in the universe that have these directive qualities and that, because these objects are human, often act in wonderful and unpredictable ways?

Barrett's insight on how we absorb the values of technique and the machine into our minds is direct and illuminating. Even though we cannot formulate it, we learn very early what the logical essence of a machine is, and consequently we learn the meaning of technique. A machine, we learn, achieves a predetermined result by automatically going through a series of steps and routines that have been built into it. If the machine is working properly, these steps do not vary from those built in by the engineers who designed it. We learn this cultural lesson of technology every time we start our car, or turn on a television set or a computer. On the command "key on," the car solves the problem of "how to start" by going through a number of prescribed and invariant steps. If the car is not defective, the engine starts. We learn that order (a sequence of steps) and the techniques used to manufacture the car itself usually "work" and that, therefore, these things are "good." This is one important way that the values of technique and technology come into our inner selves. We cannot escape it in our culture. In concluding his example of the car, Barrett says, "The last thing we want from it is that it be creative or inventive in any way. When your automobile [begins] to sound . . . as if its starting up were a matter of improvisation or invention, it is usually time to trade it in." *Technology is embodied technique. Technology—a machine—embodies technique to serve a predetermined end.*[16] Lewis Mumford offers a similar idea of a machine. Mumford discusses Descartes' method that requires that a physical system be broken down into its smallest, measurable parts, "down to the minutest particle." He then argues that this atomistic approach cannot be used to understand living organisms. To understand life that embodies intelligence, Mumford continues, we assemble parts into wholes because intelligent life is so complex that it can only be understood intuitively in the act of living. Within this context, Mumford writes that

Machines, however crude, are embodiments of a clearly articulated purpose, so firmly fixed in advance . . . that even the lowest organism, if similarly organized, would be unable to utilize fresh genetic mutations or *meet novel situations* [emphasis added].[17]

If technology is embodied technique, and if technology so constrains thought within its closed systems that even the lowest organism cannot meet novel situations, should not we in education pause to consider the devastation we are creating in our children's minds if, as I and some others believe, much educational practice reflects technological values? Should we not stop dismissing such questions as an "old idea," as abstract and theoretical, a response that itself may suggest the grip of the technological view of life on our thinking?

I must address one question that arises in a critical discussion of the technological way of thinking. Is technique absolutely bad? Technique is used in all human activities in which some end or purpose is sought. A novelist, a mechanic, an actor, and a teacher all use technique in their work. But in real-life situations, people in democratic societies usually have some choice of the ends they pursue and in the means to reach them. A teacher, for example, despite restrictions, still has wide latitude in how she teaches, some choice in what content to teach, how the class is organized, who does most of the talking, and so forth. Unlike a machine—or a technological curriculum—she is not programmed to achieve predetermined ends by standardized means. Unlike a machine, she can *set* goals and creatively work out a means to achieve them. She can invent or choose her techniques. Choice makes all the difference. This is why teaching is, first and always, an art. If we get to the point where teaching can be standardized, we will have created a more subtle kind of totalitarianism than even George Orwell could have imagined.

Art students learn technique, as Barrett notes, from their teachers. But as the students mature, the teacher-given technique is outgrown and replaced by a technique of their own creation. No predetermined technique will carry the student's painting to an artistic conclusion. Flair, talent, even genius come now into play. Immanuel Kant defined genius as the ability to produce something over and above any rules. There are no prescriptions or recipes for genuinely creative actions, Barrett believes. He concludes with an insightful remark that I wish every teacher candidate for the next ten years could explore in lively discussion: ". . . technique reaches its limits precisely at that point beyond which real creativity is called for—in the sciences as well as the arts."[18]

Might it not be, in time's long reach, that one of the finest achievements of the human mind, the invention of physical science, contains within its objective power seemingly fragile assumptions which in themselves can so limit the mind that it will function only within the barren moonscape of a tightly woven technological culture? Might not the complex and interactive science-technology connection even contain within itself the power to alter Planet Earth herself? With the destruction of much of the ozone layer in the Northern Hemisphere, for example, might not the offal of technology and material consumption be doing to the heavens what it has done in painfully visible ways to the land and air in Los Angeles? Is the Great Wizard playing games with us such that one scientific advance leads to two social-technological complexities of such magnitude the Wizard itself has no solutions? And worse, no equivalent method for creating solutions? Where is the René Descartes of the post-technological age who will teach us how to make wholes, and not fragments out of wholes? Where is the Isaac Newton of the social universe whose first law will be that there are no laws, that there are only problems-in-situations? When will we find the moral courage to face what we have wrought?

THREE DECADES OF REFORM

These two powerful ideas—the intellectual and democratic perspective espoused by the Deweyan tradition and the scientific-technological perspective with its roots in the physical sciences—provide the conceptual framework from which I shall try to make some sense of thirty years of school reform. I believe that my analysis of reform will reasonably demonstrate that reform in education has been severely distorted by the pervasive power of the scientific-technological view. The problem is not so much the "rightness" or "wrongness" of either view considered separately; the problem is one of social distortion when the power harnessed by technological means is detached from overarching social and intellectual goals envisioned by Deweyan theory. When Dewey wrote in *Human Nature and Conduct* that humans interact with their social and physical environments, and that these interactions create a culture that educates, he touched a great truth.

With these two concepts in mind, we can take a bird's-eye-view of reform since 1950 in figure 1. The 1950s suggest a context for the three following decades with which we shall be concerned. One value of this decade-by-decade listing, as aesthetically unpleasing as it may be, is to permit readers to make several "sweeps" over the list and to draw some preliminary conclusions of their own about where these reforms might be headed unencumbered by the detail a more careful analysis involves. I believe, too, that the disordered quality of the reforms listed in figure 1—indeed its helter-skelter discreteness—suggests the way reform is often experienced by harried educators and policymakers: just one damn thing after another.

Figure 1 gives a panoramic view of reform over three decades. Administrators and teachers react to the list in different ways based on my experience in schools. Administrators generally find the list of reforms reassuring. They see vitality and evidence that they are "doing something" to improve education. Teachers do not make an overall judgment or try to give some meaning to the list. They pick out specific reforms, such as the new mathematics, open class-

---

FIGURE 1. Representative Reforms and Events: 1950–1990

1950s
>   Life Adjustment Education, U.S. Office of Education, early fifties
>   (Academic revolt decrying anti-intellectualism in the schools)
>   (*Why Johnny Can't Read* by Rudolf Flesch, 1955)
>   (Sputnik orbits, 1957)
>   Publication of James B. Conant's *The American High School
>   Today* (1959)

1960s
>   New mathematics and science curriculums
>   Electronic foreign language laboratories
>   The Trump high school
>   Ungraded schools
>   Open classrooms
>   (Coleman Report, 1966)
>   Individually Prescribed Instruction (IPI), programmed texts in
>   reading, math
>   Educational television
>   Team teaching
>   Community control of schools, New York City
>   Compensatory programs in reading and arithmetic
>   (Chapter 1, Elementary and Secondary Education Act of 1965)

(*continued*)

FIGURE 1. (*Continued*)

1970s
> Behavioral objectives
> Chicago mastery learning
> Career education
> Sensitivity training
> Contracting to corporations to raise test scores in basic skills
> Accountability and testing surface
> Linear model of R and D
> Competency-based curricula, testing
> Individually Guided Education (IGE)

1980s
> State testing programs in full swing in 35 or more states
> Leadership in education
> Computers
> Effective school research
> Effective teaching research
> Plethora of reform reports and legislative regulation
> Thinking skills
> The Hunter teaching approach
> Curriculum alignment
> Mainstreaming of special education students
> The Paideia Proposal
> Concern about the professional status of teachers
> Coaching
> Assertive Discipline
> Coalition of Essential Schools

---

rooms, or thinking skills, and give personal reactions. These reactions are usually negative and can be expressed in one teacher's words who said, "Oh! I remember the time we did that one. What a mess!" The value of the list to me is the meaning it might hold for the quality and direction of reform over three decades.

The reforms in figure 1 are reasonably representative of the reforms advanced from 1960–1990. These innovations map the major features of the reform terrain we have too sleepily traversed. I shall make a short argument in support of this statement because it is open to rebuttal. Some major reforms are not on the list. The Foxfire experience in cultural journalism, for example, is not listed. This reform meets the intellectual and democratic criterion based on primary sources I have reviewed.[19] Not listing Foxfire and other progressive reforms such as the whole language approach to learning language, which has some of its roots in Deweyan theory, could be taken as evidence that I loaded the dice in favor of my idea that most reforms are technological. Limited space was one reason for not listing more reforms, but two other reasons speak to the representativeness of the array in figure 1. First, all reforms are not equal in their social and educational impact. Technological reforms are usually backed by more money and may reach millions of students. No reform that meets the intellectual and democratic criterion, for instance, has a fraction of funds or "student reach" enjoyed by the remedial programs in reading and arithmetic funded under Chapter 1 of the Elementary and Secondary Education Act of 1965. This reform is purely technological (discussed in chapter 4). Fifty billion dollars have been spent on Chapter 1 since 1965. Five million children were enrolled in these programs in 1991–1992.[20] The numbers are huge in Chapter 1 because it is a government-funded program, but this in no way lessens its impact or the damage it has done to students who most need another kind of teaching and curriculum.

The power of technological reforms is great. Even if I were to double the number of reforms that might meet the intellectual and democratic criterion and multiply the dollars invested in them and the teachers and students reached by 100, their practical impact would be far less than that of the four reforms addressed in chapter 4. In contrast, the well-funded Coalition of Essential Schools and the Re:Learning initiative, a joint effort of the Coalition and the Education Commission of the States, reached seven hundred schools in 1993 (discussed in chapter 3). Chapter 1 remedial reforms are in fourteen thousand school *districts*—virtually every system in the United States. Second, I believe the array of reforms in figure 1 is reasonably representative because I did not load the list with reforms that were likely to be technological. I did not include, for example, a number of management reforms based on systems analysis, which would have biased the list in favor of my belief that most reforms are technological. Although one or more states adopted reforms such as management by objectives, operations analysis, and program evaluation and review technique (PERT) since 1970, I did not include them.[21] Another reason for not listing management-type reforms is that I am interested in reforms that more directly influence the quality of learning and teaching. Learning and teaching are reform's pivot points. I tried to be fair in listing the reforms in figure 1. However one might disagree about the inclusion or exclusion of particular reforms, it is not possible reasonably to deny the power most of the technological reforms exert on large numbers of students and teachers.

The listing of a reform in a particular decade is not absolute. Work on the new mathematics curriculums was well underway in the 1950s, but these programs were a fixture of reform in the 1960s. The effective schools research, to cite one more example, was begun in the 1970s, but it was strong and widely used by schools in the 1980s. Many of the reforms spill across the decades. This fact makes no difference to my analysis.

But the chronological list in figure 1 is too atomistic and disordered to be useful. I must rearrange the reforms in figure 1 into logical categories based on a *preliminary* and general analysis of a reform's educational characteristics and the two major concepts that guide my critique. The reordered reforms are given in figure 2.

Reforms in the first category appear to meet the intellectual and democratic criterion at this preliminary level of analysis; reforms in the second category appear to be technological; and the reforms in the third category must be further defined through concrete examples (such as the national reform reports on education), or are so socially complex and remote from the classroom (community control of schools in New York City) that they may not easily lend themselves to analysis.

To say these thirty-four reforms were categorized in a preliminary way means they were ordered on the basis of my general knowledge before I used primary or other sources to describe the reforms themselves. If a reform does not meet the criterion for the category in which it was placed, it will be clear from the description of the reform and the analysis why this is so. Two reforms do not fully meet the intellectual and democratic criterion—the new mathematics and science programs and *A Nation Prepared: Teachers for the 21st Century* funded by the Carnegie Foundation. The new mathematics and science curriculums, for example, did not meet the democratic element in one criterion although they met the intellectual element in this criterion. Both curriculums were adopted in the more affluent communities. Rural and urban schools did not typically use these programs. The science curriculums, moreover, were developed as disciplinary-technical programs and ignored the humanistic and social import of scientific studies. These deficiencies are serious for society in an age when science is probably its most powerful system of belief.

I shall try to illuminate the nature of school reform since 1960 in the three chapters that follow. Although three decades of school reform have not moved the majority of American classrooms closer to the intellectual and democratic aims we at times embrace, reforms have arisen that reflect these values. In chapter 3, I cast a wide intellectual and democratic net to capture as many of these re-

FIGURE 2. Preliminary Categorization of Reforms: 1960–1990

Category 1
Reforms that Appear to Meet the Intellectual and Democratic Criterion

The new mathematics and science curriculums and comparable efforts in
   the social sciences such as *Man a Course of Study*
The Trump High School (National Association of Secondary School
   Principals)
Open classrooms
Nongraded schools and team teaching*
The Paideia Proposal
The Coalition of Essential Schools
The professionalization of teaching as conceived in *A Nation Prepared:*
   Teachers for the 21st Century

Category 2
Reforms that Appear to Meet the Technological Criterion

Chapter 1, Elementary and Secondary Education Act of 1965, compensa-
   tory reading and arithmetic programs for children in economically
   poor families
Chicago mastery learning reading program
The Hunter teaching approach and effective teaching research*
Individually Guided Education (University of Wisconsin)
Individually Prescribed Instruction (IPI) in reading and arithmetic
Thinking as isolated skills
Competency based curricula and testing
Behavioral objectives
Electronic language laboratories
Educational television
Computers [IBM's Writing to Read]
Accountability and testing programs used as the primary route to reform
State testing programs
Aligning the curriculum to the test (curriculum alignment)
A linear research-development-diffusion model
Effective school research
Assertive Discipline
Contracting to corporations to raise test scores

                                                            (continued)

FIGURE 2. (*Continued*)

Category 3
Reforms that are Difficult to Place in Either of the Above Categories
at a General Level of Analysis

Community control of schools, New York City
Career education
Sensitivity training
Leadership in education
Mainstreaming of special education students
Coaching
Reform reports on education

---

*Discussed together but counted separately.

forms as possible. Eight reforms will be discussed in chapter 3: the new mathematics and science curriculums; the Trump High School, which in the 1960s proposed ways to reorganize secondary schools that are worth considering today; open classrooms; nongraded schools and team teaching; the Coalition of Essential Schools, Brown University; The Paideia Proposal; and a proposal for teacher education, the Carnegie Foundation's report, *A Nation Prepared: Teachers for the 21st Century.*

Chapter 4 describes and critiques four major reforms that are classified as technological (figure 2, category 2): Chapter 1 remedial programs funded by the federal government since 1965 under the Elementary and Secondary Education Act; the Chicago mastery learning program in reading; and the Madeline Hunter approach to teaching and the research on effective teaching. The Hunter method and the research on effective teaching are discussed in one section because each of them reflects a similar view of good teaching.

I chose these four reforms for analysis because they have touched the lives of hundreds of thousands of teachers and millions of students. All of these reforms are widely used today in our schools in the belief that they will improve learning. Their adoption is taken as evidence that the schools are responding to the demand for reform. Rarely is their educational worth assessed from the perspective of a democratic theory of education.

The last reform in the technological category to which I give major attention is Individually Guided Education, developed by the University of Wisconsin. I treat Individually Guided Education as a case study in chapter 5.

Individually Guided Education sheds some new light on reform for several reasons. It is interesting as a case study because it is a vexing mix of the technological and the intellectual and democratic theories, and thus cannot be put into either category. Second, Individually Guided Education is a comprehensive reform which anticipated, by twenty-five years, today's interest in school-based decision making, school restructuring, and the professionalization of teaching. Finally, the rich qualitative studies that show how IGE was perceived and changed in schools according to the technological or progressive beliefs of teachers and principals gives some empirical support to the seemingly impractical hypothesis that the ideas and values held by teachers—their operational theories—exert a powerful influence on the substance and quality of reform.

Two other organizational details remain. Since it would lengthen and fragment the book to discuss in the text all of the remaining fourteen reforms initially placed in the technological category, shorter analyses of some of these reforms are given in appendixes B and C. A brief discussion of reforms judged to be difficult to place in either the technological or the intellectual and democratic categories (figure 2, category 3) at a general level of analysis follows. Two of these reforms—community control of schools in New York City in the 1960s and mainstreaming special education students—remain ambiguous. There is not sufficient process or outcome data to assess the intellectual impact of these reforms in classrooms. The flavor of the other five reforms is mechanistic. The pattern of reform reports and state initiatives of the 1980s, for example, did not encourage the cultivation of thought. A continuing study by the Center for Policy Research and Education at Rutgers University, for example, paints a picture of reform that is unlikely to encourage either teachers or students to teach or learn in ways that have more intrinsic intellectual and personal value.[22]

I have chosen to direct my attention to reforms that began in the decade of the sixties. The sixties generated a pervasive interest in social reform and in education. This decade may have launched a concern with educational reform that sustained itself in conflicting ways through the seventies and the eighties. But there were stirrings of reform in the 1950s. The educational reform movement of the sixties did not self-generate in a period many think of as a watershed. I think of the 1950s as a doorway to the more turbulent 1960s. The fifties saw the last gasp of the child-centered wing of progressive education with the failure of life adjustment education. This decade gave voice to the cries of the academic critics of public education who dominated the reform movement of the sixties. The overview of the 1950s, which follows, provides an introduction to the three decades of reform I shall critique in the next three chapters.

OVERVIEW OF THE 1950s

Life adjustment education attempted to reduce the dropout rate and to make high school education a practical preparation for the student's life as a parent, worker, and citizen. Its implicit aim was to *adjust* students to the world as it is. The developers of life adjustment education believed that 60 percent of our youth would profit from it. A unit title from this general education curriculum says much about life adjustment education: Basic Urges, Wants, and Needs and Making Friends and Keeping Them.[23]

A critical public response to life adjustment education and other issues broke several decades of quietude about education. Schools were severely criticized for being godless, subversive, permissive, and muddleheaded. Diverse springs in the social headwaters fed this river of criticism. Albert Lynd's book, *Quackery in the Public Schools*, suggests the critics' patient mood in 1953. Admiral Rickover, influential with the scientific manpower establishment (as was Conant), fired his salvos in 1958. Arthur Bestor's *Educational Wastelands* was a more balanced plea for schools to rediscover the cardinal position of mind in education. McCarthyism was in the air and life was tough for any school that went beyond facts and skills or the threshold of a mortuary quietness.

The launching of Sputnik in 1957 (no dog in a ball ever caused more trouble for educators than this Russian dog in space) was the climactic social-political event that created a sense of public urgency about school reform and energized the generous federal funding of curriculum projects in mathematics and science which were underway by 1957. The University of Illinois Committee on School Mathematics began its work in 1952 and the work on a new high school physics course by the Physical Sciences Study Committee began in 1956.[24] Concern with reading, then as now, was high and Rudolf Flesch aroused much public concern with his book that purported to have the answers.

The report on the American high school by James B. Conant, which he addressed to "interested citizens," was intended to bring academic rigor to the high school. Conant was most interested in the able student and in the science and mathematics curriculum.

He recommended that able students take four years of mathematics and foreign language and three years of science. Half of the four years in English was to be given to writing, which he specified by saying that each student should write one theme each week. Conant may have anticipated the spirit of the accountability movement of the seventies and the eighties when he recommended that "a school-wide composition test should be given in every grade. . ." which was to be graded by the regular teacher and a school-wide committee in the ninth and eleventh grades. Students who did not obtain a grade on the eleventh grade composition test "commensurate with their ability as measured by an aptitude test" would be required to take a special course in composition in twelfth grade.[25]

Conant believed that if more time were allocated to academic courses the quality of the learning would automatically improve, a questionable principle that was widely adopted by many states in the eighties and by the authors of "A Nation At Risk" in 1983.[26] His recommendation for the eleventh grade composition test would be called a competency test for graduation in the eighties, with the important difference that in Conant's time testing was still the prerogative of the school faculty and not the state. The use of what amounts to an intelligence test to set the passing level for the eleventh grade composition test sounds quaint today. This recommendation reflects not only a greater faith in the validity of intelligence tests in the late 1950s than is true today, but it also no doubt implicitly takes into consideration the more homogeneous ethnic composition of the student body at that time compared to today.

The *Atlanta Constitution* hailed Conant's report as ". . . educational history in the making, and of urgent interest to American citizens," which suggests the high praise his report received from the public and from educators as well.[27]

What the *Atlanta Constitution* hailed as "history in the making" thirty years ago, however, was ignored in the commission reports written in the 1980s. The practical effects of the Conant reforms were never assessed. Our educational memory was short-circuited. We see the first example of unthoughtfulness in reform. Blue-ribbon citizen panels may want more history mandated in the schools, but they ignore it in their own work.

Some of the reforms that I shall consider in the next chapter were hailed in their day, too. Journals, conferences, and conversations were preoccupied with reforms such as the new mathematics and science. Superintendents and architects collaborated in building open classroom schools. These reforms are all but forgotten to-

This 1951 photograph shows the Queen of Commercial High School and her court. Does this picture of Savannah, Georgia, students suggest the educational complacency that so concerned the critics of the time? A social complacency? Who paid for the dresses? Might this photograph not also suggest the security of a middle class not yet threatened with the massive job losses of the 1990s? Photograph from the Cordray-Foltz Collection, Georgia Historical Society, Savannah Branch.

day, their lessons lost in a dim group memory. Since I want to put the most hopeful face on reform, I shall first discuss the reforms that appear to reflect intellectual and democratic values. These innovations offer more promise to be "reform's green fields" than those in the other categories. If there are empirical grounds for hope that our schools can improve themselves, it lies with reforms that fully meet the intellectual and democratic criterion of worth.

CHAPTER 3

REFORM'S GREEN FIELDS

Although the number of reforms that met the intellectual and democratic criterion might make a pessimist of a Mother Teresa—six of thirty-four reforms since 1960—it is a sign that options other than mechanical ones exist. I *tentatively* chose eight reforms that offered some promise of meeting my primary criterion of worth (figure 2, page 35). Some schools do choose reforms whose view of learning and teaching differs greatly from the mechanical model. The school door may not be opened wide to reforms that cultivate the intelligence of teachers and students, but the door is not completely closed either.

Five of the eight reforms come from the 1960s: the new mathematics and science curriculums; the Trump High School developed by J. Lloyd Trump, University of Illinois, and the National Association of Secondary School Principals; open classrooms; nongraded schools designed around an idea-centered curriculum; and team teaching, which is alive today in a number of schools. We must walk through the 1970s, a decade of remission for progressive-type reforms, and enter the 1980s to find the last three reforms. This decade offers the Coalition of Essential Schools, perhaps one of the most comprehensive reform efforts since Individually Guided Education in the mid-sixties; The Paideia Proposal, and the report from the Carnegie Forum on Education and the Economy, titled *A Nation Prepared: Teachers for the 21st Century*, which is one example from many proposals to professionalize teaching.

I shall begin my exposition and critique of reform with the new mathematics and science programs from the 1960s. These wide-ranging efforts left their mark on the history of reform. Another reason to begin with these curriculums is that business and political leaders are pressing their concern about the quality of mathematics and science teaching in our schools. Since mathematics and science are believed to be essential to the development of new products and America's ability to compete economically, public concern about the quality of teaching in these subjects is important. In the 1960s another single concern—national defense—pushed these subjects to the fore.

THE NEW MATHEMATICS AND THE NEW SCIENCE

The University of Illinois curriculum in mathematics for grades nine through eleven presents mathematics as a "consistent, unified discipline; to lead students to 'discover' principles for themselves. . . ." The Illinois developers believed that it was important for students to become so immersed in mathematics that they would develop an *intuitive* grasp of its fundamental principles—an educational goal that was retained despite the difficulty in formulating satisfactory criteria to evaluate its attainment.[1]

The University of Illinois Committee on School Mathematics began its work in 1951. Max Beberman, the intellectual force behind the program, suggested two ideas to guide this program. First, the discovery method in the University of Illinois curriculum was to be used to encourage doing, rather than listening, by the student. Premature verbalization is discouraged. John Goodlad quotes Beberman as saying, "Precision in exposition is something we expect of the textbook and the teacher. . . . [C]orrect *action* is a characteristic of a good learner." Verbalization comes only after the student has had the opportunity to test and refine the generalization. Beberman's second idea refers to the social limits imposed by small-step, programmed texts or materials. Although Beberman was interested in using programmed-type materials for limited objectives, he was reluctant to use them in basic teaching for fear of eliminating the "electric charge" of group interaction.[2] There is a hint here that the language and social environments in which learning occurs are important. Although the curriculum is designed for all students, many students are expected to drop out by grade ten. Expenditures were estimated to be approximately $1 million annually after 1964. The UICSM project was funded by the National Science Foundation.[3]

The School Mathematics Study Group (SMSG) has no "official point of view" on mathematics education, according to its chairman, but it stresses concepts and their relationships. SMSG uses conventional topics rather than introducing new content into its K–12 curriculum. Opportunities are provided to develop an intuitive awareness of mathematics. Students are encouraged to move to progressively higher levels of abstraction and to develop a feeling for mathematical structure. The National Science Foundation awarded $6 million to support the SMSG project from its inception in 1958 until 1963.[4]

No project acronym was more widely known in the 1960s than "PSSC," which referred to the new physics course developed by the Physical Sciences Study Committee. A group of physicists in Cambridge, Massachusetts, developed this course because they believed that the standard physics course offered in high schools did not present the content or spirit of modern physics. PSSC introduced new content and emphasized understanding basic concepts in physics rather than memorization. The developers of the course tried to achieve a more conceptual understanding of physics: topics were fewer and covered in more depth, laboratory work was given greater emphasis, and supporting materials such as films were created to introduce future topics or to present experiments for duplication. Other materials included laboratory experiments and apparatus, books on special topics, tests, and a textbook. The course was more rigorous than conventional courses, according to its developers, and paid less attention to technological applications. The PSSC staff reported that between 1958 and 1963 approximately four thousand teachers participated in PSSC-sponsored institutes to learn how to teach the course. In 1962–63 these teachers taught 170,000 students, or about 45 percent of all students who took physics that year.[5]

A number of curriculum projects were launched in chemistry, among which were the Chemical Bond Approach (CBA) and Interdisciplinary Approaches to Chemistry (IAC). CBA is built on the assumption that the bonds—the ties between atoms—*are* chemistry. This course follows the 1960s developmental pattern. It was written by a group of chemists who wanted to improve high-school and freshman college chemistry by stressing the conceptual structure by which chemists organize their knowledge. The conceptual values in CBA chemistry are given practical effect by building the course around one big idea—chemical bonds—and by the developers' assumption that if a student in an introductory chemistry course knew well a few central concepts, she could relate new and old learning to these concepts and be better able to solve new problems. The course stresses theory-based logical argument through use of "mental models." In one interesting exercise the student is confronted with a "black box," which he shakes, twists, and rolls while observing the reactions of the contents within the box. He tries to match these observations with deductions made from the mental model he has chosen for this activity. The CBA course was completed between 1957 and 1963 at Reed College, Portland, Oregon. The National Science Foundation spent approximately $1.3 million in its development.[6]

The Interdisciplinary Approaches to Chemistry (IAC), developed at the University of Maryland in 1972, went against the 1960 axioms that influenced most of the major curriculum reform projects in that decade in its assumptions about the aims of a chemistry course for high school students. The course is built on a group of modules that form a unified whole rather than on a text. The modules permit greater flexibility and give the teacher the power to decide what modules are to be taught and in what sequence. The module topics include standard content such as "Diversity and Periodicity," but they also include two modules that give the course an interdisciplinary quality: "Earth and its Neighbors" (geochemistry) and "The Delicate Balance" (environmental). A second difference is that the developers of IAC believed that the students' attitudes toward chemistry were as important as their acquisition of chemical concepts. Trowbridge and Bybee quote a statement by IAC's developers that they did not want students to feel that chemistry was a dry unrealistic science "but an exciting, relevant human activity that can be enjoyable to study."[7]

The Biological Science Curriculum Study (BSCS) began its work in 1959 to teach science as a way of thinking that would be within the grasp "of all but the very weakest students at the tenth-grade level." The National Science Foundation spent $6.5 million to develop three versions of the course based on fundamental biological concepts.[8] Although each of the three versions differs in emphasis, nine themes run through each version, which include evolution, genetic continuity, the relationship between organisms and their environment, science as inquiry, and the history of biological concepts. Principles rather than the applications of biology to human affairs are stressed.[9]

The BSCS course was well received throughout the country. Two versions of the course are still available. Trowbridge and Bybee, one of whom is associated with BSCS, report that the new science curricula are more effective than their traditional counterparts, and that BSCS was more effective than any of the others.[10]

How Good Were the 1960's Mathematics and Science Courses?

Reviewers of these courses agree that the secondary mathematics and science curriculums stressed the major concepts in a discipline, and organized these subjects in the way that scholars in these fields think about them. Reviewers also argue that these courses offered students a way to use the scholar's methods of inquiry, including less tangible elements such as "good guessing" and intuitive ideas. The developers assumed students of average and higher ability could profitably study chemistry or mathematics using the scholar's specialized methods and scheme of conceptual organization.[11] Such practices reflect much of the substance and ideology that made curriculum development in science and mathematics the elixir of reform in the 1960s. They reflect, too, many of the ideas in Jerome Bruner's book, *The Process of Education*, published in 1961.[12] This book gave voice to the ideas expressed by a group of thirty-five scientists, mathematicians, and psychologists who gathered at Woods Hole on Cape Cod in 1959 to appraise science and mathematics education. Bruner's book, offered as the door opened on an active period of reform, extolled a philosophy that was followed with remarkable consistency by most of the curriculum reforms in the 1960s, a consistency that suggests the power of political and social events to direct educational reform. In many ways educators are but paper kites tethered to a short social string.

I conclude that the substance and spirit of the reforms in mathematics and science meet the intellectual side of our criterion that fundamental reform be intellectual and democratic. It is on the democratic side of the criterion, however, that most of the reforms in science and mathematics fail.

The new science and mathematics curriculums developed during the 1960s failed to meet the democratic criterion in several ways. These curriculums were developed by disciplinary scholars in relative isolation from teachers and professors of education, who had a legitimate interest in their work. The aims, content, and methods were thus based on one perspective—the disciplinary— and broader perspectives and experience had little chance to influence the *premises* on which these curriculums were developed. Second, the new curriculums were accepted by the more affluent communities for students in college preparatory programs. Rural and less affluent urban schools did not participate extensively in this reform.[13] Students of average ability were unwittingly excluded from enjoying the benefits of these courses although it was not the scholars' intention to exclude them. Finally, and most important, the scholar-developed programs in science and mathematics did not value the humanistic import of their disciplines nor did they discern the relationship of their specialized knowledge to critical social concerns—an omission that ignores the general education aim of public and private education. This omission, particularly in the case of science, seriously undermines its educational value as a liberal study.[14] The university view that values knowledge-creation through isolated and relatively pure disciplines, in other words, is counter-productive when this view is uncritically applied to elementary or secondary schools and, indeed, to liberal arts studies within the university itself.

How might we explain the omission of many essential elements in a curriculum model developed by scholars in science and mathematics? It is clear according to Dewey's theories, for example, that the *social significance* of the content taught—its general educational purpose—is critically important in a democratic society. It follows that all students, not only those who are socially privileged, must learn.

The developers and sponsors of the new curriculums in mathematics and science made an understandable if obvious error: they too easily derived equivalents between the content and methods in mathematics and science (one way of looking at the world, whose end is to build knowledge) and education (a related but different way of looking at the world, whose ends are to build a personal and social *predisposition* to the world—ways of thinking, feeling, and acting). They abstracted ideas and values from the disciplinary studies, and from this limited source constructed a loose theory of education that gave too little attention to students, to teachers, and to the proper humanistic and democratic demands on their specialized subject matter. The advocates of the new curriculums gave exclusive attention to one set of abstractions in science and mathematics, but the remainder of things—those excluded from the abstraction— were essential to the field of education and thus their ways of thinking distorted the *social* meaning of science.

Education is a larger and more complex category than any single discipline, whether that discipline be science or psychology, a condition that accounts for both its joy and its devilish frustration. Education is itself; it cannot be reduced to any combination of isolated disciplines, to management, or to something it is not.

The most serious deficiency of the new curriculums was the neglect of the humanistic and social import of their disciplines. This neglect undermined the democratic value of these studies and clouded their role in general education. I shall use science as my example. A similar line of thought applies to any subject.

Since John Dewey's philosophy is one major perspective from which I approach reform, I will use his ideas to frame science as a humanistic study possessing great social import. To give not only the content but the texture of Dewey's thought, I will use his words drawn from the chapter in *Democracy and Education* blandly titled "Science in the Course of Study," which more provocatively might well have been titled "Science as a Social Study."

Dewey criticizes the false notion that literary and historical studies are exclusively humanistic and that science is not. This view cripples the educational use of both studies.

> Human life does not occur in a vacuum, nor is nature a mere stage setting for the enactment of its drama. . . . Man's life is bound up in the processes of nature; his career, for success or defeat, depends upon the way in which nature enters it. Man's power of deliberate control of his own affairs depends upon ability to direct natural energies to use: an ability which is in turn dependent on insight into nature's processes. *Whatever natural science may be for the specialist, for educational purposes it is knowledge of the conditions of human action.* To be aware of the medium in which social intercourse goes on, and of the means and obstacles to its progressive development, is to be in command of a knowledge which is thoroughly humanistic in quality. One who is ignorant of the history of science is ignorant of the struggles by which mankind has passed from routine and caprice . . . to intellectual self-possession. That science may be taught as a set of formal and technical exercises is only too true. This happens whenever information about the world is made an end in itself. [This failure does not mean that science is antithetical to humanistic concerns], but [is] evidence of a wrong educational attitude [emphasis added].[15]

Dewey sees the rationality of science as an intellectual means to surmount the merely local and customary and to open intellectual vistas whereby the scientist's knowledge "[is] put at the disposal of all men. Thus ultimately and philosophically science is the organ of general social progress."[16]

To Dewey, science is permeated by the requirements of the social. It is not merely technical in its knowledge nor does its social significance arise, as many today believe, from the technology that may be invented from its findings, whether this technology be laser-optic surgery or laser-guided missiles. Science, to Dewey, meant nothing less than an intelligent transformation of social ends. To progress only in ends already sought is a "minor form of progress" because it improves one's technical means and leaves untouched old purposes and the hard thinking required if society is to strive for even more worthy ends. Such progress is merely technical progress and is neither social nor humanistic in spirit. After recounting the inventions of his day as examples of science's ability to perfect "control of means of action"—inventions such as the telephone and telegraph, electric motors, railways, and aeroplanes, all fruits of the industrial revolution—Dewey again warns that technical progress alone does not "modify the quality of human purposes." Given that science [Dewey means here open inquiry unfettered by imposed constraints] must transform social ends, it is education's responsibility to use science "to modify [society's] habitual attitude of imagination and feeling, not leave it just an extension of our physical arms and legs. . . . To subjugate disease is no longer a dream; the hope of abolishing poverty is not utopian."[17] Pragmatist he was. And dreamer, too.

The Deweyan educational criterion demands that what is learned in school be both intellectually and socially significant. This is a tough standard to meet, but this fact does not mean that it has little theoretical or practical importance. To be "intellectually and socially significant" means that problems are identified for study that are within the student's present experience and understanding; that pursuit of these problems leads the student to new ideas and facts; that these new ideas provide the ground from which new problems arise; and that these problems in turn open access to new subject matter. This process "is a continuous spiral."[18] But to only pursue problems is educationally inadequate if two conditions are not met. The content learned must be progressively organized into more *logical* form until, over the years from elementary school to high school, it comes close to the view held by the adult specialist in science or history.[19] But this more conceptual organization of subject matter is not an end in itself. The more conceptual understanding of a subject—what was called "the structure of a discipline" in the 1960s—is a *means* "by which social relations, distinctively human ties and bonds, may be understood and more intelligently ordered."[20]

Most of the new science and mathematics curriculums ably confronted the conceptual organization of their subjects, but they failed to see the humanistic and democratic significance of their subject matter. No subject matter, however elegantly tailored within its disciplinary boundaries, is complete if its relations to important social realities are untended.

If the scholars preoccupied with the conceptual structure of mathematics and science neglected teachers and the organizational structure of the school, J. Lloyd Trump and his associates emphasized the school and paid less attention to what the school taught.

THE TRUMP HIGH SCHOOL

The prestigious 1960 reforms of what was to be taught in schools might be compared to a hypothetical effort by a group of French chefs to improve the quality of American restaurants by offering a more sophisticated menu—from Paris. One misses in these efforts the noise and smells and the bustle in the kitchen. J. Lloyd Trump and his associates from the National Association of Secondary School Principals boldly entered the kitchen and tried to change the menu by questioning the way restaurant managers viewed their customers, scheduled time and their staffs, and organized the rooms and physical facilities. The optimism that must shine in the souls of all reformers is suggested in the authors' statement that their report "is the story of the coming of a new kind of secondary education in America."[21]

Trump believed that students need more chances to develop individual responsibility and the skills of independent study. The modern high school is too concerned with control. This overdirection means that "too many students find it difficult to [be] on their own when they reach college or go to work on a job." The "ordered regularity" of the daily schedule dulls "any lingering wonder, any curiosity" that students might feel. The school should be concerned with developing minds that have the capacity to inquire, to be critical of what they read and hear.[22]

Time is radically reorganized in this school of the future, which was conceived in 1961. Flexibility in scheduling is encouraged by dividing the day into twenty-minute modules instead of forty-five-minute periods. "Electronic devices" then coming into use would make it possible to vary a student's schedule each day to encourage sustained work in continuing projects. One essential feature of the Trump plan is the unusual way that time is allocated. Eighteen hours each week are given to large- and small-group learning, of which six hours is to be spent in small-group discussion with fifteen or fewer students. Small-group discussion will give teachers the opportunity to assess the student's ability "to handle data and solve problems" and to see how the students treat one another.[23] Twelve hours each week will be devoted to independent study. Most students would spend thirty hours per week in studying the regular school subjects. Teachers will find their time governed by the needs of teaching "rather by the insistence of the bell."[24]

Trump reports that "[a]n hour-long movie, 'And No Bells Ring,' released in 1960, met with heavy demand from schools all over the country. . ." and was widely shown on television.[25]

Teachers are not forgotten in Trump's vision of the new high school. Teacher differences will be recognized through team teaching, differentiated assignments, and salary differentials. The educational philosophy and the size of the school will determine the particular ways in which time, curriculum, and students and teachers come together. Financial rewards will be provided for talented and career teachers so that many might be able to earn "salaries of $15,000 to $20,000, and possibly more."[26]

When I compare the academic and sophisticated curriculum reforms of the 1960s to Trump's report titled *Guide to Better Schools: Focus on Change*, I am struck by the flavor of thinking in each, although the quality of this common element is not the same. The reforms in science and mathematics, for example, focused with narrow intensity on content while ignoring teachers and the social and organizational setting in which education occurs in life. Trump and his colleagues, on the other hand, are imaginatively aware of the organizational and social setting in which learning and teaching take place, while taking for granted the content to be learned. An impatience with thinking too deeply about curriculum is indicated when Trump advises schools "that many meetings spent in redefining goals merely postpones [curricular] reorganization by that much time."[27] That wheelspinning can occur in discussing goals is no reason to assert the neglect of goals as a principle. Thoughtfully chosen goals suggest criteria for content selection, learning processes, governance, and other important elements in education. I wish that the reformers in the disciplines had joined forces with Trump and his colleagues. Trump's sophisticated understanding of schools and the people in them would have helped the scholars to create a more comprehensive attack on the curriculum and the way schools are organized. This cleavage is a good illustration of the substantive differences between a competent academic approach to schools and reform and an equally competent professional approach to schools and reform. This split in reform approaches between the two groups is rooted in a false theory-practice dualism, which Dewey never tired of criticizing.

Although Trump did not pay direct attention to curriculum in 1960, he was no stranger to curricular reform. Trump headed the Waukegan, Illinois, high school from 1944 to 1947. Waukegan's high school faced a 40 percent dropout rate. Trump reflected a kind of progressive eclecticism in his reforms, which included a night school for adults, a guidance and health program, and an expanded athletic program to involve more students. Perhaps in an effort to motivate the half of the entering students who were reading below the ninth grade level, Trump introduced a fuzzy-headed course called "Self-Appraisal and Orientation" designed to orient students to the school.[28] Here we see the worst aspects of one wing of progressivism that worshipped the child and ignored his mind. Students liked Trump. In the 1946 yearbook they praised his reforms and commended him on his "democratic administration."[29]

Trump's concern with developing the student's capacity to inquire and explore, and the explicit support for this inquiry provided by independent study and small-group discussion and his other recommendations, leads me to conclude that the intellectual requirement in my criterion has been met, my criticism above notwithstanding. Trump also makes clear recommendations in his report to involve students and the community and others with a stake in reform to make it a democratic effort (which I did not detail).[30]

While the academic scholars and the humanistic psychologists wrote their dreams through the medium of new curricula in the sciences and social studies, and while James Bryant Conant and Trump spun their recommendations for the reformation of the high school in reports to citizens and administrators, another group of educators was trying to reform elementary schools. This group of educators, primarily practitioners in England and America, tried to reduce the rigidities of learning in schools by adopting an outlook and a way of teaching that is known as the "open classroom" or "open education" approach.

THE OPEN CLASSROOM

The open classroom is a learning environment that builds from the child to the subject matter. The teacher's job is to lead the student, to be sure, but to lead indirectly by using the child's normal curiosity to touch, feel, and manipulate things; to lead by building on the child's need to explore and find out by doing simple science "experiments" or by encouraging the child to read by providing a "reading corner" that abounds in interesting books. The teacher does more "pointing" than "pushing," compared to traditional teaching. Physical movement and conversation are not seen as something to be repressed until recess but as potential energy to be harnessed in activities such as counting and measuring, discussing a story, writing a spooky play and acting it out, making a topographical map, or, in the higher elementary grades, plotting data derived from an experiment in biology. There is also direct teaching and drill as necessary, but, proponents say, these take place within a context that has meaning to the student, which makes a great difference in the intellectual quality of what is learned.

A good open classroom teacher takes her kids as they are, in their uniqueness and similarities, and encourages a desire to learn through learning itself. Learning generates learning, open educators believe. Who among us, for example, can doubt the truth of this abstraction after seeing the light of earned satisfaction on the face of a six-year-old who sees the words of her dictated story take life in print as the teacher writes them on a flip chart for the world to see and invites Mary to attest to their authorship by signing it and later, perhaps, reading her story to others? Mary is learning something about symbols and sounds to be sure, but she also learns that words-on-paper should make sense, that she has some power of command with these new things, and that she feels good about the *social* experience. What can properly be called "soft" about experiences such as these? If the child acts and makes decisions within a *rich environment created by an adult* that is calculated to tap the desire to learn, the quality of learning should be high.

Vito Perrone suggests some of the directive ideas that underlie open classroom environments when he writes that unlike the post-Sputnik reforms, open education raises fundamental questions

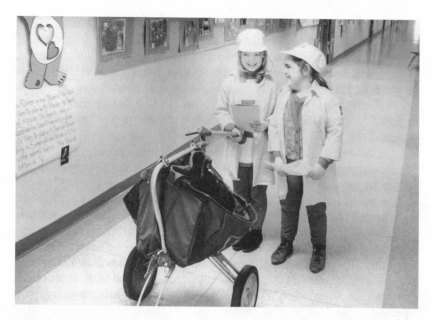

Two happy postgirls are delivering the student mail. The letters written by kids to kids are as authentic as the U.S. postal cart and the shoulder patches. Mail volume is high, writing "production" is rising, and dividends of student interest are coming in based on an informal assessment of this project. This mail activity seems to have successfully resolved the tension inherent in the progressive effort to arouse interest and make learning meaningful without trivializing content. Photograph by Laurence Kesterson. Photograph courtesy of the Owen J. Roberts School District.

about learning, childhood, and what teachers think and do. Open education raises questions about the aims of the school and reaffirms that learning is a personal matter that varies with different children. Perrone believes that learning proceeds best when children are actively engaged in their own learning in a variety of settings in and out of school. And not least, learning requires that children and childhood be taken seriously.[31] These ideas have practical force because they reflect Perrone's experience in working with hundreds of experienced teachers when he was dean of the New School at the University of North Dakota, which linked the elementary schools in that state to an imaginative teacher education program at the University.

One very strong influence on the open classroom movement in America was the experience of educators in England with the new

English primary schools that grew rapidly after World War II. Many educators and writers made near-mandatory trips to London and Leicestershire County to observe English primary schools, among them was Charles Silberman, who devotes two chapters in his book to the English schools. Silberman states that the publication in 1967 of the Plowden report, *Children and Their Primary Schools*, sparked interest in this approach to education in England and America.[32]

If we think of the Plowden report as being comparable to some of the prestigious reports on American education that were published in the eighties, the difference in philosophy is stark. One example will make the point. The Plowden Commission posed these questions: "Is there any . . . conflict between education based on children as they are, and education thought of primarily as a preparation for the future? Has 'finding out' proved to be better than being told? Have methods been worked out through which discovery can be stimulated and guided, and children develop from it a coherent body of knowledge? Do children learn more through active cooperation than by passive obedience?"[33] These questions, and the affirmative answers that the Plowden Commission gave to them, suggest the active qualities of mind and the cooperative nature of the social experience among students and their teachers that should mark learning for children six to eleven years old.

Many teachers, too, would have answered "yes" to the questions posed by the Plowden Commission if they had had the opportunity to choose a more informal way of teaching, or if they had had the chance to grow more slowly into it when the open classrooms were being tried in their school. Often this condition did not prevail as administrators built "classrooms without walls" as an architectural fad or used the idea of open classrooms to snare federal or private grants that abounded in the sixties. Roland Barth's book *Open Education in the American School* is a two-year study by a participant of how a grant coupled with an ill-considered, top-down decision by the superintendent to try open education in two urban elementary schools led to teacher demoralization and racial hostility in the school's first year.[34] At the end of two years in 1970, Barth could say that the school was successfully moving *toward* more informal classrooms. Barth's observation is made in the context of an eleven-day inservice program for parents, teachers, and aides in which the tough practical problems of working out a more intellectual and socially active way of learning were carefully addressed.[35] *Open Education* is a realistic account of the intellectual and political struggles fundamental reform entails.

The two elementary schools in New Haven, Connecticut, of which Barth wrote are not open schools today. By 1975 this phase had ended. But they are not standard schools. They were the first schools in which James Comer of Yale University worked out his "power school" idea that closely links schools to their communities and to parents.

A great deal of misty-eyed nonsense was perpetuated under the name of open classrooms as concerns with more interesting and mind-engaging ways of teaching became a fad by the early seventies. Educators regressed to romantic child-centered notions of "progressivism" in which the whims of the child too easily replaced the mature judgment of the teacher. Eschewing theory and disdainful of history, many open classroom reformers repeated the mistakes made by some progressive reformers in the 1930s whom Dewey criticized in *Experience and Education.*[36]

Reforms were underway in the high schools, too, some of which echoed the values of the open classroom. I will mention only a few whose very names prompt a feeling of loss in many who took the moonbeam ride that, in retrospect, was part of reform in the sixties. Schools such as Harlem Prep, B. Frank Brown's Melbourne Florida High School, and the Parkway Program in Philadelphia shone brightly in their time. When it began in 1969 the Parkway Program was perhaps the first "school without walls" in the country. The Metro School in Chicago soon followed and adopted the Parkway idea of using community institutions to educate. It was not long before "every major city had its special kind of 'Parkway' school. . . ."[37] The Murray Road Annex of the Newton, Massachusetts, High School, encouraged students to take responsibility for their own education while permitting students and teachers to create and manage the curriculum. The John Adams High School in Portland, Oregon, was built on an ambitious idea —perhaps too ambitious—that required this ethnically diverse urban school to organize itself into four houses of 320 students each, to provide a strong program of general education and, in addition, to educate preservice and inservice teachers, to do research, and to develop curriculum materials![38]

The Parkway Program survived, albeit as a somewhat faded image of its youthful self. The John Adams High School's life as an innovative school ended in 1981, a life span of twelve years, because students in its attendance area had to go there and their parents wanted a more traditional kind of education. Although declining enrollments and a public perception that the school was too student-centered were factors in its decline, "it would have been a huge success as a voluntary school" according to a school district official.[39]

Reform-minded public schools do not enjoy long lives. Small in numbers even in the early seventies, there are relatively few today. Nontraditional schools do not easily graft to the centralized and manual-directed education that prevails. This is a condition that the radical reformers in the Free School movement of the sixties, such as Paul Goodman and Allen Graubard, pondered. There is something about the density of our social water that will not long float humane reforms that try to make every kid a "swimmer."

Although open classrooms did not hold the attention of educators for long, I believe the idea of the open classroom as I have stated it is consistent with the intellectual and democratic criterion.

NONGRADED SCHOOLS AND TEAM TEACHING

Many of the experimental elementary and secondary schools of the sixties and early seventies tried new ways of organizing students and teachers to make school a more personally satisfying place to be. Sometimes new organizational patterns were not deliberately sought but simply came with school: when twenty-three children ages five to thirteen met four teachers in the First Street School of which George Dennison writes, "nongradedness" was present from the start in the philosophy of the school and in its small size.[40]

Nongraded schools and team teaching were devised in the 1960s to counter the curricular and teaching uniformities of the graded school. The graded school assigns pupils of the same age to one teacher: six-year olds to the first grade, nine-year-olds to the fourth grade, and so forth. Graded schools are the kind of schools most of us attended and that our children attend. This description of the American graded school, invented in 1848, is humdrum. It is the history of the graded school that is amazing.

Since one of the themes of this book is that educational reform will never be intelligent until policymakers and reformers learn a bit of history, it will not be a digression to use the rise of the graded school and its stubborn resistance to reformation as a salutary case study.

What did the graded school replace? Why a nongraded school, of course! But a nongraded school whose "class size" defies belief. Here is one example. In 1823 Boston was building schools with rooms to seat 300 students. This class of 300 was taught by a master teacher and two assistants (is this a career ladder?). Providence, Rhode Island, had a grammar school that seated 228 students on a single floor. This large ungraded classroom was taught by a master teacher and two assistants, who were responsible for teaching many subjects to students whose ages and abilities covered a wide range.[41]

As a former teacher of progressive bent, I have nothing but admiration for any three adults who had the courage to enter a room of 200 to 300 students with the intention of teaching. Given these conditions, it is little wonder that Horace Mann and other educators were impressed by the Prussian schools of the time that classified scholars by age and grade.

If Nobel prizes were given to educators whose innovations span centuries rather than a few decades at most, John Philbrick would be a Nobel winner. Philbrick created the graded school we have today in 1848 in Boston, Massachusetts. Philbrick's graded school had four floors, the first three of which were classrooms. Each classroom housed fifty-six students of similar age and one teacher. The single greatest innovation of this school was its provision of a separate room for each teacher and a desk for each student. One can imagine the anxiety reduction in teachers who pondered the new pupil-to-teacher ratios! No wonder Philbrick's school attracted national attention. The fourth floor contained a large assembly hall and the design provided for a separate principal's office. It is clear that Philbrick saw men as administrators and women as teachers. The principal, Philbrick writes, would have one male assistant "and ten female assistants, one for each room."[42]

Philbrick's school valued uniformity of curriculum and teaching, and it valued efficiency. The principal supervised his teachers to ensure that uniformity was enforced. A hierarchical, bureaucratic pattern of school organization thus entered American education to the cheers of all, in part because it was so much better than what it replaced. The graded school is the only major reform I can think of that has lasted in its original form more than a few weeks in historical time. The proponents of the nongraded elementary school wanted to break the uniformity created by the graded school of 1848.

Nongraded Schools

The idea behind a nongraded school is to permit students to progress through the curriculum at their own pace. This is one way to build on the wide range of individual differences to be found in any group of thirty-five children and to circumvent the "horizontal blocks" to individual progress imposed by the standard grades in a graded school. "Continuous progress" catches this idea. How is individual progress to be accomplished? Reorganize the curriculum along vertical strands or threads that run through the school's curriculum. These vertical strands are to be built around concepts that suggest both the content to be taught and appropriate learning activities. One concept in the social studies, for example, might be "climate, land features, and natural resources have profound effects on man," according to John Goodlad and Robert Anderson. By building the elementary school curriculum around "big ideas" that can be stated as global objectives, a framework is given to each subject and to the curriculum as a whole. Appropriate skills and values can also be related to the conceptual strands as teachers rework the school's curriculum.[43]

By organizing the curriculum around vertical strands, Goodlad and Anderson say, the content is not horizontally prepackaged by grade level, which implies that learners must pace themselves to the content. The teacher in a nongraded school, therefore, is free to use the thematic units or topics and in this way *select her own content* in accordance with the broad conceptual criteria set by the strands. This freedom also encourages teachers, proponents say, to select units that reflect student interests and needs in a way that is often precluded by textbook teaching.

The idea of the nongraded school that I have summarized requires a reconstruction in the way teachers and principals think about curriculum and teaching. That this reconstruction was not undertaken by many schools that claimed to be nongraded is a defect I will return to when I assess this proposal against my criteria for fundamental reform.

Team Teaching

"Teaching teams fit no one pattern," J. Lloyd Trump wrote in 1961.[44] Trump gives examples of team teaching that were being done in several of the "hot" experimental high schools at the time. Newton South High School, Newton, Massachusetts, divided its fifteen hundred students among three houses, each of which included students across grades ten through twelve. In this school, team teaching is a piece of a more encompassing innovation, the house plan, which is designed to personalize the students' experience in a large school and to improve communication among the faculty.[45] The other high school in Newton—Newton High School—emphasized the role of the teacher-lecturer who gives large group presentations and supervises liberal arts graduates who "step directly into teaching" by becoming members of the team for two years.[46]

Team teaching is still around and it is well done in a number of schools. The Marticville Middle School, Pequea, Pennsylvania, is one of them, a school whose work on other issues of reform I know. In this middle school, made up of grades seven and eight, team teaching is one component in a comprehensive effort to improve the quality of learning and teaching.

Marticville's students are assigned to teams without regard to the students' achievement, except in reading, where provisions are made for students who need help. I will briefly describe the seventh grade team structure and give one example of a school-wide learning activity developed by this team.

Grade 7 has three academic teams, each of which is responsible for 130 students. Each team has four academic teachers. Specialist teachers such as art teachers, librarians, or counselors "float," as needed, to teams. Each teaching team has a chair appointed by the principal and one teacher whose responsibility is staff development. Team chairs meet once a week with the principal to discuss issues relating to the school that they or the principal want to bring up. These meetings are part of a plan to involve teachers in decision making. Each team meets for two hours every six days. Topics discussed by the team rotate as needed among three major areas: staff development; guidance; and "kid day," when the team shares information about particular children who may be having problems or who may have done something of worth that should be known among the team's teachers.

The school-wide recycling project is one example of how teachers exercise initiative in curriculum at Marticville. This thematic unit became the focus for academic work and offered a way to give students some insight into the environmental concerns of their community.

The recycling project grew out of the seventh grade teams' concern to teach something important about the environment that was within the grasp of twelve-year olds. The students in the school explored the idea of recycling for one year. Some of the work in their science, social studies, and other classes were given to environmental issues. The children had many direct experiences that provided grist for the writing and oral language mill: they visited a landfill, heard their state senator talk about the mandatory recycling law, discussed the ideas related to leachate in landfills with a biology professor, wrote letters to McDonalds about their plans for recycling, and started a recycling center in the school which collected 2500 pounds of school paper.[47]

Was the recycling project "any good"? The teachers believed that the recycling unit aroused student interest and integrated some of the content from science, social studies, and the language arts, which, all things considered, is better than a steady diet of routine teaching.

Team teaching and nongraded schools take many forms, a condition that may be both their potential strength and weakness when they are sought by large numbers of schools as a kind of "reform trophy."

I find nothing inherent in nongraded schools or team teaching as ideas that would make them anti-intellectual or undemocratic. Goodlad and Anderson insist in *The Nongraded School* that a better curriculum organized around concepts, and a learning-teaching process that enhances the intellectual and social capacities of students, provide the educational reasons for a nongraded school. The Marticville Middle School's way of team teaching, on the other hand, leads to curriculum improvement, involves teachers in important educational decisions, and attempts to move beyond standard practice in helping students realize their intellectual and social capacities—all of which is consistent with my criterion for fundamental reform. I believe that nongraded schools and team teaching are fundamental reforms. There is nothing in their conception that precludes a more thoughtful and democratic approach to learning and teaching.

Despite their potential for developing schools that try to achieve a higher standard of intellectual achievement and a more humane process—a process that does not routinely slot students into impersonal learning situations—nongraded schools and team teaching were too often viewed as only *organizational* variables to be manipulated rather than an opportunity to reform learning, teaching, and curriculum. John Goodlad and Robert Anderson assessed the failure of the nongraded school in these words: "[W]e confess to deep concern over the superficiality and inadequacy of much that is being done in the name of nongrading. Many of the so-called nongraded programs are little different from the graded plans they replaced, and except for a 'levels' scheme in reading there are few changes of real significance to children."[48]

By the mid-seventies nongraded schools and, to a lesser degree, team teaching were no longer tied to the reform agenda. They passed

The merits of creating a better mix of physical space, time, teacher talents, and new technologies such as television were exciting topics of discussion in the 1960s. Team teaching and the Trump High School were attempts to make a better mix to support learning and teaching. The large group instruction room in this middle school built in 1968 reflects that era. Attempts are now being made to modify the school's traditional structure. The picture shows the room being used for an inservice meeting. Photograph by Richard A. Gibboney. Photograph courtesy of the Owen J. Roberts School District.

into history, unsung and unlamented. Other reforms replaced them. Few bothered to think about either their substance or the mechanical way they were often implemented. A lesson had been taught but not learned.

More than nongraded schools passed into the night of history. The new mathematics and science programs are all but forgotten today. Once in a while a student who had taken the new mathematics volunteers an unkind word in my class. Science teaching today presents facts in simplified form, frets over vocabulary, and all but ignores concepts prized by some teachers in the 1960s. Over 90 percent of science curriculums ignore social issues.[49] We have retreated from even the tenuous conceptual advances made by some reformers three decades ago. It is unsettling to realize how little is left from the high hopes and almost compulsive reform activity that many thought were to be the Golden Years of Reform.

Of the three remaining reforms that I tentatively believed offered some hope of engaging intellectual and democratic values, I can discuss only one in detail because of space limitations. I have chosen to discuss the Coalition of Essential Schools because it has reached a large number of high schools since 1985 and it is widely known. The long run success or failure of the Coalition will say much about the capacity of American public education to reform itself. The Coalition of Essential Schools and The Paideia Proposal met the intellectual and democratic criterion of worth; the proposal on teaching, *A Nation Prepared: Teachers for the 21st Century*, sponsored by the Carnegie Foundation, failed to meet this criterion. I used primary sources in the description and analysis of each of these reforms. Summaries of the full critique of Paideia and *A Nation Prepared* will be given after the Coalition of Essential Schools has been discussed.

THE COALITION OF ESSENTIAL SCHOOLS

Theodore Sizer understands Horace Smith, who, at fifty-three, is a proud and committed English teacher. Horace is stimulated by teaching, he enjoys teaching—and he is drained by it. Sizer not only understands Horace, he admires and even loves him, despite the corner-cutting that Horace must do in his preparation for classes and the time he can give to each student's written work. Even after all the accommodations and compromises have been made, Sizer writes, "only *five minutes per week* of attention on the written work of each student and an average of ten minutes of planning for each fifty-odd-minute class—the task is already crushing . . . ," because Horace's work week is sixty hours (emphasis in the original).[50] In *Horace's Compromise: The Dilemma of the American High School*, Sizer directly tells about the conditions within which Horace works and in doing so provides the rationale for the Coalition of Essential Schools, whose formation coincided with the book's publication in 1984.

One hundred and nine secondary schools were part of the Coalition in 1990 along with Sizer, a professor of education at Brown University, and his small staff at Brown. Sizer is clearly "chairman of the board" for this original group of volunteer schools and for approximately 160[51] schools that have joined a larger effort mounted in 1988 by the Coalition and the Education Commission of the States, Denver, Colorado, an organization of governors and state legislators whose purpose is to help state officials develop educational policy. This expanded effort is named Re:Learning. In 1993 there were 700 schools in the Coalition and the Re:Learning project in eleven states. The annual expenditure was $7.5 million in 1993.[52]

These schools are attempting a learning-centered, grass-roots effort to demonstrate that reform of high schools is possible, in part, because it is clear that the top-down imposition by states and local school boards to "teach more of this" and "test more of that" has not worked. The top-down approach has also been tried by many academics, foundation executives, and frustrated legislators in the far and recent past. It does not work according to the Coalition view. One reason it does not work is that it compounds all of the compromises Horace must make to "keep up" with the 120 kids he "sees" each day. Imposition does not work because it violates the subtle human interactions that mandates cannot redirect. It is as if aeronautical engineers designed airplanes in stubborn refusal to recognize the complexities that gravity imposes on their grand designs.

How does the "chairman of the board" keep this confederation from blowing itself up in a wild array of well-intentioned efforts to "do better"? Coherence within diversity rests on nine common principles. To base a plan for learning and teaching on non-research-based "principles" sounds quaint today. Consultants and professors by the hundreds proffer sanitized packages of skill and technique that purport to deal with elusive qualities such as motivation, skillful thinking, discipline, fine teaching, or leadership marked by vision tempered with caution. Worse, to some minds steeped in the empirical tradition of fact over idea, the principles posed by the Coalition come from "hoary old chestnuts of pedagogical commitment," Sizer writes.[53] Hardly the stuff for a refereed journal in education, let alone a hoped-for national movement. Two principles are specific: no Coalition teacher may have responsibility for more than eighty students, and the per pupil cost in Coalition schools cannot exceed 110 percent of the cost in neighboring schools.

The third Coalition principle rests on ideology, "that of a democratic faith." "It posits," Sizer says, "that in a democracy all citizens must be able to use their minds well, and must be able to function thoughtfully as critical patriots and effective members of society, its communities, and work force." Other principles embrace values that suggest teachers should teach fewer topics more deeply; that academics should be the priority of *all* students; that schools should not be impersonal places for students (hence the eighty-students-per-teacher requirement); that learning demands the active involvement of students (students are workers and the teachers are coaches); that multiple-choice examinations be replaced by essays and projects that encourage response to important questions and thus demonstrate the student's mastery of course content; and that teachers should perceive themselves as teachers and scholars in general education first and as specialists second.[54]

Students who enter high school and who are deficient in reading and writing and elementary mathematics must be retaught because such students will not be able to engage the in-depth curriculum that the Coalition schools are trying to create. Developing the mind, accepting more personal responsibility for learning, and mastering a limited number of academic disciplines is impossible for a student who struggles to read simple material. Students are expected to be taught in a way that will enable them to reach reasonable external standards of achievement. This is where Sizer's idea of demonstrating mastery comes in. Students must *show* that they have learned something by transforming what was learned into new forms. The senior students in Racine's Walden III, a Coalition school in Wisconsin, must demonstrate mastery in fifteen areas of competence by completing a portfolio on eight topics which include an autobiography, a record of books read and scores on reading tests, a written report that analyzes the mass media, a project in American history in the form of a paper that must be defended before one's peers and teacher, and six public oral presentations in a range of subjects.[55] Other schools will work out the mastery exhibition in their own way. Walden III's approach is exhaustive and a bit intimidating even to the eye of one who knows the limitations of multiple-choice tests.

Another approach to mastery is offered by the Crefeld School, a small private school located in Chestnut Hill, Pennsylvania. Crefeld has developed a comprehensive list of competencies for graduation that include content, skills, and attitudes. The descriptors along the road to mastery and excellence range from "none" or "entry," points at which the student first encounters the competency, through "working to mastery." At the point of mastery the student has completed all of the required work and can give full responses to questions or perform a skill competently on a regular basis. "Excellence," the last point assessed by Crefeld, reflects work beyond the school's requirement and may include work on an independent project or giving help to other students who are trying to master a major objective.[56]

Exhibitions and performances try to bring important and subtle elements to the fore in learning, elements too often brushed aside in the hectic pace that marks so many traditional schools. Exhibitions and performances, for example, should be authentic—life-like. A life-like quality is introduced in several ways. One way is the long time period within which performances take place, compared to traditional one-shot encounters with an objective test. Performances that assess a student's work in a course, for example, might take place over several years until mastery is demonstrated. Another life-like element is that parts of graduation exhibitions and performances take place before an audience of peers and teachers. These exhibitions, Coalition schools believe, add a social element to what otherwise is an isolated, individual effort when student achievement is evaluated by tests. Public displays of knowledge also act as incentives to achievement, and other students presumably learn something when they participate as an appropriate audience to hear what other students have accomplished.

I give this detail on how two schools have developed more realistic and educationally sensible ways to assess student progress in learning to show how deeply the ground must be ploughed and seeded to approach only one important element in the nine principles that guide essential schools. The complexity of Sizer's reform is suggested, too, by recognizing that, while teachers and principals are reforming the curriculum, developing new ways of organizing teachers, learning radically different ways to teach and to encourage students to become more independent learners, and dealing with counter-reform pressures that come from parents and often other educators in the school district while all of these reform initiatives are underway, the teachers and principals involved must still "keep school" and attend to its operational details—necessary work that itself drains the energies of good teachers and principals in more traditional schools.

The array of teaching and organizational strategies embraced by Coalition schools in their "broken front" approach to reform is impressive. Many of them are historic resurrections from the sixties as well as from the progressive era of the twenties and thirties. The bimonthly newsletter *Horace*, which is circulated to Coalition schools, mentions the following efforts in one 1988 issue: block-of-time scheduling in which history and English are taught in the

same time block of two periods to encourage correlation between
the subjects, which adopts the core curriculum idea of progressive
education; using a four-teacher team to develop a common curriculum for sophomores who are having academic problems; setting up
√a school-within-a-school to break a large school of fifteen hundred
students into smaller "schools" to personalize learning; organizing
classes as "workshops" to integrate content around themes in science such as energy and change, which is a return to the progressive
idea of thematic units; and employing team teaching and even vertical age grouping in which students from different grade levels are
organized into families that stay together throughout the four years
of high school—two imports from the 1960s. None of these arrangements is unusual in many Coalition schools. Principle 6, which sets
forth the exhibition criterion for graduation, is elaborated in the
Prospectus that describes the general conditions for participation in
the Coalition by stating that the diploma is awarded when earned
and "the school's program proceeds with no strict age grading and
no system of 'credits earned' by 'time spent' in class. . . ."[57]

Anyone who reads about the work of the Coalition schools and
its state-based Re:Learning effort and who, at the same time, believes that American high schools should improve their standard
learning and teaching practices, must come away with a feeling of
awe induced by the Coalition's efforts to move the educational
mountain and to swim so courageously against the tide of one hundred years of history that has carried schools to another shore where
they are large and impersonal, where courses and tracks increase in
tempo with the constant rise in enrollments and the increasing social and ethnic diversity of their students.

My personal feeling is more visceral. When I detach myself
from the boldness of this movement and try to imagine what it's
like in sheer practical work, I get the kind of "stomach sinking"
feelings one gets in an airplane when it flies through rough air and
drops several hundred feet in a few seconds. I wonder, for example,
if even the prestige and political clout of the eleven governors in the
Re:Learning project, and the millions of dollars in support money,
are strong enough to lift the educational mountain that reform of
secondary education requires or even to succeed with 5 percent of
the Coalition's 700 hundred schools.

My sinking feeling is not related to the problems that the Coalition has already faced. I am not thinking, for example, of problems such as the high school faculty that voted to leave the
Coalition because they feared, with some reason, that a leaner

curriculum meant losing jobs; nor of the Texas high school near Houston whose faculty and community believed that reducing extracurricular activities meant that football drill could not be done within the regular school day and who angrily rejected Sizer's personal appeal before the issue of membership in the Coalition even came before the board.[58] All of these things, along with massive state testing and local practices that evaluate teachers on the basis of "behaviors" that must be demonstrated when they teach, are important and will be faced by any reform that seriously pursues intellectual and democratic ends—very much the way the thirty experimental high schools in the famous Eight-Year Study faced and surmounted difficult problems in the 1930s only to see their teaching and curricular reforms washed away in 1941 by World War II and the "let's-get-on-with-our-lives" mood that followed the war.

Preliminary data suggest that it will take more than money and prestige to reform even one American high school. In 1993 not *one* of the 700 hundred schools in the Coalition and Re:Learning had effected *total, whole-school reform.*[59] This fits with the pattern of reform since 1960 that I am sketching in this book: not only are most of the reforms that are offered to schools by prestige institutions such as universities and foundations anti-intellectual and undemoctratic, but when Deweyan-progressive reforms are available, not even one school in a small group of *volunteer* schools is capable of assimilating the *whole* reform in a way that radically alters its educational environment! Remember, too, that virtually all of the twenty thousand secondary schools in the United States beyond the small band of 700 hundred schools in the Coalition are indifferent to the reform in any case. For them it is school as usual.

If not one school was able to renew itself as a living, integrated system, might not this fact suggest that secondary schools may be dying or are in a state somewhere between vital life and a death-like repose? Might not this condition bode ill for the very survival of public education in America? These are questions beyond the range of this book, but they are questions that are worth a day's discussion in a class or an inservice meeting. Surely Dewey's first sentence in *Democracy and Education* comes to us: "the most notable distinction between living and inanimate things is that the former maintain themselves by renewal." Renewal in biology is life. So it must also be in social life and with social institutions like schools.

Problems of this kind are deeply rooted in a technological Western and American culture. This culture reflects a stark indifference to mind and to humanistic studies; it is too much concerned with achieving narrow and immediately practical ends by using direct and technologically powerful means to achieve results (state testing programs as "reforms" are a pure example of this attitude). This technological culture has been unable to work out, on any large scale, a way of educating youth that honors democratic equality based on a belief that any normal student can learn much that is important to him and to the society that sustains him. It is the technological, "high tech" culture itself and its mindset that poses near-insurmountable obstacles to fundamental reform (and to Sizer's Coalition). I turn now to a critique of the Coalition reform itself.

The major weakness in the Coalition's approach to reform is that it severely underestimates the quality and depth of supportive education that teachers, administrators, school board members, and key community leaders require to mount and sustain their fundamental reform initiative. Never in this century have even one hundred schools successfully sustained a national reform based on intellectual and democratic principles. The Coalition seeks not only to effect radical reforms in learning, teaching, and curriculum, but it also tries to achieve radical reforms in the way time is used, the way classes are scheduled, and the way that students and presumably teachers are evaluated. And if all of this is not enough of a reform menu, the Coalition's efforts ripple out to affect existing power and prestige relationships among other schools in the system, between the Coalition school and the community, not to mention power relationships within the school system, such as those between teachers and administrators, teachers and teachers, and the Coalition school itself and the board of education. Surely such a complex practical effort needs more than nine principles as its theoretical compass and the exchange of valuable but limited "how to" information among the Coalition schools themselves.

The Coalition initiative and that of the Paideia effort as well are unique in that they are fundamental *practical* efforts. They are not idle theories spun in a university haven free from the trials of a real world; nor do they represent the dainty pickings of some academics who live off the more adventurous work of others. It is for these reasons, as well as the merit of the reform itself, that I want so much for the Coalition to succeed.

My concern is that the small, if fast-swimming, fish of the Coalition are swimming close to the ocean's surface, worrying too much about enlisting more schools to convince others of their success, or placing too high a priority on the necessary evaluation of the effort—and in doing these things are not paying enough attention to perils that lurk below, nor considering carefully how they are going to maintain strength for their long swim in very cold waters.

How can the Coalition schools maintain their strength for the long swim? How can they best work out the complex questions of teaching and school organization that they have rightly faced? I recur to a Deweyan idea for a short answer: practical action, however rich in purpose and social necessity, must be *directed by ideas that cohere, or action will ossify into unthoughtful routine and become mechanical.* Even progressive reforms can become routine and lifeless, as many of the progressive schools of the 1930s demonstrated when they ignored the complex ideas that gave them life and looked instead to slogans such as "I teach children not subject matter" or "Teach the whole child." These slogans, taken second-hand from professors of education or from reform-minded superintendents in the 1930s, did real damage to progressive ideals because they oversimplified and thus deflected the brick-by-brick reconstruction of traditional schools that progressive education demanded. Many of those who enlisted in the progressive movement had little understanding of the history from which it came or of the ideas that directed it. They had never read Dewey or the insightful critiques of progressive education by Boyd Bode or William C. Bagley, a philosopher at Teachers College, Columbia University, who believed that all students must acquire an essential core of knowledge and that many progressive schools were not teaching this essential core.[60]

John Dewey was aware that progressive education was too often superficial. His blunt advice to many of his followers in 1938 is worth repeating today. In a very short last chapter in *Experience and Education,* Dewey met the problem directly. He reiterated that ordinary experience intelligently directed is the heart of the matter and then warned that the only path to failure would be "that experience and the experimental method will not be adequately *conceived*" [emphasis added]. The new education is not an easier road to follow but a more difficult one. He continued, "The greatest danger that attends its future is . . . the idea that it is an easy way to follow, so easy that its course may be improvised . . . from day to day or week to week." Discounting the value of the labels "new" or "old" education, he ended his slim volume with these words: "[W]e shall make surer and faster progress when we devote ourselves to finding out just what education is and what conditions have to be satisfied in order that education may be a reality and not a name or a slogan. It is for this reason alone that I have emphasized the need for a sound philosophy of experience."[61]

I mean no disrespect for the work of the Coalition and its schools when I say that it will be very easy for "less is more" and "student as worker" to become the slogans for what might otherwise be the "new progressivism" of the 1990s. If I take Dewey's admonition that the 1930s progressives needed "a sound philosophy of experience" to mean an *intellectual* understanding of what they were about, I can give a general statement of what the Coalition lacks in its continuing education efforts with the teachers and principals in its schools. My impression, from reading the materials circulated among its schools and from conversations with some of the people working with the Coalition, is that the education support is too thin and too superficial. In short I believe that the chances for success would be increased considerably if the Coalition offered its workers more opportunities to read and discuss seminal ideas about such things as learning and teaching, how schools came to be as they are, and the life histories of past reforms. Most educators do not learn these things in either their teacher education programs or in graduate programs in administration. The Coalition might consider giving as much attention to developing a "reform curriculum" for its members in much the way it worked out its elegant "democratic curriculum" for youth in secondary schools.

Theodore Sizer and the Coalition imply that the nine principles based on the "hoary old chestnuts" of pedagogical commitment provide a sufficient conceptual structure from which to construct a powerful reform movement. But Sizer is too modest. If the elegance and unpretentiousness of the nine principles reflect the wisdom of "hoary old chestnuts," I would say that they are old chestnuts because they possess just enough truth not to be discarded from group memory and too much truth to be easily honored in practice. One who deals only in chestnuts would become a trader in a very stale commodity. The thing that Sizer brings to his chestnuts—and which he modestly underplays—is his learning. His learning and openness to the intellectual and social fire is what transforms stale chestnuts into something edible. Sizer errs, I think, in believing that his principles, hammered out over time and with much effort from *his* learning and experience, can be given more or less directly as ideas to others who have not hammered too much on their own experience, and who probably exhibit some of the dependency symptoms that our schools and colleges encourage willy-nilly. It is clear to me, for example, that a teacher education program that is long on technique and short on generative ideas leaves one with an impoverished experience and no hammer. The Coalition schools require some continuing education experience, staff development in the jargon, to bridge the perennial gap between doing and knowing that arises not only in reform efforts but which marks the work of schools of education as well.

The expansion of the Coalition effort to include schools in the Re:Learning project geometrically increases the logistical, geographic, and staff support complexity of the effort, and makes the need for continuing education of teachers and principals, board members, and others involved even more important and difficult. The larger size of many of the Re:Learning schools, for example, poses new challenges. In January 1988, 38 of the 52 essential schools in the project enrolled one thousand or fewer students; 26 of these 38 schools enrolled fewer than five hundred students.[62] As the number of larger schools from suburban and urban areas increase (as they must if the Coalition's efforts are to have credibility with larger schools), the need for a more in-depth, conceptual, and higher quality continuing education experience becomes critical.

An excellent high school principal who has been slugging it out with reform for seven years before his school joined the Coalition shares a similar view. Most teachers and administrators have cut their reform teeth on easy-to-learn, packaged programs, he believes, and they approach the common principles in the same way. The principles appear to be easily understood and do not appear to be complex. Teachers who agree with them do so because of "sympathetic vibes." He then says that

> this leads to a superficial understanding of the principles and all that is involved in implementing them. For example, we held three, one-half-day workshops to familiarize twenty-five teachers with the ideas underlying the Coalition. Obviously, in this brief time, the treatment could only be superficial. But the majority of the participants reacted with great enthusiasm. It was obvious that the principles aligned with their personal views of how teaching and learning should occur. The problem came with the beginning of school when these teachers began to get together. I began to hear that dreaded phrase, "I'm doing it." In other words, they were saying that they were now doing "the Coalition" in their classrooms. What they really were doing was beginning to rethink what they had always done and to alter it in terms of the principles. By no means did they have a grasp of the complexity of what the combined nine principles mean nor of the historical and philosophical content behind the principles. In other words, the Coalition ideas were being treated as another easy-to-learn program.
>
> The Coalition is not staffed to provide any more than superficial support and staff development programs. Those programs tend to be "how-to" programs for "believers."[63]

It is interesting to me—and practically very important to reform—that Theodore Sizer and Mortimer Adler, each in his own way, neglect the intellectual or idea base in which practice must be rooted. Adler places learning to teach in the hands-on category of apprenticeship in *Paideia*.[64] This placement is not illogical because Adler's theory is rooted in the liberal arts and, importantly, in a classical Greek culture that built a view of knowledge on social class lines in which the privileged classes engaged in theoretical pursuits while those in the lesser classes performed the transitory and therefore less valuable day-to-day work of life. Adler does not subscribe to this stark idea, of course, but its echo is heard in his view of teaching, which is work-in-the-world and transitory in that it leaves no theoretical mark. Sizer, on the other hand, would place teacher education within the university, but, strangely, he shares Adler's how-to view of teaching in the approach the Coalition has followed in the continuing education of its practitioners. (Sizer probably enters the broad classical stream of thought reflected in the work of essentialist philosophers of education such as William C. Bagley, from whom Sizer might have taken the idea of "essential" that figures in the name he gave his group of reform-minded practitioners, the Coalition of Essential Schools.)

It is anomalous when two men who advocate important reforms, and whose own work rests on formative ideas tempered and challenged by experience, seem to believe that ideas are less important to their followers. So I ask a question: can teachers and principals cultivate the intelligence and sensitivities of youth if their own intellectual fields lie untended?

Although the Coalition neglects the idea-base of teaching in its *process* of reform, there is no doubt that the reform itself is intellectual and democratic in substance and spirit.

THE PAIDEIA PROPOSAL: A SUMMARY

The Paideia Proposal is the work of Mortimer Adler, long known for his defense of liberal learning and the University of Chicago's Great Books Program. "Paideia" signifies the general learning required in a culture. Adler's curriculum design is organized by columns (in the manner of a Greek temple?) that depict three ways of learning and teaching. Column One relates to the acquisition of knowledge by means of didactic instruction; Column Two deals with the development of intellectual skills through coaching and

supervised practice; and Column Three enlarges the understandings developed in Columns One and Two through discussion,
Socratic questioning, and active student participation. The three
columns represent the increasing complexity in learning from
grades one through twelve. Study in other subjects such as physical
education, foreign language, manual arts, and an introduction to the
world of work round out the academic core of Paideia.[65]

Adler speaks to the democratic ethic in his plan. "Harbor no
aspirations for the fulfillment of democracy's promises or the en-
hancement of the lives of its citizens," he writes, "and you can
shrug away the sorry state of our schools today."[66] Democracy and
mind intertwine like a braided rope in The Paideia Proposal. All
children can learn. Paideia sees few limits to a child's capacity to
learn. Its idealism is socially realistic, however problematical the
response of school board members and educators might be, problems beyond the soundness of the proposal itself.

There are some contradictions in Adler's proposal. There is a
contradiction, for example, on how acceptable academic achievement is to be determined: "requisite standard of performance" is
used on page 44, which suggests a standard that is derived from
sources outside the learner, while on page 7 Adler writes that "every
child is educable up to his or her capacity," which implies another
source for determining academic achievement. I will mention one
"split" that Dewey would regard as false, thus creating an unnecessary dualism: Adler believes that teaching is a skill that can be
learned by coaching (some of it can be), but he seems not to realize
that ideas and values influence the way one teaches in the same way
that the ideas and values in his curriculum influence the learner's
actions and attitudes toward life and civic issues.

On balance, few reform proposals of the eighties so explicitly
address the cultivation of intelligence within a democratic society
and recognize, too, the failure of that society to provide all of its
children with adequate food and shelter. I believe that The Paideia
Proposal meets the substance and spirit of the intellectual and democratic criterion for fundamental reform.[67]

A NATION PREPARED: TEACHERS FOR THE 21ST CENTURY: A SUMMARY

The Carnegie Forum on Education and the Economy of the
Carnegie Foundation assembled the blue ribbon panel that wrote *A*

Nation Prepared in 1986.[68] Not one practicing teacher was on the Carnegie panel, although two teachers' unions were represented.

A Nation Prepared makes eight recommendations to build a profession of teaching. The Task Force calls for "sweeping changes in educational policy" to create a National Board for Professional Teaching Standards that will certify teachers who have met the new standards, restructure schools to give teachers more decision-making power and to create a more professional environment, introduce lead teachers with higher pay who will spearhead the redesign of schools, eliminate the undergraduate education major and offer a new Master in Teaching degree, mobilize the nation's resources to prepare minority youngsters for teaching careers, and pay teachers more for increasing school-wide student achievement and reducing dropout rates or for improving other reasonable indicators of progress.[69]

Although some isolated recommendations in *A Nation Prepared*—such as giving teachers more power to make decisions about their work—are good, these isolated goods are lost in the panel's major recommendation: improve teaching and the profession through assessments of teachers, which are to be made by the National Board for Professional Standards.[70] This is no more than the old faith of some 1920 reformers in the efficiencies that were supposedly promised by the new "science" of standardized achievement and IQ tests. I shall give one example that strips the scientific pretensions from the recommendation to assess teachers objectively based on national criteria.

Imagine five teachers, each of whom is about to undergo the revelations of modern, scientific assessment. Each teacher has a conscious theory of learning and teaching that guides her practice and that she can articulate in terms of her practice. The theory of Teacher 1 is essentially Thorndikian-Skinnerian; Teacher 2, Piagetian; Teacher 3, Deweyan; Teacher 4, Classical-Socratic; and Teacher 5, Research-eclectic. No evaluation of any of these teachers can be valid whose criteria for assessment are not generally consistent with the ideas and values embodied in each teacher's theory. The probable losers in the assessment will be Teachers 2, 3, and 4 because their theories and practices will be encompassed neither by prevailing teacher practice nor by most research on teaching. This research supports the behavioristic values of Teacher 1 as well as those of Teacher 5 insofar as the findings of the so-called effective teaching research influence the criteria for assessing teacher competence.

There are no absolute grounds on which to preclude any of these ways of teaching, with their varying views of mind and society, from having an equal chance for success in the assessment. There surely is no scientific basis for doing so. All of these ways of teaching—and blends among them—work for some teachers in some places with some students some times.

The proposed Master in Teaching degree is also flawed by the report's materialistic bias. This degree stresses practical issues in teaching, knowledge of research on teaching, and field-based experience "integrated with a demanding program of academic work."[71] Emphasizing research and "practical issues of teaching" while refusing to define what is meant by "a demanding program of academic work" raises serious doubts about the intellectual quality of this degree. Nowhere are the humane and liberal studies mentioned, nowhere does the panel say that study in the social sciences and in educational history and philosophy are essential to "reflective practice" (today's buzzword in most talk about teaching).

A Nation Prepared does not meet the intellectual and democratic criterion of worth. Ironically, its epistemological and social theories are more in step with the intellectually discredited theories of scientific management and curriculum making that were touted early in this century; this report drifts in the social waters of 1920. There is no way to get to the twenty-first century from there because Carnegie's panel skipped over some of the most enlightened progressive thought of the twentieth century.

CONCLUDING COMMENT ON REFORM'S GREEN FIELDS

Six of the eight reforms discussed fully met the intellectual and democratic criterion: the Trump High School, open classrooms, nongraded schools, team teaching, the Coalition of Essential Schools, and The Paideia Proposal. One reform, the new mathematics and science programs, met the intellectual element in this criterion but did not meet the democratic element. The professionalization of teaching, proposed in A Nation Prepared: Teachers for the 21st Century, reflects a technological approach to teaching in its emphasis on technique removed from ideas and in its belief that excellent teachers can be identified through objective assessment procedures.

Our best reason for hope that we can make better schools is that reforms like The Paideia Proposal and the Coalition of Essential Schools could even come to life in the 1980s. These efforts are swimming against the barren accountability movements of the 1970s and 1980s. It is certain, for example, that neither behavioral objectives and mastery learning, prominent in the 1970s, nor the curriculum mandates and state testing programs proposed by the education governors in the 1980s, were the soil from which these reforms grew. There are, then, other fields out there, however small and overlooked they might be, that grow a different kind of educational crop. Each of these reforms testifies, in its own way, to a faith in the intelligence of teachers and students, a belief that any normal child can learn, and a recognition that democratic social values must inform any educational effort that is both practical and conceptually sound.

If, in a valley of a thousand fallow fields, one sees a few green ones, does this not speak to the possibility of life? And if there is life's possibility, can there not be, in good time, more green fields?

But if a vital force is present in reform, it is not abundantly present. Four of the reforms are dead: the new mathematics and science programs, the Trump High School and its attempt to break the intellectual lockstep of large-group teaching, open education, and nongraded schools whose curriculum organized on conceptual strands provided coherence and continuity to learning as the child progressed through elementary school. After thirty years of reform, we are left in the early nineties with a handful of reforms untouched by the technological genie—the Coalition of Essential Schools, The Paideia Proposal, and team teaching. This is a very small cake with no icing to show for three decades of work. Even if I were to add Eliot Wigginton's Foxfire experience, which uses regional culture to teach writing and build students' self-esteem, James Comer's "power schools" in New Haven, Connecticut, and the whole language movement, the reform cake is very small indeed considering the number of people who ought to come to the party.

To look at the number of schools in the public system makes the reform picture more bleak. There are approximately 80,000 public elementary and secondary schools that enrolled over forty million students in 1990.[72] Against this giant we array the schools in the Coalition and Re:Learning and the schools working with The Paideia Proposal. There are about 1000 schools in these efforts. Even if the Coalition and Re:Learning could effectively work with 1000 secondary schools, there would still be about 19,000 uninvolved secondary schools. Paideia can do little more than wave invitingly at 60,000 elementary schools. That leaves team teaching. Since there is no valid information on the number of schools that use team teaching as a vehicle for reform, I shall assume that 10 percent of our public schools do so. [I base this percentage on practical experience, which suggests that about 10 percent of the public schools are above average, some of which are truly excellent.] This adds 8000 schools to our limited reform movement. Still something less than a landslide.

I find it difficult emotionally to accept the import of these numbers: a handful of fundamental reforms and reformers facing tens of thousands of schools and several million teachers and administrators. Even if we had twenty or so fundamental reforms, my optimism would be limited. The well-financed and widely known effort of the Coalition of Essential Schools and its Re:Learning project, for example, which is linked to state governors through the Education Commission of the States, engage only 700 schools. None of these schools has fully embraced the core of reforms entailed in this effort, such as curriculum, longer time blocks, and portfolio assessments of learning. Fundamental reform attracts fewer schools because it *is* fundamental. Fundamental reform brings to the surface honest differences among teachers and principals about what should be taught and how it should be taught, how teachers use their time, and how "tight" or "loose" their working relationship will be to colleagues. Struggles surface over power and prestige as some teachers choose reform and others do not. I recall one high school in which thirty teachers engaged reform while sixty waited and watched, indifferent or opposed. If all eventually goes well within a school, community reactions may arise in opposition to reform. These reactions may be fueled by educational, political, religious, or tax concerns. Complexity abounds. The possibilities for things to go wrong are high.

Yet we must try. We must keep trying to implement fundamental reform. This is the only way we can learn. We know so little about the possibilities and the process of reform because fundamental reform has rarely been tried in the past thirty years. We have dabbled and fiddled with reform by introducing so-called reforms that challenge nothing in the system and which reinforce existing practice (see chapter 4). Whatever the political and power and psychological dimensions of reform might be, and these may prove to be the critical elements in reform, what we know and believe and value about the most worthy ends and means of education will remain a critical constant in intelligent reform. But it is not enough to know the good. We must understand the technological ideas and values that displace the good in schools. We must understand those ideas and values that take up so much living space in our schools and in our college departments of education that alternative views of learning and teaching cannot be heard. And there is little desire that they should be heard. Surely this is the inference to be drawn from the fact that, after thirty years of alleged reform, we have a few thousand schools embracing intellectual and democratic reforms facing a mass of 70,000 schools that seem not to know that skill and idea, for example, are related elements in learning and teaching. The mechanical model of mind and learning owns the educational air waves. Most schools and university departments of education are like commercial radio and television stations beaming choppy distractions to an intellectually unengaged audience. As one all-news station boasts, "Give us twenty-two minutes and we'll give you the world." Yes, "you get the world"—in an incoherent mix of news items, each ninety seconds long, without context, commentary, or thought. But within this commercial wasteland there is local and national public radio and television. This is thoughtful broadcasting. American education, unlike public broadcasting, rarely provides an intellectual option to its students and teachers. In education, most stations "give you the world in forty-five-minute periods."

If what we believe about learning and teaching is an essential and permeating element in fundamental reform, we must understand the belief system that dominates educational practice today. As long as this technological belief system is allowed to pass without notice, without description and relentless critique, it will continue to occupy most of the educational space and make it difficult for more intellectual and democratic practices to get a hearing. In the next chapter I shall show the many and sometimes attractive faces of the technological mindset as this way of thinking reveals itself in concrete reforms that have been proposed since 1960.

CHAPTER 4

Reforms As Technology: How Technique Displaces Thought

The expert—often a psychologist—has led a long and happy life in twentieth-century education. Our faith in specialized expertise seems unshakable. One of the fathers of educational psychology, E. L. Thorndike, believed that the method *and* goals of education could be scientifically determined. Over seventy years ago Thorndike put his faith into words: anything that exists in quantity can be objectively measured. Thorndike deeply believed "that with the training of a sufficient number of educational experts, many of the gnawing controversies that had plagued educators . . . would disappear."[1] The Holmes Group, a consortium of ninety universities whose purpose is to improve teacher education, shares Thorndike's faith in educational research and social science. The Holmes Group believes that colleges of education can reform schools by requiring a master's degree in education for teachers.

Building on a strong liberal arts undergraduate program of study, the prospective teacher would study the "right stuff" in colleges of education. And what is the source of this valid knowledge for teaching? It is objective, scientific knowledge about education! "The promise of a science of education is about to be fulfilled," the Holmes Group states.[2] The research expert will lead the way.

Belief in experts who back their findings with measurement and numbers is not confined to questions about how we learn or how we should teach. Science has penetrated another social thicket—management. Many school administrators justly feel that the pressures for economy and efficiency exerted on them by taxpayers and business organizations are rivaled only by the biblical tale of Job's trials. These perennial pressures for efficiency in education set the stage for the entrance of another expert, the scientific manager. "Scientific management" came on the scene in 1910 in the person of Frederick Taylor, and it is no exaggeration to say that his time-and-motion studies took the business and educational community in easy surrender by 1930. Although full-blown scientific management was out of style by then, its techniques endured in education management.[3] Taylor's basic principle of scientific management required that a job be broken into smaller, component tasks that were carefully sequenced to attain the goals of greater worker efficiency and productivity. Since this principle also characterizes most of the reforms that I shall judge to be technological later in this chapter, it is worth looking at more closely. Few will deny that breaking something into its component parts and linearly sequencing the parts has the charm of common sense about it, which is one source of its appeal then and now. The Chicago mastery learning program in reading, for example, "broke" reading into 273 discrete subskills. This led to fragmentation in the teaching of reading; subsequently the subskills were reduced to 150, presumably a better number.[4]

The spirit and some of the substance of scientific management are captured in the five steps of its methodology. Taylor's first step was to carefully observe the work of the most skillful workers. He next defined and timed with a stopwatch the various movements of the men as they performed what Taylor perceived to be the component parts of the job, such as making parts in a machine shop or loading pig iron on railway cars. The stopwatch symbolized the new approach to management based on measurement. Second, the motions and tools required to do a particular job efficiently were standardized and required for all similar jobs in the plant. Taylor claimed that time-and-motion studies coupled to job standardization had certain psychological-social benefits: since the job standards had been determined objectively and scientifically, they reduced worker laziness and prevented disputes over what constituted a fair day's work. Third, specific tasks were defined each day for each worker. Taylor used teaching to justify his task idea. "No . . . teacher would think of telling children in a general way to study a certain book or subject. It is . . . universal to assign each day a definite lesson beginning on one specific line and page and ending on another. . . ."[5] The planning department gave each worker a job card that described in detail what he was to do, how he was to do it, and exactly how much time he had to do it. Functional foremen, who taught the workers how to do the work on their job cards, were the fourth element in Taylor's system. Work was very specialized. Each man was to perform a single leading function. There were seven types of functional foremen, all of whom were "expert teachers" chosen for their knowledge and skill in special areas. These foremen or supervisors had titles such as the gang boss, speed boss, repair boss, time clerk, and disciplinarian. The last major element in scientific management was the planning department. The planning department ran the plant; not the manager, superintendent, or foreman. The planning department developed the "science of the job [and made the] many rules, laws, and formulae to replace the judgment of the individual workman."[6] At Bethlehem Steel, for example, workers were moved from place to place by clerks with elaborate maps of the yard before them "very much like chessmen are moved on a chessboard. . . ."[7]

Taylor believed that there was "one best method" to do any job and that "first-class men," those trained in his objective methods, could do the job and earn more. If we accept the assumptions and implicit values in Taylor's approach, he was correct. Worker productivity in loading pig iron at Bethlehem Steel rose from twelve tons to forty-seven tons per day. The worker's scientifically computed bonus for this work was a daily pay increase of 60 percent, from $1.15 to $1.85. But human factors limited Taylor's dream: only one man in eight was capable of loading forty-seven tons of pig iron each day.[8]

If we consider scientific management as a technological interpretation of *aspects* of the scientific method, such as observing and measuring, the educational descendents of Frederick Taylor can be seen today. Programmed texts and teaching methods, competency-based education geared to a sequenced array of subskills with "mastery tests," reflect a faith in finding and objectifying the "one best method." These sequences can be taught to thousands of teachers by today's equivalent of Taylor's "planning departments," federally funded research and development centers and regional laboratories, or by university professors, who often act as entrepreneurs. Most of these packages promise efficiency and increased "worker productivity"—increased scores on standardized tests. The principals and supervisors who are already in place in the schools act as "functional foremen" in a Taylorean system to ensure that the prescriptions on the newly developed curricular "job card" are carried out. One pure example of a curriculum made by reincarnations of Taylor's planning departments is Individually Prescribed Instruction (IPI) in reading and arithmetic, developed by the University of Pittsburgh Research and Development Center in the early sixties and disseminated to schools until 1976 by Research for Better Schools, a regional laboratory in Philadelphia. IPI's approach broke reading and arithmetic into a long series of subskills. Student learning was evaluated through mastery tests based on discrete skills. These mastery tests neglected thinking. The intellectual content in IPI arithmetic was virtually nonexistent when this curriculum was assessed by criteria based on Deweyan-progressive theory (see appendix A). (Individually Prescribed Instruction is critiqued in appendix B.)

One other echo of Taylor's system of scientific management in education today should be noted. I am struck by the parallel in physical movement between clerks moving workers about the yard at Bethlehem Steel "like chessmen on a chess board" and the migrations of a thousand or more students every fifty minutes in a high school. The students' work stations are the classrooms, the principal is the all-seeing clerk-of-the-yard, and the teachers are Taylor's functional foremen chosen for their knowledge and skill in a specialized area. There is logic in this chessboard movement, as there is in Taylor's system, if one accepts as given a separate-subject high school curriculum with 150 or more subjects tiered into three or more levels of "difficulty" by tracks.

Frederick Taylor's belief that a job could be broken into sequenced steps that could be standardized reflects the technologist's indifference to coherence. This indifference to coherence leads to fragmentation, whether the technologist is concerned with factory jobs or subjects in the curriculum. The technologist in a factory breaks a job into a series of sequenced motions; a technologist in a university research and development center breaks reading or arithmetic into a sequenced series of behavioral objectives and subskills. The whole is lost in the confusing clutter of motions, objectives, and skills. Clutter also surrounds us when we try to understand

FIGURE 3. Nineteen Technological Reforms Regrouped into Families

Family A: *Reforms That Focus on Content Pieces or Isolated Skills for Greater Efficiency*

Chapter 1 (Title 1), ESEA, remedial reading programs for children in economically poor families
Chicago mastery learning reading program
The Hunter teaching approach and effective teaching research*
Individually Guided Education
Individually Prescribed Instruction in reading and arithmetic
Thinking as a set of skills
Competency-based curricula and testing
Behavioral objectives

Family B: . *Reforms Whose Attracting Feature is a Machine*

Electronic language laboratories
Educational television
Computers [IBM's Writing to Read]

Family C: *Reforms That Focus on the Organizational-Management Dimension*

Accountability and testing programs
State testing programs
Aligning the curriculum to the test (curriculum alignment)
A linear research-development-diffusion model
Effective schools research
Assertive discipline
Contracting to corporations to raise test scores

---

* *Counted as two reforms*

something larger than a job or a single subject—something like school reform, for example. To make a path through the clutter of reforms, as one might do with children's toys left in disarray, I have grouped them into three families in figure 3.

I shall discuss the first four reforms in Family A in this chapter. The first reform—the federally funded remedial programs in reading and arithmetic—provide an excellent practical example of a technological reform. These programs were begun in the 1960s as part of the war on poverty. Virtually every school district in the United States participates in this program, in part because the cost is borne by the federal government. If the quality of this reform is low, and five million children were enrolled in 1991–92, as I document below, the overall quality of American education suffers. The second reform, mastery learning, is widely accepted by educators as one way to ensure that basic skills are being taught. The popularity of the Chicago mastery learning program in reading, for example, rested in large part on the assumption that reading was a matter of learning basic skills in a sequence and testing frequently through criterion-referenced tests. I describe and critique the Chicago mastery learning program in reading and review the controversy among researchers about whether or not the assumptions on which mastery learning rests are verified by students' achievement in the basic skills. The last two reforms, Madeline Hunter's approach to teaching and the research on effective teaching, are discussed together because the teaching practices they recommend are similar. Hunter's approach had been widely adopted by state and local educators where reform has included the improvement of teaching coupled to a uniform system for evaluating the effectiveness of teaching. The clarity of Hunter's approach and her claim that the methods advocated are supported by research appeal to teachers and administrators who are pressed by either their state legislatures or local school boards to improve students' test scores. Although hard data on the use of the Hunter-effective-teaching model are not available, it is widely believed by educators that the Hunter model is a national phenomenon. I can document the use of the Hunter-effective-teaching model in some states. The model has been used to improve teaching as one element in school reform in Pennsylvania, where 60 percent of the state's 501 school districts have trained teachers in its use. Other states, such as California, Washington, South Carolina, and North Carolina, use the model in teacher professional development centers or to increase the effectiveness of their schools.[9] Based on these data and my personal experience with educators at national conferences, I would conservatively estimate that two to three hundred thousand public school teachers have been exposed to the Hunter model from the approximately two million teachers in the country. If I assume that each of these teachers teach thirty children (while ignoring the one hundred or more students secondary teachers teach each day), the Hunter model may reach six to ten million students. Any reform that reaches several million students should be critically examined.

Since behavioral objectives are an essential part of most technological reforms, they will not be discussed apart from the reforms themselves.

Individually Guided Education is the most comprehensive and systematic reform developed since 1965 (other than Theodore Sizer's Coalition of Essential Schools, which was launched in 1985). I shall treat it as a limited case study in the next chapter. This reform combined the brains and prestige of the University of Wisconsin with the power of federal and foundation funding to build a learning-teaching approach around the unique ways individual students learn. Individually Guided Education anticipated by twenty-five years today's interest in school-based decision making, school restructuring, and the professionalization of teaching. Its mixture of failure and success, of the technological and the intellectual and democratic, say much to us that we need to hear if reform is ever to be fundamental rather than technologically trivial. By treating IGE as a case study, I have a bigger loom on which to weave some of the technological and intellectual threads that have been spun out in the preceding chapters. The rich descriptive studies of IGE's use in schools also throw some practical light on what happens to a reform in the hands of teachers and principals.

One other procedural detail remains. Most of the other fourteen reforms will be discussed in summary form in appendixes B and C. This procedure is necessary to reduce the book's length and because further discussion in the text would not add significantly to the ideas and practical implications for reform I am trying to develop. Although some of these reforms are of little intellectual and practical interest today, such as educational television or IBM's "Writing to Read" program, other reforms discussed in the appendixes are of interest. The introduction of the business model, for example, in performance contracting to corporations to raise test scores, a radical reform in the early seventies, has echoes today in the calls for school choice and privatization. Competency-based curriculums and testing, on the other hand, are alive today. Competency-based education is not so much a discrete reform, such as mastery learning or the federally funded remedial programs, as it is an intention by policymakers to assure that certain things are being learned. In acting on this intention to assure that learning is taking place, policymakers and educators often draw on the philosophy and technology of the reforms I shall discuss in this chapter.

One major reform of the 1960s is stronger politically and financially today than it was in its vigorous youth over twenty-five years ago. Known as "Chapter 1 programs" in the jargon, this federally initiated program is aimed at children living in poverty. Chapter 1 programs try to bring "up to speed" children who have difficulty learning to read and write and to do elementary arithmetic. Approximately $50 billion have been spent since 1965 in this remedial effort.[10] I estimate that twenty million children have been enrolled in Chapter 1 programs since their inception. Despite the strong political and financial support for Chapter 1, its educational health is uncertain. How can this be? I try to explain the anomaly of this reform in the discussion that follows.

THE PROMISE AND THE FAILURE OF FEDERALLY FUNDED REMEDIAL PROGRAMS

Few of Lyndon B. Johnson's War on Poverty programs have enjoyed a longer life or more billions of dollars than the effort to teach children who were falling several years behind their age mates to read and write and to learn elementary mathematics. Begun in 1965 this program will involve five million children and cost $6.2 billion in the 1991–92 school year where every dollar is a federal subsidy to the fourteen thousand participating school districts (about 90 percent of school districts in the U.S.).[11] This program in "compensatory education" is formally known as Chapter 1 of the Elementary and Secondary Education Act of 1965 (originally Title 1).

If ever there was a massive and sustained reform in education about something socially important and, at the same time, whose "cure" was politically sweet, it is the Chapter 1 remedial programs in reading and mathematics. I say this remedial effort is "politically sweet" because almost every school district in the nation gets a piece of the money pie. For years these remedial programs were regarded by federal and local officials alike as slow-moving streams of money into congressional districts. The concern was with local compliance to the limiting federal regulations and very little concern was given to the quality of the learning and teaching that these billions of dollars were paying for. This indifference to education quality changed in 1988 with the passage of the Hawkins-Stafford amendments. The road to better quality is still obscure as federal, state, and local officials dance around the practical ramifications induced by this desire for quality. I want to touch on this quality issue because it shows how complex "doing better" can become in school reform and that common sense is sometimes a poor guide as to what direction a particular reform might take. I shall then deal with the question of how successful this compensatory program has been and whether it is, when the smoke of politics and good intentions rolls from the field of reform, good for children.

Chapter 1 compensatory programs were scheduled to expire or to be reauthorized by Congress in 1988. As part of its preparation for this decision, Congress reviewed a number of studies on the effectiveness of this program. Studies showed that the students in Chapter 1 programs made slight achievement gains (to be specified later) when they were compared with similar students who did not receive this program. This small gain, however, was not enough to close the gap between these so-called "disadvantaged students" and their more "advantaged" peers. Lawmakers and advocates of Chapter 1 wanted more attention to be paid to the quality of the program. As a result of these concerns, the House-Senate conference committee established a new standard that academic expectations for Chapter 1 students should not be "substantially different from those expected for other students of the same age or at the same grade level."[12] To this point generosity and common sense prevailed.

The United States Office of Education held hearings on the program improvement requirement in the law and on other issues. The law requires local school districts to determine the "effectiveness" of their program based on "realistic outcomes that can be measured."[13] One outcome must be measured on standardized test scores although other measures may also be used. So far so good. But then the USOE had a strange thought on the way back from this forum in which the local schools and their state educational agencies agreed only that they did not want the federal government to set the standards for "good programs." States wanted the standards to be set at that level while local districts believed that they could best set the standards. Here is where the strange thought of the USOE enters, after having been, I assume, kicked around a bit by the other two competing interests. The USOE subsequently issued regulations in which the federal government chose *not to require high standards in Chapter 1 programs* because, inexplicably, the "regulations did not require any state or local agency to go beyond the minimum standard contained in the federal regulations [which said, in effect, that even the equivalent of *fractional* percentile gains would be accepted as evidence of satisfactory program improvement]."[14]

When USOE regulations that do not support the intent of the legislation—an anomaly in itself—are coupled to other provisions in the legislation and in the regulations which require that schools not making satisfactory progress in achieving their stated outcomes be "targeted" as needing special help to improve by being publicly identified as failing, we have a real Catch-22. To avoid the *percep-*

tion of public failure, local and state officials may set low but achievable standards, which is the bureaucratic definition of a "good program" because they will not be "targeted" for program improvement. *A deliberate choice for mediocrity can circumvent the legislation intended to eliminate it!* This may be happening: in 1991 two states set high standards based on test scores and, more important to a broader definition of quality, only one state is requiring its schools to include three goals not based on standardized test scores alone.[15]

However this issue of improving the quality of reading and mathematics learning for millions of children is resolved between the federal government and the states and local schools, it is encouraging that the need for better programs is at least being addressed in an important reform effort that was twenty-eight years young in 1993. It is encouraging, too, that success indicators may be used by the states that include outcome measures such as the degree to which Chapter 1 students are encouraged to do more voluntary and independent reading from the rich store of books on adventure, fairy tales, and biography that are easily available in most elementary school libraries. We read, in the last analysis, because we have a desire to read; and, by reading, we teach ourselves to read. There is no better teacher of reading than a real library book and a student with a desire to enjoy it.

Despite the good intentions of educators and the billions of dollars that have been spent on these compensatory reading and mathematics programs, the results in learning have been very disappointing. Students in these remedial programs make little progress, as the summaries of research on the effectiveness of this reform clearly state. Children in these programs do not "catch up" with other children in schools, which means that these compensatory programs have failed to achieve their major objective (and one must recognize, too, the idealism in this intention and the extreme practical difficulty that this intention poses for educators).

The best-designed studies comparing students who received "treatment" in Chapter 1 remedial programs with children who did not receive these services show gains of one to three percentile points at best—small "results" that disappear after the third grade. What do gains of a few percentile points mean in the world of reading? They translate into a "few more sight words [learned] or a little more speed doing arithmetic computations," which will hardly open the door to a better life for a child struggling in poverty.[16] The major study by the System Development Corporation conducted be-

tween 1976 and 1979 suggests that the overall gains reported for Title 1 students, small as they were, came from students who were
only moderately disadvantaged and scored high enough to be pro-
moted from the program in one year. "Students who received Title
1 for all three years of study entered Title 1 at a low level of achievement . . . and their achievement did not improve as they received
Title 1 services," the author reports.[17]

Lorin Anderson and Leonard Pellicer reviewed fifteen years of
research on Chapter 1 remedial programs and concluded that in
twenty-five years we have not learned how to teach these students
in a way that permits them to achieve at a level comparable to most
of the other students in our schools. "Rather than truly compensating or remediating these students," they write, "we have contented
ourselves with merely slowing the rate at which they fall further
and further behind. We continue to justify continuing huge financial commitments to programs that simply don't work very well,
year after year after year." They call this rigid adherence to learning
and teaching practices that have failed decade after decade "inexplicable and tragic."[18]

What is more tragic than the unnecessary failure of many of
these students—unnecessary because this failure has been virtually
unacknowledged in any practical way until 1988 by either the Congress or by state and school officials—is that 40–75 percent of the
students who are placed in these remedial programs never "graduate" to learning in a regular classroom, but are doomed to the pur-
gatory of "remediation" for all of their school lives. Approximately
half of those students who score high enough to leave remedial programs return on the next testing date. The evidence for this chain of
failure is so compelling that Anderson refers to these students as
"lifers."[19]

The chain of failure in remedial programs that were conceived
and generously funded for over twenty-five years to break the cycle
of school failure raises this question: what was the nature and quality of the learning and teaching that these normal but underachiev-
ing students experienced in Chapter 1 remedial programs? These
children, in great need of learning first to *want* to learn to read by
experiencing the excitement of a good story, were given boring
drill-for-skill teaching. Even if it were possible to erase low achievement in the language arts and mathematics for 90 percent of these
students, which may be possible, drills in isolated skills dominated
by fill-in-the-blank kinds of "learning" exercises will never discover it.

If someone you loved were a Chapter 1 student in desperate need of learning to read and write and to do arithmetic, I will cite some of the conditions, documented by descriptive research studies, under which this loved one would be expected to learn. In the typical Chapter 1 program teachers believe that their students live in '"intellectually deficient' home environments, lack self-esteem, are unable to work without supervision, and are 'slow learners'." The work that is given to students is often *below* their present level of achievement, which makes it difficult to pass standardized tests (which are the only way to move out of the remedial program). Thinking is not part of the language or mathematics learning because the emphasis is on learning of skills and facts. Students most often work alone, filling in blanks and doing exercises on dittoed worksheets and workbooks that come with the commercial reading program. Teachers circulate among the students to monitor the isolated workbook exercises and to offer help. Students rarely have the chance to interact with their teacher or with other students by asking questions or making comments about the content supposedly being learned.[20] The natural use of language, in other words, is not used to teach language, yet this is how everyone learns language and learns to become increasingly proficient in its use, whether the person is a teacher, a mechanic, a novelist, or a student.

What does it mean to do workbook exercises day after day? Here is one example for grades one to three from a commercial reading series. The skill to be learned is the short vowel. The student fills the "holes" in the words in the following sentences. "Dr_p the d_st cl_th, dr_p the m_p! It's time for f_n, so work m_st st_p."[21] This little exercise, and thousands like it, makes no sense from either the perspective of language (natural language does not come with "holes" in it, with "parts" deliberately omitted to tax the reader's or listener's ability to make sense of nonsense), or from the perspective of teaching, where meaning is an essential precursor to learning. Reading engages the eye and the ear. To give children exercises in plugging artificial holes in language is like asking them to view badly spliced films day after day while believing that this experience will eventually help children to enjoy full-length movies (I thank James Comey for this comparison).

What does the drill-for-skill way of teaching language (not learning language) mean to students who go through its endless exercises month after month, year after year? When the technological mindset takes over language there is no end to the levels into which reading is sliced and vertically layered like a pound of sliced ham waiting for new life in a hoagie sandwich. There is no end to the isolated skills to be learned, and there is no end to the "instructional materials" helpfully and profitably supplied by the commercial publishers. Frank Smith, a linguist, contends that this fragmented way of teaching language bores students and teachers and impairs the learning of *all* students, even those unscarred by living in poverty. Here is his description of an expensive and limiting set of "instructional materials" published by the Macmillan Company.

> The complete package of Macmillan primary grade materials for . . . students making their way up the eighteen levels from kindergarten to the end of fourth grade consists of ten student texts, seven workbooks, nine practice books, ten sets of practice masters, seven sets of comprehension and writing masters, three readiness tests, seven initial placement inventories, ten assessment tests (each in alternative A and B forms), four testing/management resource books, and three achievement tests plus sets of student profile cards and class profile cards at each grade level. Supplementary material across the eighteen levels includes seven skill development charts, four vocabulary development charts, ten solo books, and ten "Extras! For Reinforcement", three sets of ABC cards, five sets of phonic picture cards, five sets of word cards . . . three packs of games, seven records or cassettes and five tutorial programs.[22]

To keep the poor teacher from losing her way through this pile of helpful materials, the publisher of this complete reading program provides ten teacher's manuals.

Overteaching is common in these totally planned reading programs for typical students, and tendencies are even more exaggerated in remedial programs such as Chapter 1 where the unexamined assumption is often "give the students a stronger dose of the skill instruction that did not work in the first place." One example of overteaching from the Macmillan series will provide texture to the phrase "drill-for-skill." Smith reports a story called "Rico and the Red Pony," which introduces students to the color red. This very short story, Smith writes, has seven literal comprehension questions, "five 'interpretative thinking' questions ('Why did Rico yell when he saw a car or a bus?'), five 'critical thinking' questions ('Why do you think Rico had the pony if he didn't like it?'), and three 'creative thinking' questions. . . ." Two pages of drill and workbook exercises continue this line of questioning. Tellingly, Smith says, "there are more questions than there are sentences in the story, more paragraphs of guidance for the teachers than there are pages in the story, and the ritual is repeated day after day, week after week, and year after year."[23] This is the technological mindset at work!

The widely-held professional and lay belief that learning to read and write consists of learning a disjointed series of subskills one by one, testing frequently, and proclaiming that passing these subskills tests is mastery does not work. Educators involved with Chapter 1 seem not to have heard that the Report of the Commission on Reading, in its conservative statement titled *Becoming a Nation of Readers*, questioned the emphasis on subskills, the use of "mastery tests," and requiring students to work their way through a hierarchy of skills one by one. "This may be one reason," the Commission continues, "that many children manage to pass the mastery tests without learning to read very well"; subskills are never integrated with "real reading," namely, reading stories and books.[24]

Chapter 1 and most remedial programs will continue to fail and deny millions of our children the joy of reading—until the issues of learning and teaching and curriculum that I have touched on are *seriously* faced and discussed. Chapter 1 is, after all, for children, and not a money chute. Yet some of the good summaries of research on Chapter 1 treat learning and curriculum issues as empty boxes to be moved around and correlated to test scores. Reviews of Chapter 1 programs, for example, too often deal with the superficial aspects of learning by citing such characteristics as the use or nonuse of aides, the varied interpretations given to "generic models" by schools, the coordination of remedial programs with the regular curriculum, the quality of the Chapter 1 staff, and the small size of Chapter 1 classes. Remedial classes typically mirror the worst drill-for-skill and frequent testing elements in programs such as those offered by Macmillan and most other publishers. This impractical way of teaching is, in turn, supported by many researchers, parents, teachers, and principals, not to mention governors and legislators. I see virtually nothing, for example, in the twenty-five years of research on the "effectiveness" of Chapter 1 programs about how students feel: Do they like to learn these subjects? Do they want to learn more? What books and other kinds of reading do they voluntarily choose to read during their stay (and after their stay) in the multibillion dollar Chapter 1 effort? What are the teachers' ideas and intuitions about the good and bad and the problematical effects of these experiences on young and older learners? I do see percentiles and normal curve equivalents, but surely they cannot by themselves tell us much about the intellectual, emotional, and social qualities that the emotion-charged experience of being singled out for "special instruction" has on children. I do not hear, in the scientific blandness of the research on Chapter 1, either the voice of quiet compromise that marks *Becoming a Nation of Readers* or the acute voice of the humanely concerned critic one hears in Frank Smith.

The "Feather Bird" Error in Chapter 1 Programs

Although federal officials and some state directors of Chapter 1 compensatory programs are generally aware of the need to improve the quality of these programs, the pervasive influence of the technological mindset among many researchers and state and local educators is severely underestimated by federal officials. There is more than a technological tinkle among the voices who speak about "effective programs," a phrase that itself masks a skills and technological bias in the very way this research topic is stated. I shall give some examples below to support this assertion.

Robert Slavin recommends, for example, that the "federal government should provide support for the dissemination of effective programs to Chapter 1 schools using the National Diffusion Network as one means."[25] If "effectiveness" is the criterion and if "effectiveness" is defined primarily by numbers, as lay and political opinion presses for, we sink deeper into the technological pit. Nineteen of the twenty-five "effective" programs listed in the 1990 edition of *Educational Programs That Work*, published by the National Diffusion Network in "Section G: Basic Skills—Reading," are drill-for-skill models—the very approach that has failed in Chapter 1. One typical curriculum from this set is "Programmed Tutorial Reading" (PTR), which purportedly shows satisfactory gains for students who have taken this course. Slavin lists PTR as a program that should be disseminated nationwide by the federal government.[26] What is Programmed Tutorial Reading? The description in *Educational Programs That Work* states that PTR is "an individualized, one-to-one tutoring program for slow learners or potential reading failures regardless of economic or demographic background." PTR supplements the regular program through "specially trained, carefully supervised paraprofessional tutors who implement its highly structured content and operational programs."[27]

> The teaching strategy is based on established learning principles and uses many elements of programmed instruction—frequent and im-

mediate feedback, specified format, and individualized pace—but, unlike programmed instruction that uses the fading process, proceeding from many initial cues to the minimum needed for success, PTR uses the brightening process, in which minimal cues are followed by increased prompting until complete mastery of the reading task is achieved.

Children receive a *tightly* organized 15-minute daily tutoring session, during which they read from classroom basal readers supplemented with special texts dealing with comprehension and word coding and decoding. Tutors are trained to follow, *verbatim*, the content and operational programs contained in the Tutor's Guide. These specify in detail what, when, and how to teach the content material and also *limit tutor's decisions* about children's responses. Integral to the PTR methodology are its special recording procedures, which not only indicate children's progress, but also prescribe *exactly* which separate items must be reviewed until mastery is achieved. Constant reinforcement or praise is also an essential part of the instructional technique, while overt attention to errors is minimized [emphasis added].[28]

Estimated costs and support services are explained and the name and address of the person to contact in the Utah school district that developed this exemplary curriculum are given to encourage the diffusion of Programmed Tutorial Reading throughout the country.

The technological bias in curriculum materials and teaching methods that is implicit when the criterion of "effectiveness" is used is supported by another Slavin recommendation, which he believes will make Chapter 1 programs "better" when "better" is defined solely by improvement in test scores. He endorses the computer-assisted program for Chapter 1 students in reading and mathematics developed by the Merrimack Education Center, Chelmsford, Massachusetts,[29] which provides "individualized, structured, and sequenced drill and practice and tutorial services" for students.[30] The description of this curriculum in *Educational Programs That Work* states that children are placed in "the appropriate instructional level" based on their "measured strengths and weaknesses." Students receive thirty minutes of daily "individually tailored basic skills remedial instruction." The instructional materials in this curriculum

have been organized in a series of age/grade curriculum strands that are available on both computer-assisted instruction (CAI) and paper/pencil form. Two-thirds of class time is spent in small group or tutorial sessions with the teacher. The remaining third is spent in interaction with the CAI system. Information is presented to the students in small chunks. Depending on what type of response a student makes, the computer takes an appropriate step—for a correct response, reinforcement and new material; for an incorrect response, a tutorial with additional practice. The teacher can assign the student a special drill for remediation when necessary. The computer management system keeps track of each student's progress, and generates reports for use by [the] teacher and administrators.[31]

As if all of this instructional precision and implied certainty is not enough, the Merrimack developers assure prospective adopters that procedures and a "management technical assistance system exist" to guide the implementation of this effective Chapter 1 experience in learning. These technology activities have been identified as a National Diffusion Network Lighthouse Center where educators are instructed in "software and courseware" as well as "hardware" and cooperative purchasing, data base management, and comprehensive planning.[32] With all of the "software" and "hardware" concerns of the Merrimack Center, it is difficult to know whether one is witnessing a breakthrough in Civil War naval technology or is lost in an attractively designed store that sells haberdashery and plumbing supplies.

If approximately 75 percent of the "exemplary" programs listed in the basic skills section (Section G) of the 1990 National Diffusion Network book are technological drill-for-skill approaches, there is a desirable and marked change in educational philosophy when programs are listed for the gifted and talented children (Section J). Approximately ten programs among the twenty-three listed appear to depart from the mechanical and atomistic skill-based pattern of teaching. The Child Development Project, for example, attempts to shape students' social and moral attitudes through a "caring community" based on democratic values; the Folger Library Shakespeare Festivals teaches Shakespeare through actual performances of his plays, which is a participatory and historically accurate, and accessible way, to meet these works; the well-known Philosophy for Children program uses stories and discussion to create a "community of inquiry" for children in grades three through seven to infuse reading, writing, speaking, and listening with reasoning; and the Urban Arts Program makes art direct and personal by learning about art and developing aesthetic judgment through workshops where art is created, displayed, and performed.[33]

The change in *spirit* cannot be missed when we develop programs for our "good students," for those more privileged who are

not slotted into the dry-as-bones skill approaches we deem necessary for those less privileged who get the blessings of Chapter 1
"treatment." If we take the *spirit* of these programs as our guide, is
there any educator or researcher who can say with certainty that
seeing plays (live or on film), discussing them, acting in them and
eventually writing and reading plays might not be a good way to get
"disadvantaged" students to read and write and, more important, to
want to read and write after all of the "mastery tests" are behind
them or, better, if mastery tests are never allowed to dominate the
way students learn? Can art not be used as something interesting in
its own right and be *made* into an environment where rich thematic
units in social studies and science, for example, offer interesting and
varied opportunities to experiment, to grow plants, to paint murals,
to listen to others read and to discuss what has been read, to read
and to write in a context of finding out, a context that is "thicker"
and more rich than worksheets or behavioral objectives? *Where is
the research, the comparisons, on curriculums such as these for
"Chapter 1 kids"*? Are we merely comparing dead cats with dead
cats and wondering why they do not move? Might there not be a pervasive bias in what curriculums get developed and in what curriculums get researched? Might we not, in raising these questions, be
face-to-face with that old mindset that makes mind into a machine
and knowing into predetermined sequences of skills? Might we not,
in raising these questions, be face-to-face with a value bias in what
ought to be developed and researched for those in most need and,
through this bias, are we not also unthinkingly limiting our policy
options to do better for those children who have trouble learning to
read and do arithmetic? Are we not caught in an unseen intellectual
and educational cul-de-sac whose very familiarity supports a belief
that all educational streets must end in a semicircle?

However inviting and warranted the ideas and values—and
the expectations—may be for socially and academically privileged
children, it is beyond reasonable refutation that we offer far less educational quality to our children who are in most need. Fifteen of
the twenty effective programs that Slavin cites, for example, are
drill-for-skill programs.[34] Even if these programs do increase test
scores as Slavin claims, I cannot but question the high personal and
social costs we must pay for these modest score gains in student
boredom, in implicitly teaching students that drills and mastery
tests are what reading and language are all about, and in the uncon-
scious decision of many of these students to read only on demand
because they never had a chance to experience the joy and adventure

of exploring ideas and the feelings of people in real books. What Chapter 1 may be buying with its billions of dollars is an even larger audience for commercial television, alluring video, and Nintendo. The needless loss in the cultivation of intelligence and sensitivity that drill-for-skill programs exact, and our desire to develop, research, and propagate even more of these failure-ridden ways of learning, defies rational explanation. Our desire to pursue failure might best be explained by a deep cultural belief that wholes can only be known (and taught) by splintering them into unrecognizable pieces. Our desire to pursue failure—to invest in more of the very thing that has failed for twenty-five years—suggests a modern belief in magic not unlike that which the Aztecs invoked when the Spaniards arrived. Although some writers believe that the Aztecs might have prevailed over their enemy with pointed sticks and rocks, the Aztecs persisted in using a failed strategy. When the Spaniards arrived, youths were sacrificed. The Spaniards advanced; more sacrifices were offered. This advance-sacrifice pattern was followed until the "Aztec priests were slaughtering youths and maidens as fast as they could lay a hand on them."[35] Nothing worked. At last the Aztecs brought out their secret weapon: a man dressed in a feather suit that struck terror in any army that knew the supernatural meaning of the frightening feathers. The only problem the Aztecs faced was that the Spaniards did not flinch; they did not know the meaning of the feather bird. And several hundred foreign invaders turned the population of an entire continent into slaves or corpses.[36] The Aztecs never had the opportunity to use what they may have learned from their "field experiment" with sacrifices and the feather bird. What will it take in sacrifices and feather birds to break the Aztec pattern in Chapter 1?

But there may be one bright spot in the Aztec sky of Chapter 1. That spot may prove to be Success for All, a kindergarten through grade three program developed by Robert Slavin and his colleagues at Johns Hopkins University. Time will tell. I am encouraged by some of the progressive and holistic language elements in this program. Students listen to stories read by the teacher and discuss them, for example, because this is one sound way to develop a listening and speaking vocabulary—and this activity is interesting and motivating in its own right. Efforts are made to encourage what I call "natural language use" in the classroom and which Success for All incorporates as the "developmental use of language" in everyday classroom life. The motto in this program seems to be "Teach well and prevent reading failure" to reduce the excessive load of school-induced failure which unnecessarily shunts thousands of students into sterile remedial and special education classes.[37] If this program reflects a change in Slavin's implicit technological theory of education it will be a good thing. I am pleased that the Johns Hopkins group did not take seriously most of the "effective" Chapter 1 programs that Slavin listed in 1987.

But we cannot trust one group to do it all. The Hopkins group has had an educational center of gravity that is very close to the traditional educational research position that holds, in effect, "if the numbers come out right for an innovation, the innovation is 'good'." We need more alternatives. I would like to see, for example, what David Elkind, a psychologist in the Piagetian tradition, might develop with a group of colleagues. Or would not a Bank Street College of Education approach to Chapter 1 kids be interesting? I wonder, too, if Lawrence Schweinhart and his colleagues at the High/ Scope Foundation might not come up with a curriculum that would nurture the mind and feelings of students and teachers and reduce our skill fixation in doing so? Might not the idea of "student initiated activity" within a teacher-created framework, an idea Schweinhart uses well in early childhood education, be productive? Children are freed by this idea to explore and inquire unconstrained by a narrow focus to get the correct answer as quickly as possible[38]—a condition that exists in most Chapter 1 programs, one that absolutely demolishes thinking and the positive feelings that go along with a more unhurried, exploratory way of learning. In our frenetic pursuit of skills, we have achieved neither skills nor thought nor good feelings that most students *do* develop in a challenging and supportive educational *environment*.

CONCLUDING COMMENT ON CHAPTER 1 REMEDIAL PROGRAMS

Consider only a few of the facts that I have presented in my discussion of remedial programs in reading and arithmetic for children who are achieving two or more years behind their age-mates: here is a federal program, carried out by the states and local schools that is over twenty-five years old (itself a record of long life for an educational reform), on which at least $50 billion has been spent, and which has touched the lives of millions of economically and educationally needy students—*to no demonstrable satisfactory educational or social end!* Technically valid research studies show only slight achievement gains for Chapter 1 remedial students. Descriptive studies of what life is like in these programs find that students rarely have a chance to interact with a teacher, that teachers often give them work that is *below* their present achievement level, an action that is consistent with the low expectations teachers and administrators hold for these students. Teachers believe that these students are "slow learners." Learning to think is displaced by students plodding through reams of fill-in-the-blank "skill sheets." Forty to 75 percent of the students who are placed in these remedial programs never get out. The chain of failure is so great, as I stated earlier, that one researcher refers to these kids as "lifers."

It is difficult to contain one's outrage, to use a phrase John Goodlad sometimes invokes in his studies of high schools and teacher education programs, at the low quality of the educational and social experience that students in Chapter 1 have endured. Although the summaries of the research that I have read tellingly ignore the personal effects on students' attitudes toward themselves and toward learning, I do not see how outcomes in these important and not-easily-measured dimensions of education can be anything but negative. A punishing environment punishes. It is as simple as that.

Of all of the programs that I use to illustrate the pattern of reform across three decades, Chapter 1 of the Elementary and Secondary Education Act of 1965 is probably the most significant because it touches virtually every school district in the nation, and because it has endured so long and has touched the lives of perhaps twenty million students over the years, five million in 1992 alone. The time is tragically past when Congress and educators can regard this "politically sweet" reform as a money chute from Washington to the hinterlands. If ever the technological mindset was at work, coupled with political expediency and a moral indifference to the children most in need of our caring and the very best educational *environments* our minds and imaginations can create, it is the children in Chapter 1, who ask for little and who have received even less. Let us hope that the first glimmer of more humane and intellectually challenging programs that have begun to emerge spread like the morning light. Federal and state policy should encourage the development and *comprehensive* evaluation of these programs which promise so much. We need to hear much less about the restrictive programs published by the National Diffusion Network, whose publication is innocently mistitled *Educational Programs That Work.*

If Chapter 1 offers a limited educational diet in an attempt to "remediate" what policymakers judge to be the students' deficiencies, the Chicago mastery learning program in reading adopts a similar philosophy of learning and teaching for urban students in regular classes. Although the historical path taken by each of these reforms is very different, the learning outcomes are similar. One important difference between them, however, is that the stormy life of Chicago mastery learning resulted in a public display of no confidence in the reform's power to deliver what it promised.

THE TECHNOLOGICAL MINDSET IN BRICK AND GLASS

MASTERY LEARNING CHICAGO STYLE

Benjamin Bloom, Distinguished Service Professor of Education Emeritus at the University of Chicago, and the theoretician behind mastery learning, offers two idealistic and humane ideas that capture the core of mastery learning as he sees it: give students the time they need to learn something under favorable educational conditions and most of them, 80 percent, will achieve at the level gained by the top 20 percent. There is considerable evidence, Bloom writes, "that mastery learning procedures do work well in enabling about four-fifths of students to reach a level of achievement which less than one-fifth attain under non-mastery conditions. . . . The efficiency of correctives and the additional time needed are direct functions of the quality of the diagnostic-progress feedback testing—the formative tests."[39] This is it. These are the core ideas on which mastery learning rests.

The ideas that undergird mastery learning are stated in another way by Bloom. He says that all students can learn much more than they now learn if instruction is approached "sensitively and systematically," if students are helped at the time difficulties occur, and "if they are given sufficient time to achieve mastery, and if there is some clear criterion of what constitutes mastery."[40]

Because I believe that ideals as well as ideas are essential to any practical way of thinking about education, and because I believe that Bloom's idealism has been filtered out of the more general interpretations of mastery learning (as I shall show), I want to continue with this unnoted idea dimension within mastery learning. Although I believe that Bloom is a behaviorist through and through, it is remarkable that some important and most unbehavioristic ideas break through Bloom's epistemology like water shooting from an artesian well in a desert. Bloom speaks about students having "peak learning experiences," an idea he borrowed from A. H. Maslow. Peak learning experiences are "so vivid that students will recall them in great detail many years later." These vivid experiences are often unrelated to the objectives in the curriculum. Although Bloom believes that students do not often have "peak learning experiences," he hopes for more by saying that we may learn "how learning in the schools can be vivid and one source of fulfillment for most of our students. . . ."[41] Bloom is aware, as many of his professorial and practitioner followers are not, that the feedback-corrective component (loosely, frequent reinforcement) in mastery learning can lead to student dependency on this feedback in which the students want ever-increasing amounts of it. Bloom, therefore, wants independent learners with the abilities and attitudes which will be useful in dealing with a wide range of life situations.[42] Finally, there is this shocker that I do not recall reading anywhere in the literature on mastery learning, and which I believe is lost on many who practice mastery learning. *Mastery learning, Bloom believes, is effective to the point at which it eventually becomes unnecessary.* While mastery learning techniques may be needed at some stages in learning, "over time these [favorable conditions] may be gradually discarded."[43] Mastery learning, therefore, as it is viewed by its developer, is to be seen as "starter feed" for educational chicks, which is to be ingested only until more nourishing fare can be eaten.

Bloom's vision for mastery learning is broad. He believes that mastery learning "can be one of the more powerful sources for mental health" by reducing the anxieties associated with school failure. "Mastery learning can give zest to school learning and . . . develop a lifelong interest in learning," Bloom writes. He believes that continual learning should be the major goal of the educational program.[44]

Bloom turns to some of the practical considerations in mastery learning in his book *All Our Children Learning.* "The specification of objectives and the content of instruction," Bloom says, "is one necessary precondition for informing . . . teachers and students about the expectations." Translating the specifications for what is to be learned into "evaluation procedures helps to further define what it is that the student should [learn]," Bloom continues. One useful procedure is to "break a subject into smaller units of learning," such as a chapter in a textbook that might take one or two weeks to learn. Bloom believes that learning can be layered into a hierarchy of tasks that range from facts to abstract ideas to the analysis of complex theoretical statements. Brief diagnostic progress tests (criterion-referenced tests) are then constructed "to determine [if] the student has mastered the unit and what, if anything, the student must still do to master it." The diagnosis should be accompanied by a "very specific prescription if the students are to do anything about it." Small groups of two or three students working together for an hour or so a week on their prescriptions seems to give good results. The kinds of help provided to students, according to Bloom, include tutorials, rereading original materials, working on specific pages in other textbooks, audio-visual materials, workbooks, or programmed texts.[45]

This brief excursion into Bloom's thinking on mastery learning suggests the quality of his educational vision. How do the practitioners of mastery learning, or others in the academic community, view Bloom's creation? If "truth happens to an idea," as William James believed, what "truth" was imparted to the idea of mastery learning by the Chicago public schools in 1979?

Joseph P. Hannon, the Chicago superintendent of schools who initiated the mastery learning reading program, linked it to a continuous-progress curriculum of 1400 objectives. These objectives are "hierarchically sequenced between [reading] levels," which number thirteen. Criterion-referenced tests are used to assess mastery of the 273 reading objectives. The Chicago mastery learning instructional materials include a series of "learning packets" that include all of the necessary materials for mastery learning: structured teaching activities, pupil practice materials, formative tests, and corrective exercises. The Chicago program is tied to a competency-based promotion policy that requires elementary students to pass 80 percent of the objectives in each of the thirteen levels. Those who do not meet this criterion are retained for one year.[46]

By 1980 the Chicago mastery learning materials were officially published. Short of visiting a mastery learning class in Chicago, we can get a feeling for what the students and the teachers encountered in this version of mastery learning by reviewing one unit for the third grade. I encourage the reader to "take in" these materials and try to imagine how a third grader in Chicago might deal with them while simultaneously trying to imagine what it might be like to teach in this program. I offer this admonition, projecting a failing of my own, because I resisted the opportunity to "really get into these materials," in part because it is superficially more rewarding to deal with high-flying generalities. Let us now get below the idea level of a Bloom and a superintendent of schools, to see what life was like for the kids and the teachers who were following this mastery learning program.

Chicago Mastery Learning Reading is a kindergarten through grade eight curriculum that teaches reading through thinking skills. "These materials encompass a logical sequence for skill development in Word Attack, Comprehension, and Study Skills," its developers write.[47] The thinking skills for grade three include Comparisons, Making Sense, Cause and Effect Relationships, Reading for Detail, and Categorizing. I shall walk us through most of the third grade unit on Categorizing. The content of the unit deals with categorizing animals and objects in certain ways. The major steps in the unit will be numbered here for convenience. These lessons are taken from *Excerpts from Chicago Mastery Learning Reading* distributed by the program's publisher.[48]

1. Initial Instruction—First Teaching Activity

A. [The teacher is told, in the spirit of a teacher's manual, that this activity is to show students how things may be grouped into categories. Two large-group blackboard exercises are led by the teacher in which the students are asked to group two sets of ten objects into the appropriate categories. The students are told that each set of objects is a category and they are asked to come up with a label for each category. Food is the correct category for the first set, animals for the second.] [The next part, B, is a direct quotation from the instructions to the teacher.]

B. Tell students that today we will read a story about animals, past and present, and that in the exercise which follows the story, we'll be asked to divide animals into categories which show how they are alike in some way. As we group the animals we'll fit them into categories by asking what kind of skin they have, and where they live or spend most of their time.

Some animals have feathers (birds), others have scales (fish), and still others have fur or hair. Some animals live on land, some in water, and others spend most of their time in the air. . . .

C. [Vocabulary words from the story the students are about to read, "Animals, Past and Present," are introduced, such as *prehistoric, extinct, Ichthyosaur,* as well as words such as *resemble* and *tremendous* that might not be in the children's vocabulary.]

We don't expect a single child to know
how to categorize, or even what a category is.

The first page tells the teacher the basic
outline for presentation with examples
to give to the class.

Student Activity Sheet #1

Animals, Past and Present

Did you know that animals have been around the earth for
a very long time? How long do you think? Would you believe for
about 350 million years? If you have ever been to the Chicago
Field Museum, you have seen one of the very earliest animals that
lived on earth. He is very, very big. He stands about 40 feet
tall! You can't miss him as you walk in the front door of the
museum. Although he's big, and looks as though he could devour
you, he's actually very quiet. He's not alive, and neither is any
animal like it alive today. You could say that he is extinct.
This means that no animals of his type or species are still being
born, or will probably ever exist again.

He is also called a prehistoric animal. He lived before man
began to make a written record about what was happening on earth.
Some of the very early prehistoric animals are called dinosaurs.
These are very large lizard-like animals.

The Tyrannosaurus Rex (tə-ran-ə-sor-əs reks) was the largest
meat-eating dinosaur that ever lived on land. His name means
"master lizard". From the top of his head to the tip of his tail,
he could grow to nearly fifty feet long. He weighed up to 12 tons,
larger than even the largest elephant. His short front legs and
his large hind legs made him resemble a tremendous lizard.

The dinosaur at the entrance of our Field Museum is a replica
of this type of dinosaur. A replica is a close copy of something.
But, if dinosaurs are prehistoric animals and are extinct, how do
we know what they really looked like? Man has found fossils, parts
of plants or animals sealed within the earth which still reveal
what life resembled many years ago. Using these fossils man has
been able to draw or make replicas of animals which lived in the
past.

Another animal from prehistoric times is the Ichthyosaur
(ik-thē-ə-so(ə)r). Its name means "fish lizard". This is an
extinct animal which lived in the water like a fish does, and
which also was shaped like a fish.

A third prehistoric animal was the Pterodactyl (ter-ə-dak-t-l).
Its name means "wing lizard". Some of these animals had wings that,
when stretched out wide, measured 25 feet from end to end. These
were the largest flying animals that ever existed. Can you imagine
how you would feel if you were walking home and one flew over
your head landing on the sidewalk in front of you? Never fear,
these animals are also extinct. These are all animals of the past.

4

First, a story to read aloud. The story is
complex, but the story itself is not the
lesson. The only purpose of the story is
to introduce dinosaur ancestors of
mammals, fish and birds. This prepares
students for the first activity, where
they categorize animals by type.

CATEGORIZING

Student Activity Sheet #1 (cont'd)

There are many animals living on our earth today. Some
live on land or in the water, others fly in the air. You will
be given a list of animals which live on our earth today. We
can divide this list of animals into categories which show that
they have something in common. Some of these animals belong to
a category called mammals. They feed their young babies with
milk, have hairy skins and live on land (the group of water mammals are an exception to this, including dolphins and whales).
Another category called fish live in water and have scaly skin.
The third category, birds, have feathers and wings and usually
can fly in the air (an exception is the ostrich, a bird so large
that he is unable to fly. The ostrich may weigh up to 300 lbs.)

Look at the activity sheet that follows on the next page. An
animal list is provided and three categories are pictured in the
drawing. To what category does each of the animals in the list
belong? How can you tell whether it is a mammal, a fish or a
bird, or what the animal name means? Refer to the story, "Animals,
Past and Present" or to the dictionary if you aren't sure. Then
put each animal's name under the correct category in the drawing.

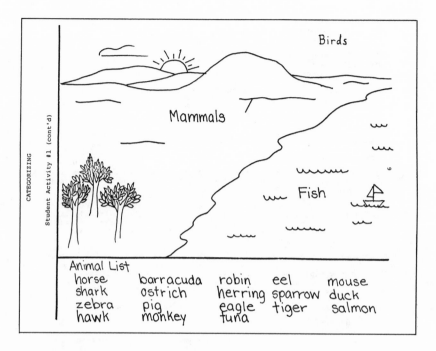

Birds

Mammals

Fish

Animal List
horse   barracuda   robin   eel   mouse
shark   ostrich   herring sparrow duck
zebra   pig   eagle   tiger   salmon
hawk   monkey   tuna

The initial activity provides a visual
image to support the deductive process.

Put fish in the sea, birds in the air,
mammals on land.

Someone might even have to use a
dictionary to see what a barracuda is.

The second activity shows the direction
in which the unit is moving:
categorizing in two dimensions at once
without the visual image.

CATEGORIZING

Initial Instruction

Second Teaching Activity

Instructions to teachers:

A. Chart making is a method of concisely organizing and categorizing
   information. In the first teaching activity students were asked
   to categorize information by utilizing one set of criteria to
   determine whether a specific animal belongs to a group called
   birds, fish or mammals. In these chart making activities which
   follow, students will be asked to group animals again using the
   previously studied criteria, plus one additional criteria, such
   as whether the animal is large or small, or whether the animal
   is generally used for food or not.

   Explain to students that this lesson will deal with ways of categorizing or grouping animals. Ask students to think about how
   they grouped their list of animals in the previous lesson as
   birds, fish or mammals. Review with them the set of criteria
   for determining the group to which each animal belongs.

B. Write the following list of animal names on the blackboard:

   Animal List

mouse	hippopotamus	goldfish
elephant	shark	eagle
guppy	pigeon	hamster
robin	barracuda	ostrich

   Then draw this diagram on the blackboard:

Animals	LARGE	SMALL
Birds		
Fish		
Mammals	7	

We ask the students what's *large* so
they can practice categorizing.

Second Teaching Activity (cont'd)

Point out to pupils that you have made a chart which will answer two types of questions about the animals from the animal list. First, what kind of animal is it (a bird has feathers and wings and normally can fly in the air; a fish usually has scales and lives in water; and a mammal is a land-loving furry or hairy animal)? Next, what size is it, is it an animal which is small, or is it a large animal?

Pronounce the animal names on the list, and allow pupils to comment about them or to describe them if they are not familiar to all the students.

Fill in the chart on the blackboard as a group activity. Discuss why each animal fits into a particular slot in the chart by meeting two criteria which tell what type of animal it is (bird, fish or mammal) and what size it is (large or small).

C. Explain to pupils that you will ask them to categorize animals again. This time they will have to decide what type of animal it is, bird, fish or mammal, and whether we generally use it for food or not.

Before beginning the chart which follows, discuss farming and fishing with students. Explain that fisherman capture seafood, and that farmers raise vegetables, fruits and animals for us to eat. Explain how cattle and sheep are domesticated and raised for food by ranchers.

Ask pupils to name some animals which are not used for food. Point out that many insects and wild animals are not generally consumed as food in this country, but may be eaten by a few people here, and may be a popular food elsewhere. Some examples: fried ants, snails (escargot), shark and horse meat.

Explain to pupils that on the chart which they will do next (Student Activity Sheet #2), the animals will be divided into the bird, fish and mammal categories and into two additional categories; animals used for food, and wild animals, animals not generally kept on farms or ranches, or sold in most grocery stores as food.

Pronounce and review the words from the animal list. In classes needing guidance in the activity each choice can be discussed by students together, then written on their own charts after the appropriate responses have been decided and agreed upon by all.

Students may also fill out their charts independently, then check their work by filling out the same chart on the blackboard as a group.

Animals	Animals Used for Food	Wild Animals
Birds		
Fish		
Mammals		

Animal List

canary	hawk	skunk	shark	piranha	eagle
eel	chicken	trout	rabbit	sheep	bass
cow	salmon	duck	elephant	pheasant	bluebird
giraffe	hippopotamus	tuna	barracuda	turkey	pig

Again, a chance to practice skills. This time, instead of large and small, it's which is used for food and which is wild . . . What about salmon?

This is a comprehension lesson, so we don't care that much about the salmon. We care about the thoughts one would think to make that decision.

If a kid says "I went out fishing last summer, and I caught the biggest salmon of the day—it's a wild animal," he's right.

The kid next to him says "Yes, but I'll bet you put it on a grill and ate it for food. So it's an animal used for food." He's also right.

The child who says "For food or wild but I don't know why," is not engaged in the thought processes necessary to solve the problem.

Within each unit is
a Formative Test.

The child performs in the same basic
format as in the activities. CATEGORIZING

Formative Test

Directions:

Read the paragraph and complete the exercise which follows:

GOING CAMPING

One day three brothers, Ronnie, Anthony and Robert began planning a camping trip. They had to decide what to take and who was
going to get it all together. Ronnie was especially interested in
the kinds of equipment they should take, so he said, "We have to
have the right equipment, so I'll collect it, because I'm the only
one smart enough." Anthony didn't care about that; what he liked
was eating. "I'll get the food and cooking stuff, so we don't
starve." Robert was most interested in not freezing. "I will be
the one to get something to keep us warm."

These are some of the things that they finally took on their
trip:

tent	pots and pans	water
blankets	rope	canteen
flour	sweaters	raincoats
bread	milk	sleeping bags
flashlight	kerosene lamp	knife
fishing rod	matches	hats

List each of these below the name of the person who brought it
on the camping trip. Note that some things may fit into more than
one category. One thing has already been filled in under each name.
You are to complete the lists for each boy.

Ronnie	Anthony	Robert
kerosene lamp	bread	sweaters

10

The Teacher's Manual provides the right
answers, the mastery level, and
specific scoring instructions.

CMLR's essential component—the one that makes it work—is the remedial instruction. It approaches the learning in a different way.

The (Corrective) Additional Activity might be pictorial instead of verbal, concrete instead of abstract, manipulative instead of auditory.

CATEGORIZING

Additional Activity #1

I. Look at each group of four things listed in the boxes below. Three things in each group should be together because they are alike in some way. One does not belong with the others. Put a line through the one which <u>doesn't</u> belong in the same <u>cate-gory</u> as the others. The first one is done for you.

1. doll kite yo-yo ~~peach~~ ___toys___	2. goldfish cow shark eel _____	3. balloon dress coat pants _____
4. tricycle book motorcycle bus _____	5. brick corn carrots apple _____	6. house apartment clock igloo _____
7. sparrow bluebird kangaroo pigeon _____	8. four 9 III Sally _____	9. crayon eraser chalk pencil _____

II. Look at these boxes given above. Then choose the correct <u>category label</u> which tells how these things are alike and why they are grouped together. Write the correct category label on the line below the list in each box.

Category Labels:

food	birds	things used for writing
numbers	toys	things you ride
clothes	fish	places where people live

12

The remedial instruction reverses the approach and uses inductive reasoning.

In this unit the first approach is deductive: boxes are labeled and students figure out what goes in each.

Students figure out what doesn't belong, and what label describes three items but not the fourth.

Matching Words

Find the word in the second column that belongs with a word
in the first column. Write the letter in the space provided.

___g___ tulip   a. animal

_____ 1. April   b. color

_____ 2. apple   c. state

_____ 3. Christmas   d. fruit

_____ 4. baseball   e. month

_____ 5. spinach   f. holiday

_____ 6. Illinois   g. flower

_____ 7. Chicago   h. toy

_____ 8. red   i. sport

_____ 9. elephant   j. vegetable

_____10. doll   k. city

Directions:

Write your name at the top of your
paper. The directions say: Find the word
in the second column that belongs with
each word in the first column. Write the
letter in the space provided.

Look at the example. The letter G has
been written in front of the word tulip
because tulip and flower belong
together.

Now do the rest of the page in the
same way.

Discussion and Assessment of the Chicago Mastery
Learning Materials

The *Excerpts from Chicago Mastery Learning Reading* (CMLR), assembled by the publisher, from which my examples are taken, states
that CMLR "teaches reading through thinking skills" which carries
the burden of teaching comprehension in this curriculum.[49] Thirty-
two lessons in word attack and study skills complement the
comprehension-thinking skills component. The lesson examples in
categorization, one of the ten thinking skill units for the third grade,
reflect the content in this unit.

I have three major criticisms of CMLR: CMLR takes a superficial stance toward subject content and to reading itself, CMLR ignores student purpose in its activities, and CMLR is cavalier toward
meaning. Before I discuss these criticisms, I want to bring in the
publisher's view of CMLR. The comments of Donald W. Robb,
Charlesbridge Publishing, the successor company to the first publisher of CMLR, show that mastery learning can be interpreted in
richer ways than those used in the 1980 version.

> In its inception, *Chicago Mastery Learning Reading* was de-
> signed to be one component of a total reading program: instruction in
> the kinds of thinking processes typically employed by good readers. A
> complete reading program would, of course, also include a rich selec-
> tion of children's literature. The rationale for this approach is the be-
> lief that skills in isolation, as presented in most workbooks, or as ends
> in themselves, are of minimal value. Rather, students need an oppor-
> tunity for instruction in strategies and ample opportunity to apply
> those strategies, with increasing independence, in the reading of good
> literature or of content area textbooks.
>
> Now revised and published by Charlesbridge Publishing as *IN-
> SIGHTS: Reading as Thinking*, the program retains the highly suc-
> cessful organization of the original: carefully sequenced prerequisite
> skill development, embedded learning strategies, and alternative
> strategies for corrective instruction. Used in thousands of classrooms
> across the country, *INSIGHTS* is highly regarded by many teachers as
> an essential element of their reading program. For many teachers *IN-
> SIGHTS* supports the goals of an integrated curriculum, since stu-
> dents can apply the strategies in their reading of literature and in the
> reading of non-fiction materials related to science, social studies,
> health, math, and other curriculum areas. Reading passages in the *IN-
> SIGHTS* units, as well as application activities in each unit, encour-
> age this transition to integrated reading. Because *INSIGHTS* reflects
> research in critical thinking processes, units are designed to assist

students in constructing meaning—that is, using information in the text they read along with their own prior knowledge and experience to understand and connect actively with an author's message.

Effective reading involves the automatic and simultaneous blending of a variety of processes and strategies. The purpose of *IN-SIGHTS* is to help students internalize these processes into a personal repertoire of thinking strategies and to encourage them to draw on these strategies for purposeful reading.

Thinking, thinking in life, always involves knowledge, purpose, and meaning. Knowledge is the grist for thinking, purpose supplies the drive, and meaning makes thinking coherent and supplies the context within which knowledge and purpose can do their work. Even if something like thinking skills exist in the world removed from particular subject matters, such as spotting an error in a blueprint or writing a legal brief, this is not a sufficient condition to believe that "categorization" or "analogies" is one of them. Categorization, for example, does not appear on one well-thought-out list of the components in critical thinking, although it might show up on another list of over twenty-five hundred possibilities of the ways in which one might think.[50] The artificiality of the "stories" in the 1980 version reflects an indifference to content, purpose, and meaning, which the new version tries to remedy. Notice, for example, that the story on dinosaurs—a potentially gripping study for many children—is denigrated in the developers' note in the left hand margin when they write that "the story itself is not the lesson. The only purpose of the story is to introduce dinosaur ancestors of mammals, fish and birds." It would not take much imagination to develop a thematic unit on dinosaurs which would integrate reading, writing, talking, listening, and science in an interesting study. There might even arise in this thematic unit a meaningful opportunity to "categorize" in which case the question of whether "categorization" is or is not a "thinking skill" becomes moot.

Another example of epistemological disassociation in this curriculum arises with the corrective test, whose purpose is remediation (page 116). The developers assume that an alternative inductive approach to labelling categories of things is "corrective" and desirable when the deductive process fails. On what grounds might this be so? Only because "inductive" may appear to be opposite and separate from "deductive," although in scientific and other kinds of reasoning they may occur in one thinking process? The larger question that cries out for remediation is the disjointed story content and its social and intellectual irrelevance. Might not, for example, sheer boredom be one possible cause of failure on the criterion-referenced test? Another example of this kind of reasoning occurs in the Second Teaching Activity (page 112) mentioned in the developers' marginal note. The unit is moving toward "categorizing in two dimensions at once without the visual image." Why is this desirable? How does a "visual image in two dimensions" relate to the psychological-social process of learning language?

Why is it that we insist, despite failure after failure, to so tightly wind the educational clock in sequenced systems of sub-skills that the clock stops? And Chicago's mastery learning clock stopped. The Chicago Board of Education abandoned CMLR in August 1981 after spending $7.5 million in what began as a "continuous progress" curriculum in 1964, although it was not until 1974 that school officials completed the required 525 criterion-referenced tests.[51] A local education-research and advocacy organization, Designs for Change, said that 75 percent of Chicago's ninth graders were reading below grade level. The report blamed over-reliance on CMLR as contributing to these results. Opponents claim that the program dampens children's enthusiasm and ability to read by presenting reading as a set of fragmented subskills.[52] But it was a layman, George Munoz, president of the Chicago Board of Education, who may have said it best. CMLR became a crutch for teachers, according to Munoz, who relied too much on mechanical techniques. "[A]dministrators put too much emphasis on the mechanics of reading," Munoz continued, "and not enough on *reading itself.* The object became mastering mastery learning and not on mastering reading or math" [emphasis added]. Benjamin Bloom agreed. Stating that mastery learning is not only a series of work skills, Bloom added that "it has to involve reading. Unless a kid reads a great deal, he's not going to learn reading very well. . . ."[53]

But the failure of CMLR goes deeper than a reliance on mechanical sequences of skills. Most of those in the research and academic community rely still on a perspective on learning and teaching that is behavioristic, a system of belief akin to the philosophy of E. L. Thorndike and B. F. Skinner, including that of Benjamin Bloom. We keep trying to wrestle learning to the ground, to overcontrol with "explicit systems." We keep trying to build ever more elaborate psychological pumps to force educational water to run up hill. The pumps fail and hundreds of thousands of children drown in the deluge, only for a later generation to see another pump builder come along and try the same trick with new materials and the same old promises. To try to teach reading without real books and lots of reading, writing, and talk is an aberration that only God can comprehend—or the more humble among us who have not lost their common sense. When young children use language at home, to cite one bit of commonsense evidence, they organize and sequence vast amounts of information, learn hordes of new words, learn the cultural codes of speaking (taking turns, for example), and they inductively generate a grammar for the language they are "swimming in." *Children are by nature systematic learners.* Yet theorists in the tradition of behaviorism generally ignore this holistic learning.

Until we accept another idea—a more valid theory of language *learning* as a natural psychological and social process which a good school can build on—we will continue to fail. Why do we resist theories which hold that learning is "meaning-centered and social . . . that the best vehicle for language development is language itself, 'using language to fine tune language', " as one writer put it? One holistic curriculum in language asserts that using language does not mean breaking it down into parts and proceeding part by part. Whole language theorists such as J. Harste and K. Goodman remind us that language is used "to make meaning, to accomplish peoples' purposes; [that] language always occurs in a [social] situation, and these situations are critical to the meaning that is being made."[54] CMLR had no meaningful social situation or purpose beyond itself as a curriculum, which is one reason it failed. Skill practice that is done outside of real reading and writing, without a desire to tell someone something or to understand what another has written or spoken, makes learning more difficult because it violates the social nature of language use. "Our problem is not how to teach language," according to Susan Lytle and Morton Botel, "but how to enhance the language learning already taking place."[55] If the educational pump builders would heed this message they might still build pumps, but instead of trying to make water run up hill they would enrich and accelerate its horizontal flow.

The following observations by John Dewey, written in 1916, resonate with modern theory in learning language. When we send or receive a message, Dewey says, we qualitatively enlarge or change our experience. To communicate with another human *means* that one "has to assimilate, imaginatively, something of another's experience. . . . All communication is like art." Dewey does not ignore the power of the social environment to educate, as too many theorists and educators do today. "Any social arrangement that remains vitally social, or vitally shared, is educative to those who participate in it. Only when it becomes cast in a mold and runs in a routine way does it lose its educative power." But Dewey cautioned, ever mindful of the "real world," that the mere existence of a group (one thinks of a teacher or a group of students or a school faculty) does not mean that desirable social relations exist. "A large number of social relationships in any social group are still on the machine-like plane," he writes. "Individuals use one another [to get] desired results, without reference to the emotional and intellectual disposition and consent of those used." Such uses may reflect technical superiority or power, but they form no true social group. Giving orders [or developing sequenced-skill curriculums] may effect results, but it does not "effect a sharing of purposes, a communication of interests."[56]

CONCLUDING COMMENT ON MASTERY LEARNING

Chicago Mastery Learning Reading is a technological curriculum. This judgment is reasonably supported by the description of one complete unit of instruction on categorization and the discussion and assessment of these materials. It is clear, for example, that the Chicago program ignores significant content in its efforts to teach reading comprehension, that its approach is tightly sequential, and that teachers are managers of a system created by others rather than creative adapters or developers of a curriculum. The publisher has tried to address these problems in a new version.

As is true of all of the technological curriculums or teaching methods that I have discussed so far, the promises and the invocation of seemingly solid and persuasive words and phrases such as "mastery," "all students can learn," "individualized," "lifelong learning," "fixed performance standards," "feedback and correctives," not to mention the appeal of "thinking skills," sound better and promise more, far more, than they can deliver. By invoking some of the *images* of an intellectual and humane education, images that seem to touch deep springs within ourselves, such as "personal" or "thinking," technological curriculum developers cash in on the credit built up by educators in the progressive tradition. One source of the appeal of these technological curriculums is that, like a professed nonbeliever who still attends church occasionally, they have it both ways. Technologists offer the promise of efficiency and measurement but, without guile, they cannot help but echo some of the values in the progressive tradition. Many policymakers and educators eagerly pursue the purported efficiency and clarity of these programs, giving scant attention to the humanistic echoes. But academics like Benjamin Bloom feel more deeply. When Bloom, for example, speaks of "peak experiences," learning as fulfillment, or of the danger that feedback and correctives can create dependency in students for immediate satisfactions, he truly believes it. But he cannot escape the metaphysics of his materialist system, so empirical research and numbers and isolated variables lead him to think in terms of small-step learning, hierarchies, diagnostic-progress tests, and specific prescriptions. Bloom's need for a scientifically grounded theory of school learning snuffs out the humanistic and intellectual echoes that lie within him. *Flowers cannot grow on the hard rock of scientific materialism.* Progressivism is a larger, more inclusive category that *may* at times take in some form of mastery learning (or Madeline Hunter's model or the research on effective teaching), but Bloom's implicit metaphysics (and that of the others), is not big enough to take in the ideals of progressive education in the Deweyan tradition. One is a pinched view of humans and of learning, the other an open and more optimistic view of the human capacity to learn.

For an advocate of a contrary position to say that scientific materialism offers a "pinched view of human beings" may be suspect on its face, but compare some of the evidence before us. Contrast the view of language and comprehension taken by the developers of *Chicago Mastery Learning Reading,* for example, with the holistic theories of language and language learning (not teaching alone) and those of Dewey that I mentioned earlier. The difference between them is no quibble—it is a chasm of Grand Canyon scale. Or consider the matter of criterion-referenced testing, which is broadly influenced by behavioristic philosophy and by societal pressures for accountability. Criterion-referenced tests are not intrinsically bad, but they too often become invalid and trivial, as we saw in Chicago mastery learning. The pilot's ability to safely land an airplane, for example, during a flight review, is a valid criterion-referenced test. But consider what the technological mindset usually ignores in school settings: "if you wish only to know how well a curriculum is achieving *its* objectives, you fit the test to the curriculum; but if you wish to know how well the curriculum is serving the national interest, you measure all outcomes that might be worth striving for," asserts L. J. Cronbach.[57] Once more we see the social dimension in education coming to the fore in yet another way from those mentioned earlier. Even if the test scores significantly increase in a given reading or mathematics program, but an assessment of "other outcomes worth striving for" suggests that students do not like the subject, or that students are becoming dependent on learning crutches such as immediate knowledge of results, I would say that this is not a good program however much it might be acclaimed by those who watch the educational Nielsen ratings.

A Critical Review of the Research on Mastery Learning

How well is mastery learning doing in the world beyond Chicago? I will turn to Robert Slavin who, however much he believes that a high "Nielsen rating" is the criterion for goodness, is at least careful about the design qualities of the research he summarizes, something that many of those who do research ignore, as Derek Bok, former president of Harvard University, bluntly points out.[58] Because those who practice educational technology believe in objectivity and numbers, it seems only fair to apply these criteria to determine if mastery learning increases achievement.

After eliminating methodologically unsound studies, studies that did not use a control group, studies that used experimenter-made tests rather than standardized tests, and studies whose duration was less than three days [!] or four weeks, Slavin's critical review of valid studies on mastery learning in reading or mathematics found no greater achievement gains for mastery learning students than students in the control group. "For most educators," Slavin states, "the uncontested finding that year-long studies show no greater effects for mastery learning than traditional methods on standardized measures should be the end of the story."[59] The studies that showed no difference were on group-based mastery learning programs with correctives or enrichment to supplement the group instruction as they do in the Chicago mastery learning program.

The story did not end with Slavin's adverse report on mastery learning in the *The Review of Educational Research*. If anything it heated up. Prominent proponents of mastery learning, such as James Block and Benjamin Bloom, responded to Slavin's research synthesis. Block notes that it is the twentieth anniversary of mastery learning [1988] and says that it is not surprising that a concept in education that lasts this long should draw potshots. Block cites "83 quasi-longitudinal studies . . . [which show] that mastery works."[60] Slavin replies in a subsequent issue of the same journal to Block's citation of 83 longitudinal studies by saying they are scientifically worthless. To say that this year's third graders are doing better than last year's—Block's meaning of "quasi-longitudinal"—is invalid, Slavin argues, because educators have inflated standardized test scores by such expedients as increasing promotion standards, teaching test-taking skills, and in other ways. Since mastery learning is often introduced as part of a higher standards–curriculum alignment plan, it is impossible to separate the effects of mastery learning.[61] Bloom wades into this scientific dispute hoping that "Slavin will declare a truce in his opposition to mastery learning."[62] Bloom's comment may have been sparked by one of Slavin's criteria for good research, which required that studies span at least four weeks, a criterion that Bloom did not meet. Studies that produced large effects, and which are often cited by Bloom and others in the "pro" mastery learning literature, "were conducted in three days, one week, two weeks, three weeks," Slavin laments.[63] I will leave this debate here, although it says much that practitioners need to know, and too often do not know, about the slippery nature of the phrase "research says."

Intellectual capriciousness and disregard for the coherence of subject matter are evident in the Chicago mastery learning materials. This curriculum invokes the appeal of thinking skills and promises a "logical sequence for skill development" in reading—words calculated to appeal to educators. But what Chicago mastery learning actually offers is a superficial series of atomistic exercises that are unrelated to either thinking or reading. Chicago mastery learning illustrates the anti-intellectual nature of the technological mindset. The atomization of content is so complete one might be excused for believing that the developers set out to shred it. It is impossible for children to make anything sensible from this unit. Thinking is neglected. Teachers and students are required mindlessly to submit to the remote control of their classroom exercised by the curriculum's developers. A surreal atmosphere permeates this enterprise, an enterprise where thinking becomes unthinking, where teachers purvey nonsense, and where students are implicitly expected to find meaning when adults have taken it away.

Although it would be extremely difficult to show that intellectual and democratic values shaped the Chicago mastery learning program (or Chapter 1 remedial programs), one has to acknowledge that Benjamin Bloom did catch glimpses of this landscape. He described a part of this landscape when he talked about peak experiences, as I stated earlier, and when he expressed his hope that learning in school might become more vivid and fulfilling for most of our students. Bloom, in a sense, bracketed his faith in psychological and educational science when he made these statements. The two reforms that I shall discuss next, Madeline Hunter's approach to teaching and the research on effective teaching, more fully embrace the attempts of researchers to study teachers and teaching scientifically. Although Hunter, too, makes statements that modify her essentially scientific view when she says teaching has some artistic threads woven into its scientific fabric, these statements seem not to carry the depth of feeling I sense in reading Bloom's book, *All Our Children Learning*, however much Bloom's belief in scientific methods ultimately undermined his hopes.

SCIENTIFIC BLUES: M. HUNTER'S TEACHING MODEL AND THE RESEARCH ON EFFECTIVE TEACHING

Madeline Hunter did something General Robert E. Lee could not do: she attacked from Harrisburg, Pennsylvania, the state capital, with the cooperation of the friendly forces in Governor Richard Thornburgh's office and his troops in the Department of Education, and took Pennsylvania by storm. Whether Hunter took Gettysburg does not matter because, by 1985, she held most of Pennsylvania.

If Pennsylvania were only one of a few states to adopt the Hunter model, its importance might be minimal. But the Hunter model is a national phenomenon. Although no survey has been made on the number of states that have adopted the model in the name of reform, most educators would agree that the Hunter model is used by schools in virtually every state. Its use in 1987 by at least 60 percent of Pennsylvania's five hundred school districts has been authoritatively reported.[64]

One of the major ideas that influenced the reform agenda of the 1980s was the research on effective teaching. Effective teaching research is influential because it tells teachers, in clear language, how to teach. These teaching behaviors can be easily converted to explicit criteria by which to evaluate teaching.[65] This pleases those who want teachers to be more accountable for what they do. Hunter's teaching model reflects this teaching-evaluation tie-in because it has a supervisory [evaluative] component for administrators to use. In figure 4 I give a summary of what the effective teaching research says good teachers do. The researchers write that "many of these functions [teacher behaviors] appeared earlier as the elements of the 'Lesson Design'" developed by Hunter.[66] It is reasonable, therefore, to believe that the teaching behaviors on this list reflect Hunter's view of what teaching should be.

I draw this list of teaching behaviors from the 1986 edition of the *Handbook of Research on Teaching*, published by The American Educational Research Association and written by two well-known researchers. The chapter in which these behaviors are listed was reviewed by three other researchers whose own research conforms to the assumptions on which effective teaching research is based. Figure 4 lists the six "fundamental instructional functions," as reported in the *Handbook*, with some detail under each of the six.

A note in the *Handbook* suggests that for older or more knowledgeable learners the size of the step in the teacher's presentation can be increased, that less time can be spent on teacher-guided practice, and that the amount of overt practice can be decreased and that "covert rehearsal, restating, and reviewing" be done instead.[68]

The authors point to some limitations of the effective teaching research. They say that the explicit teaching procedures offered are good only for learning things that can be taught in a step-by-step way. What content can be taught in a step-by-step way? A number of examples are given. "[T]hese procedures apply to the teaching of facts that students are expected to master so that they can be used with new information in the future," the researchers state. Examples include arithmetic facts, vocabulary, English grammar, the factual parts of science and history, and the factual and explicit parts of "electronics, cooking, and accounting." General rules can also be taught using procedures supported by this research. These rules can be applied in new situations or to solve problems. Using teacher behaviors based on this research, students can learn to apply scientific laws, solve algebraic equations, or tune an automobile engine.[69]

The researchers are frank to say that the rules for teaching they propose cannot be used for "ill-structured" content subjects in which the content to be taught cannot be reduced to explicit steps or with content that lacks a general skill which is applied repeatedly. "[T]he results of this research are less relevant for teaching composition and writing term papers, analysis of literature, problem solving in specific content areas, discussion of social issues, or the development of unique or creative responses." Almost all subjects have well-structured and ill-structured parts, the researchers write, and "explicit [direct or didactic] teaching can be used for teaching the well-structured parts."[70]

Thus far I have presented the list of research-based teaching behaviors that are widely used in reform efforts to improve teaching or to make teachers more accountable through evaluation systems

FIGURE 4. Desirable Teaching Behaviors Based on Effective
           Teaching Research

---

1. *Daily Review and Checking of Homework*

2. *Presentation*
   Provide short statement of objectives
   Proceed in small steps but at a rapid pace
   Highlight main points
   When necessary, give detailed and redundant examples and
       instructions

3. *Guided Practice*
   Initial student practice under teacher guidance
   All have a chance to respond and to receive feedback
   Guided practice continues (usually) until a success rate of
       80 percent is achieved

4. *Correctives and Feedback*
   Quick, firm, and correct responses can be followed by another
       question or a short acknowledgement of correctness; i.e.,
       "That's right"
   Hesitant correct answers might be followed by, "Yes, Linda, that's
       right because. . ."
   Guided practice continues until the teacher feels that the group
       can achieve the objectives of the lesson

5. *Practice is Directly Relevant to the Skills/Content Taught*
   Practice until the responses are firm, quick, and automatic
   Ninety-five percent correct response rate during independent
       practice
   Students alerted that seatwork will be checked
   Actively supervise students

6. *Weekly and Monthly Reviews*
   Systematically review previously learned material
   Give frequent tests
   Reteach material missed in test[67]

---

that are based on the teaching behaviors identified by this research,
and I have enumerated the kinds of content in which the researchers
believe these teaching behaviors apply and do not apply.

One final dimension to this research on effective teaching
must be mentioned: What are the sources for the teaching behaviors

summarized in figure 4? The writers give three primary sources: one study of forty fourth-grade teachers in mathematics, the findings of which are consistent with six other studies that covered a range of grade levels and which the authors believe are noteworthy, and the elements in Hunter's lesson planning guide which she derived from a list of "components of instruction" developed by Robert Gagné in 1970. These sources are also compatible with another source. The teaching steps recommended by this research are very similar to those proposed in "How to Instruct," the authors say, prepared in World War II by the War Manpower Commission.[71] The scientific validity of the teaching behaviors in figure 4 rests on these three sources.

This summary of the research on effective teaching suggests its content and the values that underlie it, although there are variations in interpretations among those who use it or write about it. The source I used is authoritative and is a statement of the official research view by virtue of its having been published and reviewed by the the American Educational Research Association. The teaching recommendations derived from this research are those accepted by Hunter and to which she refers in my description and critique of her teaching model that follows. I will first present the seven elements of instruction in Hunter's plan of teaching.

1. Anticipatory set—develop a mental set to focus the learner's attention on the lesson
2. Objective and purpose—state explicitly what is to be learned
3. Input—task-analyze (break the content into small steps)
4. Modeling—show the learner what is to be learned or how something is to be done
5. Checking for understanding—find out if the students know what they are to do and have the skills to do it
6. Guided practice—practice and drill what is to be learned under teacher supervision
7. Independent practice—learner practices lesson after the teacher is sure that the student will not make serious errors[72]

Although this simple list of the elements of good teaching may be unacceptable to some educators, it is fair to say that Madeline Hunter, a lecturer in education at the University of California, took America's school administrators by storm. They perceived a long-sought clarity in Hunter's way of thinking about teaching that they could find nowhere else. Does the Hunter approach offer more than clarity? I turn to a description and critique of the Hunter way of teaching.

The news from California looks good. Science has unlocked the complex cause-and-effect relationship between teaching and learning. Madeline Hunter, designer of a teaching approach based on these scientific findings, is about to speak. "Teaching [is] one of the last professions to emerge from . . . witch doctoring to become a profession based on a science of human learning, a science that becomes the launching pad for the art of teaching. Only recently . . . has long-established research in learning been translated into cause-effect relationships of use to teachers. Only recently have teachers acquired the skills . . . using these relationships to accelerate learning."[73]

She continues: "[My] model is equally effective in elementary, secondary, and university teaching. [I]t applies to every human interaction that is conducted for the purpose of learning. [F]aculty meetings . . . Rotary Club meetings . . . school board meetings . . . are all improved by [the] application of the principles of human learning."[74]

Hunter describes the elements of lesson planning based on the principles of learning. These seven elements, she says, are "helpful in interpreting the effectiveness . . . of direct teaching and in identifying what is needed should lessons be ineffective."[75] These and other elements are used by teachers to make decisions about teaching. However, fearful that some teachers may slavishly follow the elements, Hunter advises caution: "Simple techniques of teaching have limitations; principles of learning are not absolute; and real-life teaching has a way of blurring the neat distinctions of laboratory theory."[76]

Hunter states that the seven elements of lesson planning provide the base for her approach to teacher supervision. She explains the learning theory on which her model is based, citing Ivan Pavlov in an example, and recalls a finding of Wilhelm Wundt's that the beginning and end of any series are easiest to learn. "The knowledge has been around for years, but it was in terms of pigeons and rats, or in terms of the psychological laboratory. . . ."[77] She reviews key topics in her learning theory, such as positive and negative reinforcement, massed and distributed practice, and task analysis to break learning into a step-by-step procedure.[78]

Her talk ends 20 minutes later. The ambiguities of teaching melt away. The invocation of science and the clarity of the speech carry the day. The audience seems to feel that Hunter has put lights on the road to better learning and teaching.

I am not so sure. I am uneasy. Terms such as *task analysis, specific objectives,* and *cause and effect* have a mechanistic ring to them. So do terms such as *positive and negative reinforcement.*

In accepting Hunter, might we not be buying simplicity and a false clarity about teaching that displaces a more fundamental concern about learning? Might we not be buying a subjectively based model of teaching in the guise of science?

Hunter's Model from a Scientific Perspective

Hunter claims both that her model will improve learning because it is based on research and that she has unraveled the connections between learning theory and the teacher behaviors that result in better learning. I take issue with these claims on several grounds.

First, Hunter has not produced the research evidence to support her claim for improved learning. It is not in publications where it might reasonably be expected to appear. In her chapter titled "Knowing, Teaching, and Supervising" in *Using What We Know About Teaching,* she offers no supporting research citations and no bibliography. I find no research to support her claims for improved learning in *Mastery Teaching.* Nor does she provide any research evidence to support her claims for higher achievement in *Teach More—Faster.*[79]

One would think that in the 19 years since *Teach More—Faster* was published, Hunter or others would have produced a series of studies across the twelve grade levels in a representative sample of subjects that would cast some light on her claim. Without a pattern of such studies on important cognitive and affective learning outcomes (not merely some limited time-task relationship), it is difficult to see the science in her model.

Second, the lack of any pattern of research to support her claim for improved learning also confounds Hunter's starting point: "scientific" learning theory. Hunter's model starts with learning theory, moves to prescriptions for teaching, and, finally, to claims for increased student achievement. Ignoring the fact that her learning theory is based in part on research with lower animals that lack the capacity to create a language and a culture, her view is inconsistent with at least one major theorist who embraced a generalized method of science.

John Dewey held that a finding might be scientific in psychology or in sociology, for example, but not be scientific in education until it has been tested in educational practice. Until that happens, psychological learning theory is only intermediary and auxiliary.[80] Hunter conceptually equates psychology and education. Without a pattern of evidence that her psychologically based learning theory increases learning in school settings, it can be argued that the validity of her learning theory is educationally suspect, however well it may be accepted in other fields.

Third, without a solid pattern of evidence to support the claim for improved learning, there is no scientific basis for the Hunter Model; the links she infers (I cannot use the term *cause and effect*) between learning theory and rules for teaching have not been demonstrated. Even the basis for the model, learning theory, can be questioned if the criterion for testing in educational settings is applied.

I use scientific criteria to critique the Hunter model only because she, herself, invokes them. But merely to apply scientific criteria to this or any other model of teaching and learning (or supervision) misses important substantive educational questions. Science tells us at best what is, not what ought to be. If one applies some "ought to be's" to the Hunter model from the value perspective of a more intellectual and holistic theory, substantive questions can be raised about the model, regardless of whether it is proved to be effective in practice.

Hunter's Model from a Philosophic Perspective

Comparing the Hunter approach with that of Dewey reveals two major deficiencies in the former: First, the content of the model is primarily about technique and the training program uses a didactic teaching process that requires mostly fact-recall responses from participants; both content and training are nonintellectual. Second, the model itself is nonintellectual and mechanistic and thus will not improve the quality of education.

According to Dewey, the primary aim of teaching is to cultivate thought. Dewey relates thinking to learning, methods, content, interest and motivation, and aims. Dewey makes a unity from essential pieces.[81]

Hunter, in contrast, does not clearly assert that the primary aim of teaching is to cultivate thought. By not building from this essential aim, Hunter misses a chance to formally unite the basic elements of her teaching model with thinking.[82] Thinking is not organic to the Hunter model in two important respects.

Some supporters of the model say that the inclusion of Bloom's Taxonomy of Educational Objectives counters my criticism that the model is nonintellectual. However, the Taxonomy did not influence Hunter to set explicit intellectual aims for her model, nor to incorporate it in the model's major elements or in the techniques she discusses in *Mastery Teaching*. In the important area of transfer of learning, Bloom explicitly cites *thinking* in the Taxonomy as fundamental whereas Hunter, writing on the same topic, omits thinking.

Hunter writes about sixteen techniques, of which use of the Taxonomy is one. The Taxonomy's influence is not discernible on the other fifteen techniques, such as "teaching students to remember" and "teaching for transfer," to which it might be expected to relate. Writing about transfer, Bloom says: "If we are concerned with the problem of transfer of training, by definition we would select intellectual abilities . . . as having greater transfer value."[83]

Hunter, in contrast, omits thinking when she writes about transfer. She labels transfer a principle of learning, talks about positive and negative transfer, and goes into great detail about its four attributes without ever mentioning thinking.

Hunter's content consists primarily of technique: technique uprooted from the ideas of a comprehensive educational theory. Ideas give techniques flexibility and direction and provide a basis for their intelligent use. Ideas in a theory provide criteria for what is worth teaching, for knowing when a thing is truly learned, and for giving general direction to learning and teaching so that one does not get lost in a forest of technique.

Pithy findings from psychology, which Hunter calls propositional statements, do not cohere into a satisfactory educational theory. Psychology is not education.

Dewey's admonition on technique is worth recalling. He says that nothing has brought pedagogical theory into greater disrepute than handing out models and recipes to be followed in teaching. "Mechanical . . . woodenness is an inevitable corollary of any theory which separates mind from activity motivated by a purpose."[84] "Purpose" is more than a behavioral objective.

Thus, the aim of Hunter's model is not the cultivation of thought, and thinking does not pervade it. We are left with technique unrelated to the aim of cultivating intelligence. The gaps and omissions in the model relative to thinking are characteristic of atomistic and mechanistic theories in which complex wholes are broken into disparate pieces with the result that critical qualities of the whole, such as thinking, are lost.

The Training Process

The learning process used by most trainers of the Hunter approach is also nonintellectual because it consists of didactic presentations to passive teachers. This judgment is based on a review of the training materials and talks with teachers and administrators in three Philadelphia-area school districts that received Hunter training.

My impressions of the learning process are confirmed by Jack Corbin of the Pennsylvania State Education Association, who has conducted over forty regional forums involving three thousand teachers, many of whom had been trained in the Hunter model and who freely discussed the model.

The teachers and administrators I talked to, including those who support the model, agreed that the trainers lectured on the techniques to be taught; asked trainees to memorize these techniques and their subparts; used self-checking quizzes (on points such as the five factors in motivation); and dealt, in two instances, with trivial factual content: fifteen-minute demonstration lessons on two kinds of jellyfish and the surfaces of the teeth. Teachers agreed, further, that there was very little critical discussion or active participation by the trainees.

One teacher, who liked some of the techniques, said, "They practice what they preach. They model everything they say." I infer that her idea of what the model is was influenced by the learning process used by the trainer.

A high school principal echoes this teacher's feelings about the quality of the inservice training sessions on the Hunter model in this account.

> As a member of the first group of trainees in our county, I participated in a nine-day program taught by a Hunter associate in two two-day and one five-day sessions. The most vivid recollection of that experience is that the trainer practiced what he preached. A lesson objective was always stated, each lesson was begun with an anticipatory set, active participation was required ("Raise your hand if . . . ;" "Show me one finger if you agree with the answer;" "Turn to your neighbor and repeat what the first element of instruction is," etc.). Every skill was modeled and then practiced under the instructor's guidance. The trainer also made use of metaphor to explain the importance of understanding the elements of effective teaching (e.g.,

"Would you want to fly in an airplane in which the pilot had a feeling about how to land the plane but didn't understand the step-by-step procedures?"). I also remember that questions were usually not answered, unless they dealt directly with the material being learned. Questions about how the model relates to other educational issues were brushed aside with a "We don't deal with that." A special effort was made to avoid questions about how the supervision model related to evaluation of teachers.

My school district appropriated $100,000 for a five-year staff development program in which every teacher and administrator in the district would undergo a five-day workshop in what was being called the Essential Elements of Instruction. These workshops were taught by district personnel who had been trained by one of Hunter's associates.

Four years later in our school district, the Madeline Hunter model has gone by the way of so many other top-down reform efforts. Although the training sessions continue, one seldom hears any reference to the model, whereas, in the early days, administrators were required to use the model in their supervision efforts, to conduct follow-up and refresher sessions in their schools, and many teachers talked about the model when they spoke of their work in the classroom.[85]

The listen-don't-talk-tell-me-what-I-said quality of Hunter's learning process is nonintellectual. The process excludes seminal ideas, critical discussion, use of the imagination, and critical comparisons among different perspectives in teaching. There is, in sum, little thinking.

What these trainers do is not the responsibility of Hunter. Hunter, in fact, has expressed "horror" at what some people have done to her decision-making model. There is irony here, however. This training process reflects many of the didactic and passive qualities of teaching and learning criticized by John Goodlad and Theodore Sizer.[86] To use a wooden teaching process to teach technique, and to say that this is a fundamental effort to improve the quality of American education, is to believe that water can dilute itself.

The practical problem of the training process stems from a faulty idea: teach directly for results and ignore the intellectual quality of the process. This idea splits ends from means; it is managerial, not educative. Here is a more powerful and practical idea: quality inheres in ends only insofar as quality inheres in means. It is the quality of the intellectual process that counts.

Hunter wants teachers to be decision makers. If the content is technique and the learning process is listen-recite, is not this decision making within very narrow, technique-bound limits? Is it not, therefore, a technical decision-making model that views teachers as technicians rather than as professionals? And isn't the model therefore better for teaching discrete facts than for teaching continuous and interconnected concepts?

Is the model, for example, the best choice in helping students understand *Huckleberry Finn*? Is technique the best basis to develop the ideas in the novel about racism, friendship, and social criticism? Or to develop the idea of the changing character of imperialism over the past two hundred years? Or to develop the idea that science is a way of thinking based on some assumptions that in themselves are not "proven"?

Might not the model's bias for behavioral objectives; for discrete lesson planning removed from the flow of learning over days and weeks; for breaking learning into small, sequential steps (task analysis); and for (implicitly) teacher-dominated, total group teaching suggest that conceptual topics can be neatly boxed in advance to eliminate the ambiguity, time, and the forward-backward-forward qualities of real thinking?

What It All Means

When the content and the learning process used by trainers in the field are critically viewed through the lenses of Dewey's theory of learning and teaching, the following conclusions are warranted:

- The content of the model consists primarily of techniques unrelated to a coherent body of educational theory.
- The training process didactically presents techniques that are unrelated to ideas and uninformed by reading or discussion.
- Teachers are implicitly viewed as technical decision makers, not as professional decision makers.
- The model accepts the educational status quo, in part, because it excises teaching from its social context, and it offers an incomplete and atomistic rather than a more complete and holistic account of learning and teaching.
- Because the model is nonintellectual and mechanistic, it is not a fundamental response to the problem of quality in education.

I will conclude my critique of the Hunter model where we began—with research. There is one longitudinal study of the effectiveness of the Hunter way of teaching done by two researchers, Jane Stallings and Eileen Krasavage, that is worth summarizing. It is the best test in the literature of the Hunter model because its design is technically sound, it spanned four years, and it ensured that the teachers in the experimental school (the "Hunter school") were teaching in accordance with the effective-teaching prescriptions. Hunter herself provided some of the training for the teachers.

Two elementary schools in Napa County, California, serving economically poor communities were involved. The schools were selected because they had the most students eligible for Chapter 1 remedial help. One school became the Hunter school, the other the control school. The students in the study were in kindergarten through fourth grade, 450 in all. The teachers were given *intensive* instruction in Hunter's techniques of teaching and classroom management between 1982 and 1986, the years in which the study was done.

How well did the students in the Hunter school do? Stallings concludes that "the sobering fact is that during the four years of the study the [Hunter school] children did not achieve higher scores than did children in the control school in either reading or mathematics." What may be more surprising to some readers "[is] that control students gained as much or more than [Hunter school] students in reading and mathematics." Other researchers who have reviewed this study, such as Lorin Anderson and Robert Slavin, conclude that the data "paint a dismal picture" and that the study "provide[s] little support for the instructional effectiveness of the [Hunter] program. . . ."[87]

I am somewhat surprised at these results. I would concede to Hunter in a debate that her way of teaching might well show significant gains on standardized test scores in reading and arithmetic, imperfect measures of intellectual learning that these tests are, on the ground that her model is made-to-order for drilling students in facts and skills, which are what these tests measure. I would concede this possible "gain" and still reject her model on philosophical and psychological grounds because we simply do not learn important things, like learning to comprehend and speak a "foreign" language by age three or so, or how to reason, in the neat, step-by-step way that she and many other researchers reared in the tenets of behavioristic psychology believe we learn.

Barak Rosenshine and Robert Stevens, who wrote the chapter on effective teaching research which I cited earlier, admit as much. "Ill-structured subjects," they say, "such as writing papers or solving problems in chemistry or history are not amenable to the ministrations of this research because these subjects cannot be reduced to explicit steps or they lack a general skill which is applied repeatedly." One might be forgiven for asking what all the fuss is about if effective teaching research is not generally useful in cultivating thought and if, on the other hand, Hunter's version was not better than standard methods of teaching even basic skills to children in one well-controlled study?

That the research on effective teaching and Hunter's model negate thinking or, at the least, confound the importance of thinking in teaching *and* learning, is evident on the face of it from the teaching behaviors endorsed in figure 4. Does one need a research study, or is a Ph.D. in anything necessary to know that thinking is negated when a teacher is told to respond to "hesitant correct answers," that is, answers which are not clearly understood, by saying "Yes, Linda, that's right. . ." and to continue with the *teacher giving the answer* to Linda (see Correctives and Feedback)? Or is a "ninety-five percent response rate" in seatwork (Independent Practice), which means filling in blanks in worksheets, a way to nourish thought and feeling if this kind of busywork takes 50 to 75 percent of students' time in grades one through seven according to descriptive studies of classrooms.[88] One would think that university professors who do this research would want to cut such time-serving to about 15 percent at most, rather than to encourage it. I know that as a former elementary teacher and as a university professor, if I got a 95 percent "correct response rate" (notice the technical echoes in these words) in what I taught, I could not be teaching much that was intellectually or socially important, and that I would be coming close to the line that separates indoctrination from education.[89]

We need only to flip ahead five hundred pages from Rosenshine and Stevens's summary of the research on effective teaching to another chapter in the *Handbook of Research on Teaching* to see a strange phenomenon at work in the "science of education." This contrasting chapter discusses some of the research on learning mathematics that had been done since the *Second Handbook on Research on Teaching* was published a decade earlier. Two experts on mathematics education, Thomas A. Romberg and Thomas P. Carpenter, who teach at the University of Wisconsin, wrote the chapter. The tie between their chapter and the Rosenshine-Stevens chapter on effective teaching is not only that both chapters deal with educational research, but that Romberg and Carpenter include a critical analysis of the research on effective teaching in mathematics in their review. Another tie is that Rosenshine and Stevens anchored their report in seven major studies, at least one of which dealt with mathematics.

In their summary statement about effective teaching research in mathematics, which Romberg and Carpenter call "scientific" within quotation marks, they say this research has, first of all, "failed to provide teachers with a list of tested behaviors that will make them competent teachers and ensure that their students will learn." There are other major problems with the research findings on effective teaching: scores on standardized tests (the criterion of goodness in this research) and fancy statistics such as "residualized mean gain scores" have become proxies for what teachers should aim for and for what is worth knowing.

Second, even when the effective teaching researchers do find something effective, their rules only apply if a teacher teaches in a more traditional here-is-how-you-will-learn style, a style that does not encourage thinking. These few rules may make traditional teaching more efficient, but they *cannot make teaching very different from what it is*, something that Romberg and Carpenter believe is necessary.

Third, because no coherent set of ideas guide this research and there is no theory, the explanation of any relationships that are found must be circular and contained within the empirical findings alone. The findings, in other words, cannot escape from themselves. This kind of thinking is very much like putting fertilizers on split-plots to see which plot grows better corn while denying to one's self the beneficial knowledge of chemistry and how corn plants ingest and use nutrients.

Fourth, since a class of twenty-five children do not constitute one homogeneous "group brain" which the teacher prods into learning, the promise of relating teaching to individual differences is ignored, to sound a note from Individually Guided Education (for which Romberg developed an excellent mathematics program).

Romberg and Carpenter conclude their summary of effective teaching research by saying that if researchers lack a set of organizing ideas to guide their research, they must collect facts about teaching, and all of the facts collected, therefore, seem to be equally important. We come back to facts once more—facts removed from idea. Although fact-collecting is a part of the scientific process, they say "one hesitates to call the resulting literature scientific." They add, however, that some of the findings from effective teaching research are important and need to be kept in mind as new programs are developed.[90]

I have argued that research on effective teaching is not scientific, whatever else it may be. Research on teaching reflects schools of thought, loose philosophies and collections of unexpressed assumptions about what learning and teaching "are." I am comfortable with this state of affairs. It is the only honest intellectual and practical stance we can take since we do not have a science of education. I am not comfortable with the thought-stopping reaction of practitioners and policymakers when researchers invoke the magic phrase "research says. . ." and, in this invocation, falsely impute a *scientific aura to a theoretically incoherent set of findings that too often reflect a mechanical and anti-intellectual view of learning and teaching.* There is no science without intellectual coherence. Research on effective teaching is harmful because it unnecessarily limits the intellectual and social growth of teachers and students. "Teach More—Faster," the title of one of Hunter's books, is a good example of technique imposing limits on human development, which is probably rooted in the finding promulgated by the research on effective teaching to "teach in small steps at a rapid pace." Many good teachers who have never, unfortunately, read John Dewey or Jean Piaget or Jerome Bruner would, nonetheless, respond to this nonsense as these thinkers might by saying, "No, the slogan is wrong. How about 'teach less, more slowly'," implying that learning is something to be savored like a fine meal and cannot be hurried without destroying those fragile yet essential qualities that make it something worth doing in the first place.

Other evidence also supports my point that the research on effective teaching is not scientific, as the researchers imply, because they ignore research that contradicts their data. Rosenshine and Stevens write that systematic instruction (notice how this school of thought takes over words that have a high "cash value" in a technological society—words like "systematic," "effective," and "efficient") does not result in humorless or regimented classrooms, and that the teachers are warm and flexible and allow students freedom of movement. That most teachers are caring and warm to students I believe is true. But the import of their paragraph, loaded with adjectives, that the emotional climate in highly structured classrooms is positive can be seriously challenged. One of the major findings in John Goodlad's study of one thousand classrooms is that the emotional tone is flat, neither markedly "up" nor "down," and the color,

I suppose, is battleship gray.[91] That these classrooms were highly structured is absolutely true. Yet Rosenshine and Stevens ignored this rigorous descriptive study for their own fragmentary findings. In the "personal physics" that prevails in too large a segment of the education research establishment, one is free to ignore "gravity" if it confounds the ideology that energizes and shapes one's own research.

CONCLUDING COMMENT ON THE HUNTER MODEL AND THE RESEARCH ON EFFECTIVE TEACHING

The teaching approach of Madeline Hunter and the research on effective teaching are not scientific—for no other reason than that each of them ignores contradictory data, as I have demonstrated. These prescriptions for teaching offer only fragmented empirical facts about teaching garnered from one point of view. These facts are not scientifically grounded for a second reason: they are, at best, isolated facts about the world devoid of a coherent and empirically warranted set of ideas which alone can give them scientific meaning and practical flexibility. Each of these reforms can more properly be viewed as loose philosophies, as schools of thought, even ideologies. They represent techniques removed from idea, techniques removed from a critical consideration of worthy ends that teachers and students ought to pursue. They were born and live within the imploding boundaries of the technological mindset.

Dewey's comments about the prescriptive method of Johann Herbart is as true of these two schools of thought as it was of Herbart's. Herbart's method, Dewey wrote, "was the schoolmaster come to his own. This fact expresses at once its strength and its weakness." Herbart's method, Dewey continues, represents the pedagogue's narrow view of life. "The philosophy is eloquent about the duty of the teacher in instructing pupils; it is almost silent regarding his privilege of learning." Herbart "exaggerates beyond reason" the usefulness of a rationally formulated method. "It insists upon the old, the past, and passes lightly over the . . . genuinely novel and unforeseeable."[92] Herbart takes, in brief, everything educational into account except its essence—vital intellectual energy trying to make sense of its environment.

What research shall we believe? What is the true philosophy? Where is the Sir Isaac Newton who can take a penetrating philosophy and order heaven itself before our believing eyes?

TECHNOLOGICAL CURRICULUMS: MOVING BACKWARD
INTO THE FUTURE

The four technological curriculums discussed in this chapter—Chapter 1 remedial programs funded under the Elementary and Secondary Education Act of 1965, mastery learning, Madeline Hunter's way of teaching, and the research on effective teaching—promise learning outcomes they do not deliver. Chapter 1 promises to bring children who are two or more grade levels below other children up to grade level in reading and arithmetic. It does not. After billions of dollars and two and one-half decades, the gains of Chapter 1 students on standardized tests of isolated skills—tests which *do* assess the skills these students have been taught—one would need a psychometric microscope to see the tiny gain in scores. This evidence is in plain view for any policymaker or federal or state educator who cares to look. The local educational establishment, itself unseeing, lured by the "free money" and the inertia of past practice and an uncritical attitude toward its work, persists in prescribing the same old medicine of workbook-type drills in reading skills. If the practical *actions* taken by these educators could speak, the voice might say: "We educators know what these kids need: direct and efficient instruction in the skills of reading. This we give them without mercy. The fact that the children do not learn is not our fault. These children bring many personal and social pathologies into school with them because many of them live in poverty. The way to end-run these disabilities is to increase the dosage of our skill medicine. The medicine will work. If we had twice the money and twice the time to spend on these kids, the remedial medicine would show results. The medicine we give is good . . . the medicine we give . . . the medicine. . . ." The voice fades as yet another "pathological generation of students" enters Chapter 1 programs to get the medicine it does not need or deserve.

Chapter 1 does teach something. It teaches most children that reading is a boring affair that cannot compete with television or videos, that school is not a useful place to spend time, and that they are stupid because they cannot read very well. Chapter 1 teaches these things not alone through its nicely sequenced hierarchy of skills and behavioral objectives and tests, but indirectly through the classroom environment it creates. What is learned is not that which is directly taught in the teachers' lesson plans. The classroom environment of Chapter 1 distorts the rich resources of oral and written language which should be used to increase the students' understanding and feeling about life and the world. Chapter 1 distorts the learning environment by defining language as skills very much the way a funhouse mirror distorts a human face and makes it something it is not. This distortion of language is fed by a belief that human beings, who often are poor, are in some mysterious way different from others in the species; they have a social gene that blocks learning. The whole environment of Chapter 1 is designed for learning failure. No wonder it cannot show results on even low-level tests of reading skills. The innocent students fail, of course, but the teachers, too, suffer failure. The teachers' failure seeps into this foggy environment, which makes it even more difficult to create a coherent and rewarding learning climate, a climate human beings require if they are to learn, and if they are to teach as well.

Although I believe that Chapter 1 programs in general do little more than create a most restrictive educational environment based on a mechanical theory of knowledge and learning, other observers are less critical. Richard Elmore and Milbrey McLaughlin, for example, while they criticize the decision of local educators to make Chapter 1 a pull-out program that fragments the school day, see benefits in this program that escape me. They say that "many exemplary local projects emerged" which were disseminated to others by the federal government. Elmore and McLaughlin say that the evidence "is less heartening" on whether or not Chapter 1 benefited its students when the achievement test data are reviewed. In their final statement, they write that

> it is not accurate to say that because a federal policy produces weak aggregate effects . . . , reform is necessarily a failure. The verdict must be much more cautious. In fact [Chapter 1] produced a wealth of practical insight at the school and district level into the special problems of educationally disadvantaged children. This insight probably would not have occurred without the introduction and targeting of federal funds. Over time . . . many states and localities developed positive ways of responding to [Chapter 1] requirements that not only allowed but encouraged effective educational practice. . . . [93]

Finally, these authors see an "administrative maturity" in Chapter 1, which means a less restrictive federal view of regulations and the ability of local schools to "translate those requirements into effective educational practice."[94]

By not making the educational worth of Chapter 1 programs the pivot idea of their analysis, Elmore and McLaughlin lose the essential educational idea that Chapter 1 programs provide an impoverished environment for students who most need a rich and stimulating learning climate. No degree of "administrative maturity" can compensate students for the intellectual and emotional barrenness that characterize most Chapter 1 programs. The review of Chapter 1 research by Anderson and Pellicer, which I discussed earlier, is close to the truth when they say that huge financial expenditures have not altered the chain of failure in these sterile programs. This amazing pursuit of failure, decade after decade, is, they say, "inexplicable and tragic." If the failures of Chapter 1 have produced, as Elmore and McLaughlin hope, insights into the needs of poor and low-achieving students, I am at a loss to know what they are. These insights have not, in any case, leavened the mechanical and harsh quality that characterize most Chapter 1 programs. This quality is all that matters to the millions of students who must suffer them, and to a society that cannot afford to leave unrealized the potential of these children because they are, first, human, and only second, poor. *I cannot escape the feeling that Chapter 1 is educational malpractice on a grand scale.*

If Chapter 1 remedial efforts represent the generic qualities of the technological mindset, Chicago mastery learning, Madeline Hunter's way of teaching, and the research on effective teaching are specific examples of its application to solve some of the practical problems of learning and teaching. None of these widely adopted reforms has come close to delivering on its promises.

Chicago mastery learning, as I have tried to show, vaporizes reading and learning to read in the heat of contrived units on thinking skills such as categorization, criterion-referenced tests, and a decontextualized skill approach to reading. No reading or thinking was taught in Chicago mastery learning and none was learned. The president of the Chicago Board of Education, who attended the demise of this widely advertised program, saw what many educators do not see: the mechanics of reading cannot substitute for reading itself. Although I quoted Munoz earlier, his statement that the "object became mastering mastery learning and not mastering reading or math" is so insightful and precise that it warrants repetition. An error of this magnitude can only be made by ideologues who believe they have the "one best method" and are, therefore, closed to any critique or alternative way of learning and teaching. That this intellectual blindness was masked by a contrived aura of science, objectivity, and efficiency makes the error worse. Chicago mastery learning not only vaporized reading as reading, it abused the faith that many educators and laymen attach to any work they believe to be in the traditions of real science.

The Hunter teaching method and the research on effective teaching also bask in the imputed rigor of real science; that is, the legitimate gains made in the past three hundred years or so in physics, chemistry, and biology. Hunter offers only more technique and no seminal ideas to a generation of teachers drowning in technique. How the denial of ideas, drawn from the humanities and thoughtful writing in education, is to leaven the anti-intellectual quality of our schools and of our inservice and preservice professional education programs is ignored by proponents of the Hunter method and the prescriptions for teaching based on research for effective teaching. When educators continue to embrace the premises of these systems, this is itself powerful evidence of the pervasiveness of the technological mindset and of the virtual irrelevancy of intellectual concerns in matters related to the professional development of teachers or to the intellectual development of their students.

Some of the limitations of the research on effective teaching are stated by the authors of the summary which I quoted earlier. If its prescriptions for learning and teaching are unsuitable for writing a paper, or for such things as "problem solving in specific content areas," or for a discussion of social issues, is not the incapacity of this research for developing the intellectual capacities of teachers and students painfully evident? What is left for its ministrations are the teaching and learning of isolated facts and skills. This research and the Hunter method thus ignore what is essential to any education worthy of the name. One cannot think without knowledge and the imagination to devise ways to solve problems—aims that are incorporated in a Deweyan approach to learning and teaching—but one can learn facts and skills by the dozen without being troubled by thought in technological philosophies of education. This statement suggests the appeal and the tragedy of research based on behavioristic theories of what learning and educational science should be. Their appeal lies in the fact that they challenge nothing in the existing state of educational affairs yet, because the prescriptions for practice they offer claim to issue from scientific study, there is the implicit suggestion of goodness and newness in their prescriptions. In this way busy educators mislead themselves that they are serving reform when they adopt curriculums and teaching methods based on this mechanistic philosophy of research whose roots lie in the seventeenth century and the rise of modern physical science. Both the researchers and the practitioners share a similar belief system. It is this shared belief in the values of a mechanistic theory of learning and teaching that permits them to go backward into the future.

In the next chapter I present one 1960s reform, Individually Guided Education, which might have taken more schools forward to a better future. Although Individually Guided Education contains contradictory ideas about learning and teaching within itself, it anticipated by two decades today's concern with restructuring schools and giving teachers more decision-making power in the daily life of schools. I present Individually Guided Education as a case study whose life history can teach us some new and important lessons about fundamental reform. These lessons were ignored in their time because of faddism and the unthoughtful push of the herd to ever seek the new by tinkering with the prescriptions of a (false) science of education.

Examples of Progressive Practices Creeping into Traditional Schools

This picture may have been an anticipation in 1946 of today's buzz word, cooperative learning. Or perhaps this image depicts a standard recitation with a student in the teacher-pitcher's box. In the sunset of the progres movement, I see this picture as one that captures the power of small group work and the desirability of students taking greater responsibility for their learning. Note the ferns on the sill and the bird cage that suggest a teacher's effort to create a pleasing physical environment. Photograph is from the Cordray-Foltz Collection, Georgia Historical Society, Savannah Branch.

This photograph catches an instant in one teacher's transition from traditional to more progressive practices. Progressive influences are suggested by the heterogeneously grouped and individualized reading program. Movable furniture has been used to achieve a more personal and comfortable atmosphere. The territory being left behind is marked by the school rules (upper left) which include admonitions to raise one's hand and to be quiet so the teacher can talk. Hand-raising is not required in small group work. Note the basal readers and the notation on the board about creative writing along with that standby the spelling test, and a "handwriting paper." Since the early 1970s when this picture was taken, the teacher has moved on to whole language. Information and photograph courtesy of Phyllis Snyder and the Owen J. Roberts School District.

Amidst the screwed-down desks of the traditional school a thematic unit seems to flourish. The second student-written chart from the left states the "center of interest" as a theme: "how geographic conditions affect man's way of life and his use of his environment" in the Lowlands. Another chart lists science interests. Student work abounds. Other progressive elements include dramatization, the model house, and art work which gives play to talents other than the verbal. Not least the "big idea" in the theme drives the study. The teacher is unobtrusively in this 1946 picture which may suggest a teaching attitude—or merely a lack of space in the crowded room! Photograph is from the Cordray-Foltz Collection, Georgia Historical Society, Savannah Branch.

A Chapter 1 aide and a student play games in this federally funded remedial reading program in the 1970s. No formal experience in reading was
given. Although this approach is atypical, it does reflect an attempt to incorporate feelings and interest in what is generally a harsh skills program.
This example also shows the dangers of hazy, ill-informed efforts to be
"progressive." Feelings alone are distracting; skills alone are deadly. Information and photograph courtesy of Linda Sue Bauer and the Owen J.
Roberts School District.

A teacher talks to one of three students in a writing group. The seeming casualness that often becomes part of the learning medium in progressive classrooms can be seen in the girl who is sprawled over two desks. This casual attitude gives many teachers and citizens fits because it appears to be undisciplined—and it may be. The teacher assures me this is not the case. Note the girl working independently and the table of electronic gear (rear), a sign that the 1960s have swept through. This classroom was probably among the more progressive in the school. The photograph was taken in the mid-1970s. Information and photograph courtesy of Linda V. Nitsche and the Owen J. Roberts School District.

I like this picture because it is joyful and celebrates a school community coming together. The time is 1946 in Savannah, Georgia, and the students and parents of the Price Street School are enjoying Mayday. In urban places today, and in our large consolidated school districts where fleets of yellow buses are the physical sinews of the school-social system, true school communities are difficult to establish. Community is one part of the old that we should strive mightily to make part of the new. Photograph is from the Cordray-Foltz Collection, Georgia Historical Society, Savannah Branch.

CHAPTER 5

How Teachers' and Principals' Ideas Defined the Quality of a Major Reform

The power of our ideas to shape practical actions is easy to overlook amidst the public pressure on educators to achieve results. I take some comfort, therefore, when a distinguished black federal judge sees fit to call the attention of one of his colleagues, who was recently appointed to the United States Supreme Court, to the power of one's ideas in creating a good law. Judge Higginbotham wrote these words in an open letter to the new justice.

> You must always focus on what values [are brought] to the task of interpreting the Constitution. Our Constitution has an unavoidable—though desirable—level of ambiguity, and there are many interstitial spaces that as a justice of the Supreme Court you have to fill in. To use Justice Benjamin Cardozo's elegant phrase: "We do not pick our rules of law full blossomed from the trees." You and the other justices cannot avoid putting your imprimatur on a set of values.[1]

Reform, too, has its ambiguities and its "interstitial spaces to be filled in" by one's ideas and values. A conclusion from the previous two chapters might be that we cannot pick our reforms "full blossomed" from a university or federal tree despite over thirty years of failed effort to do so. Practice and idea live together in the world. It is impractical to think or to act otherwise. The story of the several lives lived by one reform, Individually Guided Education, provides the texture and detail that supports the Deweyan notion that practice and idea are most alive when they work together in the flux of everyday life.

There are several rich resources to be tapped that will illuminate Individually Guided Education as a comprehensive reform and as reform writ large. There is, first, a deep developmental-descriptive literature about IGE. If IGE were a play, we have the playwright's intentions, notebooks, and revisions as the play was being written. We have, too, the accounts of the educational drama critics in the form of qualitative field studies, which tell us how the play was performed and understood by audiences in the cities and towns of the hinterland. And, finally, IGE is seminal because it carries within itself the contradictory strands of both progressive and technological ideas and values. These two strands, in my view, function as mirrors that reflect clear images of the teachers' and principals' guiding ideas and values about learning and teaching. Practitioners interpreted and thus reshaped this packaged reform as they conscientiously tried to follow what they thought IGE demanded. Stated another way, IGE acted as a Rorschach test that empirically revealed something as intangible as educational theory. My analysis will demonstrate the practical power of ideas in education and in reform—an idea itself that is almost contemptuously dismissed by too many in our profession, whether they be practitioners in the public schools, teacher educators, researchers, or professors of educational administration.

There are three stories to be told about Individually Guided Education. The first story is told by researchers who observed teachers and children, and principals and superintendents working with this reform in the daily life of schools. This is a good story and it tells much about the different—and conflicting—lives a reform leads once a school takes it in. The second story about IGE is the story of its developers' intentions. What did Herbert J. Klausmeier and his colleagues at the University of Wisconsin Center for Cognitive Development want IGE to do for teachers and elementary school children? I shall make some judgments about the research story and the story of the developers' intentions, which will be the third tale about Individually Guided Education.

Before I tell how the beliefs of teachers and principals influenced the educational quality of Individually Guided Education, I shall sketch the content of IGE as a reform. This overview of IGE suggests, too, why this reform, born in 1965 and still alive in a number of schools in the 1990s, is worth treating as a definitive case study of reform.

OVERVIEW OF INDIVIDUALLY GUIDED EDUCATION

Individually Guided Education is a comprehensive, all-out reform effort. IGE is the "most comprehensive program ever undertaken by a federally funded R & D center or regional educational laboratory," writes Herbert J. Klausmeier, who was its guiding force at the University of Wisconsin. "It was the only attempt to restructure a level of schooling [elementary] in its entirety," Klausmeier continues.[2] Although Klausmeier wrote these words in 1990, it is a fair description based on my review of IGE primary sources. Two important IGE components, how learning is to be personalized and how the elementary school is to be fundamentally reorganized, are described below.

The developers of IGE wanted learning to be more personal and individualized. They designed an instructional planning process that they believed would permit elementary students to progress at their own pace. Each student would be placed either in an instructional program tailored for her or in an existing program. The student's level of achievement, learning style, and motivation were to be noted through criterion-referenced tests, teacher observations, and work samples. Individualization was to be encouraged by varying such elements as teacher assistance to the student, peer tutoring, the kinds of printed and electronic materials used, and the time spent in activities such as independent study, small- or large-group instruction, or student-led or adult-led group work. IGE sets objectives for each child to attain over a short period of time (two to three weeks), the attainment of which was to be assessed by "mastery tests or some other criterion."[3]

This description suggests the flavor of IGE individualization. Individualization was to be achieved through a content-neutral planning process in the fashion of a flow chart in which objectives were set for the student, elements were varied as described above, and learning was assessed. If the student did not attain mastery, the teacher reassessed the situation (including the student's characteristics), set new objectives, and proceeded as described, using different approaches such as peer tutoring or small group work to assessment. A student who attained mastery moved forward to new content repeating the setting-of-objectives–instruction–assessment process.[4]

The most radical component is IGE's reorganization of the elementary school. The traditional organization, which placed students in a grade based on age, was replaced by a nongraded school in which teachers taught in teams. In this plan three to five teachers taught a group of 100 to 150 students whose age spread over several years, such as a group of eight-, nine-, and ten-year-olds. Instructional aides and a student teacher rounded out the team membership, depending on local circumstances. Team leaders, a parent representative, and the principal made up a committee "that replaces the principal as the sole education decision maker at the building level." This instructional committee set school objectives, interpreted and implemented educational policy, coordinated the work of the teaching teams to assure curricular continuity, and managed "the use of time, facilities, and resources that are not managed" by the teams.[5] In some schools team leaders received differential pay.

The developers of Individually Guided Education were not content with throwing a defensive punch at the status quo. They wanted to personalize learning and to create more professional roles for teachers by giving them decision-making power in curriculum, in setting school aims, and in coordinating the work of the teaching teams. This is why it is important to study a reform that is over twenty-five years old. Individually Guided Education was an ambitious reform effort. It shares this characteristic with other reforms of the 1960s such as the new mathematics and science programs and with contemporary reforms such as the Coalition of Essential Schools. Like many of the earlier reforms, IGE often failed to realize its aims in schools, for reasons I shall later explore. But Individually Guided Education shares another characteristic with reforms that become visible nationally: it was backed by an impressive array of human, institutional, and fiscal resources. I shall touch on some of these power dimensions of reform, which are essential to the development, dissemination, and research that made IGE a formidable competitor in getting money and in attracting the attention of several thousand schools. Reformers seek venture capital for a nonprofit enterprise. Without it, most national reforms would be still-born.

Individually Guided Education was backed by the institutional prestige of the University of Wisconsin and the development and research talent a major university attracts. The Wisconsin Research and Development Center for Cognitive Learning, which developed IGE, was one of the most productive federally funded research and development centers in the country. Between 1965 and 1980 it produced almost one thousand research studies, theoretical papers, and pilot studies.[6] This center attracted professors from law, engineering, and education. For good or ill, most reforms are incubated in universities. The four reforms, for example, that I discussed in the last chapter were developed in universities or strongly influenced by research conducted by university professors. If reform in America has a technological cast of mind, all of the responsibility does not lie with the teachers and administrators in the public schools.

The comprehensiveness of Individually Guided Education as an idea is suggested by some of its expenditures. The Sears-Roebuck Foundation, for example, gave $1.3 million to introduce preservice and inservice teachers to IGE; the federal government contributed $1.6 million to support schools that were adopting IGE.[7] Based on these and other data reported by Herbert J. Klausmeier, I would conservatively estimate the cost of IGE to be $6 million.

I believe that a careful assessment of Individually Guided Education may help us move beyond the fog and babble of reform. IGE is a serious and comprehensive effort to reform elementary schools. As with the eight reforms discussed in chapter 3, IGE was backed by talent, money, and powerful social institutions such as foundations, the federal government, and a major university. Money talks, but prestige speaks softly and is more often listened to, for better or worse. The power of prestige may be an overlooked element in the larger picture of reform: is reform in America overly directed by the personal and institutional prestige of a reform's sponsors? One recalls, for example, how James B. Conant's reform proposals for high schools took the country by storm in the early sixties. Conant's prestige as a former Harvard president and ambassador to Germany gave his proposals a gloss that their intrinsic worth did not warrant. From today's perspective, Conant's proposals are seen as superficial and as supporting the status quo rather than challenging it. IGE is old enough to have some gray hair and, in those years, to have amassed a unique and rich developmental and research literature that can help us understand reform. IGE came closer than most of the eight reforms assessed in chapter 3 to effecting an honest partnership between practitioners in the schools and the development and research staff in a university. Practice and theory tried to work together. Thus tethered, theorists do not fly so high as to become enfeebled for lack of oxygen, and practitioners do not fly so low that the smallest hill looms large before them as a mountain.

THE REAL STUFF? INDIVIDUALLY GUIDED EDUCATION IN ADOPTING SCHOOLS

Are most reforms doomed to shine like stars in the minds of their developers only to disintegrate when they encounter something as benign as the ordinary public school? Or do these reform stars pass through the brighter sky of some schools to enable the teachers and children there to do better the good things they always did? The authors of a well-crafted study of six exemplary IGE schools pondered these questions.

Thomas S. Popkewitz and his colleagues spent four years observing the practices of teachers and principals in six schools that were judged by its developers to be exemplary implementers of Individually Guided Education. This fact is important because schools often claim to be adopting a reform that its developers would not recognize as a reasonable implementation of their reform. I shall be concerned with four of the six schools Popkewitz studied because the beliefs and actions of the teachers and principals in these schools bring to the fore two fundamental and contrasting perspectives on school reform: the technological perspective and the intellectual and democratic perspective. Three of the schools implicitly viewed IGE as a technological reform and "acted it out" in a way that was consistent with this belief; the fourth school viewed IGE as an intellectual and democratic reform and acted in a way that was consistent with this belief. Popkewitz labels the first group of three schools "technical" based on their beliefs and actions. The fourth school I shall label "progressive" based on its actions and beliefs rather than "constructivist," the label used by the researchers. The other two schools Popkewitz studied served poor urban students. The story of these schools is depressing because what is offered in the name of learning to these children is vacuous and hurtful, and repeats the dreary tale of Chapter 1 programs I discussed earlier. These urban schools exceed in psychic damage anything that even the technological mindset can inflict on middle-class children. The urban poor in these schools are believed to come to school with nothing and the school offers them nothing. Popkewitz calls these schools "illusory" with good reason.

To characterize a school as "technical," or as a school that embraces the "technological mindset," is to clothe vital action with abstractions. And schools are "action places" where one's "theory" is rarely talked about. Educational theories in schools "push" action from behind rather than "pulling" action up front like horses harnessed to a wagon. The hardworking teachers and principals in the three schools Popkewitz characterizes as technical reveal the push of a system of beliefs.

The Clayburn Elementary School is located in a poor rural community in which more than 50 percent of the students live below the official poverty level. More than half of the low-income students are black and are bused to Clayburn to achieve racial balance. "The road to the school passes small plots of okra, small plantings of cotton, and fields where a few cattle graze," Popkewitz writes.[8] Clayburn enrolls three hundred students and ten teachers.

Clayburn's principal is forceful. He believes deeply in an individualized curriculum. The teachers, too, see themselves as successfully implementing IGE. A national survey of how IGE teachers perceived the degree of IGE implementation placed Clayburn's teachers 21st out of 158 schools reporting.[9]

The mindset held by Clayburn's teachers and principal is revealed in the following account of the researchers' observations. Faced with the task of developing objectives for reading and language arts, the teachers turned to teacher manuals. "From these [manuals], they derived a list of objectives for the language arts curriculum that referred to skills such as the use of margins, and mastery of spelling rules and punctuation. During subsequent meetings, the list of objectives was put into a logical sequence and disseminated. . . ." A Clayburn teacher described the process by saying, "The objectives that we have in reading are the Scott-Foresman objectives. In math, they are the ones from Silver-Burdett, right straight from the manual. . . . There are 107 . . . skills. That's what they are tested on."[10]

But isolated skills wrapped in behavioral objectives are not only for the poor. One technical school, Belair, located in an affluent community, approached objectives as did Clayburn, only here an imaginative teacher gave these objectives an epistemological twist that would amaze philosophers the world over. A researcher who observed Belair reports this teacher as saying that "no separate set of behavioral objectives is needed beyond the 'concepts' . . . organized in a systematic and hierarchical order. *'The behavioral objectives are the concepts,'* he says. The concepts to which he refers are the computational skills of mathematics" [emphasis added].[11] Maplewood Elementary School, the third technical school, serves a suburban, blue-collar community "that underwent a growth spurt after World War II, when the move to the suburbs began. . . ." Maplewood is in the first ring of old suburbs dominated by reasonably-priced housing and old shade trees. Teachers describe the residents as skilled and semiskilled tradespeople. Parents are concerned about their children's education.[12]

Maplewood was built in 1971 on the open-classroom plan to encourage flexibility in the ways and times students and teachers came together and to create a more personal school environment. A central office administrator encouraged the principal of Maplewood to consider IGE. The principal believed that the school's physical layout was compatible with the goals of IGE and "recruited teachers for the new school by explaining [its physical features] and the goals of IGE to the candidates." He recruited teachers whom he believed were capable of teaching in an IGE school. Maplewood has three IGE units [teaching teams], each of which serve children drawn from two conventional grades.[13]

An observer is struck by the continuous movement of Maplewood students "from teacher to teacher within the unit, and out of the unit to physical education, music, and other specialized instruction." Teachers are constantly on the go collecting papers, checking student work, and giving assignments. Teachers know that hard work is necessary to get results and believe that they are correctly implementing IGE. Maplewood students score above the national average on standardized tests of achievement.[14]

Curriculum and teaching are closely linked to behavioral objectives. Students are systematically tested on sets of subject objectives until the mastery level of 80 percent correct answers on post-tests is achieved. Students are grouped and regrouped based on their achievement level in the major subjects: reading, language arts, math, spelling, and study skills. Student progress through the sets of behavioral objectives is carefully recorded. This old system was to be computerized in 1982. Popkewitz and his two fellow researchers see this move as significant. "It commits the staff to the kind of 'systems' approach to instruction offered by IGE" while, at the same time, it takes money to do it. Two teachers were to be trained in computer programming and an aide was to be employed to run the computer.[15]

The "management of systems" dominated the talk of teachers in the technical schools in their school-wide instructional planning meetings, and concern with procedural and management problems influenced the conversations of students as well. The teachers' concern with procedures pushed ideas from the conversations. A teacher-team meeting in Maplewood dealt only with procedural details such as schedules, testing dates, and how tests [not teacher observation and judgment] were to be used as diagnostic devices to prescribe individual student instruction. "Pupils and teachers talked about school work in terms of page numbers, columns, and letters, rather than in terms of ideas or skills. In some children's conversations the importance of test scores outweighed the . . . ideas being studied. The task was to get a mastery score." Popkewitz gives this example in one of the technical schools: "A new child came over. 'What do I do after B-1?' he asked. The teacher said, 'Go into the purple book'."[16]

It is commendable that some teachers, limited in their teacher education studies by a scrambled array of courses in the techniques of teaching that neglect organizing ideas, intuitively felt "that something was wrong" in a school where a curriculum became an exercise in clearly defined procedures. One Clayburn teacher expressed such feelings, but notice how she casts her concerns in the technological language of procedure: "Classroom procedure is fine, but I want to be more than just a manager all the time, you know. . . . Last year it was a big thing that my room was so organized and managed that I could leave for an hour and my kids were great, they were occupied. . . . [I] still needed to be there, because I think they need the interaction [with] somebody on some of those skills. They could still learn, I mean they could still pass the test, but they . . . didn't get the depth they needed on some of those skills."[17]

"A ton of theory" could be packed into this teacher's statement if one picked up on Dewey's idea that practice is always richer and more complex than any theory can capture. When this searching teacher says, for example, that "they didn't get the depth in skills" without her help, she is still unthinkingly defining the curriculum as skills and defining teaching as what she can do to assist students to learn these isolated skills—the basic ideas and values on which her classroom rests are not questioned. And how could she articulate the ideas that lie in the basement of her implicit knowledge if, for example, she knows nothing about the knowledge-assumptions of behavioristic psychology made by such power-houses as E. L. Thorndike and B. F. Skinner? After all, her methods courses in college were probably based on this psychology. How could this teacher have learned about scientific management and Frederick Taylor if the study of history is rejected as impractical for teachers? In this teacher's comment we have concrete and eloquent support for the idea that technique unrooted in ideas becomes sterile and mechanical because ideas alone give technique intelligent flexibility in practice.

The technical schools ignored the conceptual component that the developers of IGE believed to be essential in an elementary school curriculum. The managerial nature of the curriculum and teaching in the technical schools left teachers with "little or no professional autonomy over . . . their work . . . [and for children] concern with tests and levels of achievement replaced insight into the ideas offered by the curriculum."[18] Intellect lost out to a wasp-like swarm of skills to be taught to the demands of efficient procedure.

But technological efficiency did not totally displace creativity and thought in the technical schools. It was there; teachers encouraged creativity when it appeared, but they did not cultivate it. One might say that creativity and thought grew like a flowering weed on the perimeters of daily classroom life. Its appearance was a bit of a surprise. The beauty of its flower was taken in by a quick side glance, but no one rushed to the edge of classroom life to pull it out and vigorously shake the few grains of soil from its shallow roots. The students' imaginations were given play, most often in language arts and sometimes in mathematics. More able students who had finished their skill work wrote short essays on the topic "My toes are terrific because. . . ." The writing seemed clever and free to an observer. The teachers and the principal in the Belair school enjoyed a hilarious story written by a sixth-grade boy about an unlucky knight who helps to subdue the "semi-barbarian Welsh." Each page has one sentence which begins with the word "fortunately" or "unfortunately." Teachers expressed concern about the limiting skill curriculum in interviews and said they wanted to encourage children to be more creative and thoughtful. But a curriculum dedicated to removing learning deficits and to teaching children to reproduce the proper "behavior" in response to tests of skills leaves little time or energy for the students to play with making meanings from their school experience. The emphasis on worksheets in the three technical schools limited thought.[19]

Given the tugs and pulls between skills and thinking, writing and filling in blanks on skill worksheets, what is the larger picture of education painted by the three technical schools?

Individually Guided Education in Three Traditional Schools: What Does it Mean?

Individually Guided Education gives isolated teachers in schools a modern technology to "rally round." The morale of IGE teachers is good. Teachers see IGE as a successful cooperative effort that offers more promise than any teacher's individual attempt to improve learning and teaching. IGE provides a complete system of goals and procedures, and a common technical vocabulary with which to talk about the innovation.

One technology in IGE that supports the beliefs of the teachers in the technical schools is its Instructional Planning Model, presented in Figure 5. This model is the primary technological element in IGE. The instructional planning model is rooted in systems theory and behavioristic psychology. The model contradicts the other element in IGE which reflects more intellectual and democratic values. (This contradiction in theory is critical to understanding IGE. I shall return to it in the two following sections.) Steps 4 and 6, for example, play into the beliefs of technically oriented teachers. When these steps require the teachers to set the instructional objectives for each child that are to be covered and assessed in a *short period of time*, they sanction the unexamined technological theory of teachers (which is already "pushing" their actions from behind) and virtually assure that reading and arithmetic will be reduced to discrete and measurable skills.

Popkewitz and his colleagues found IGE to be an undesirable form of social control. The technology of IGE, when used as an end in itself for education, *resulted in a loss of control over ideas and work by both students and teachers.* Since this conclusion follows from much of what I have already presented about education in the technical schools, I will give a brief account of the researchers' beliefs. First, efficient ways to process students was a primary concern; teachers became more concerned with the technology of IGE, such as setting objectives and record keeping, than they were about substantive issues of what to teach to whom and how to teach it. Second, excellence meant spending time on tasks—looking busy.

FIGURE 5. The Individually Guided Education Instructional Planning Model

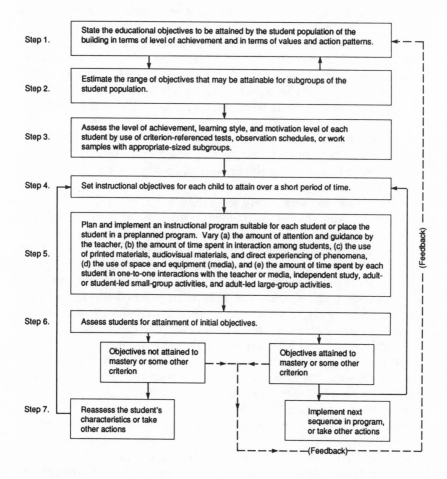

Step 1.	State the educational objectives to be attained by the student population of the building in terms of level of achievement and in terms of values and action patterns.
Step 2.	Estimate the range of objectives that may be attainable for subgroups of the student population.
Step 3.	Assess the level of achievement, learning style, and motivation level of each student by use of criterion-referenced tests, observation schedules, or work samples with appropriate-sized subgroups.
Step 4.	Set instructional objectives for each child to attain over a short period of time.
Step 5.	Plan and implement an instructional program suitable for each student or place the student in a preplanned program. Vary (a) the amount of attention and guidance by the teacher, (b) the amount of time spent in interaction among students, (c) the use of printed materials, audiovisual materials, and direct experiencing of phenomena, (d) the use of space and equipment (media), and (e) the amount of time spent by each student in one-to-one interactions with the teacher or media, independent study, adult- or student-led small-group activities, and adult-led large-group activities.
Step 6.	Assess students for attainment of initial objectives.

Objectives not attained to mastery or some other criterion

Objectives attained to mastery or some other criterion

Step 7.	Reassess the student's characteristics or take other actions

Implement next sequence in program, or take other actions

(Feedback)

(Feedback)

Source: Thomas A. Romberg, ed., Toward Effective Schooling: The IGE Experience,(Lanham,Maryland: University Press of America, Inc., 1985), p. 22.

*The Individually Guided Education literature refers to this process as the Instructional Programming Model.

This was true for both students and teachers. Third, content to be learned was standardized. Fourth, "standardized" meant those things that could be easily measured. "'Understanding a story' meant being able to respond to five questions which had precise, unambiguous answers that a child could identify on a dittoed sheet." Fifth, preplanning and measurement eliminated spontaneous comments and questions from students that often lead to valuable and meaningful learning when they were redirected by a sympathetic and skilled teacher. And, sixth, content was broken into objectives that were sequenced by others in isolation from the learner and the teacher. The objectives were without context or meaning, which makes the selection of intelligent means difficult if not impossible. Human work in the real world is an interplay of practical skills, context, and thought in which both "what is to be done" and the "means whereby work is to be done" make sense to the worker.[20] (I have elaborated the sixth conclusion to make it more concrete.)

Individually Guided Education in the technical schools might be viewed as a beautiful vase, well-crafted and elegantly colored, that promised to preserve the flowers of competence and efficiency, except for one thing that was beyond the educators' and parents' visual field: the vase was empty. One flower that was not in the vase, for example, was that bright students finished the limited skill objectives quickly with little to challenge them beyond more hierarchically arranged and sequenced objectives. But the metaphor of the vase and flowers cannot capture the image of IGE. IGE in the technical schools cut more of a geometric figure with straight lines and sharp angles and its color was gray with bright yellows and reds bursting forth only when a student might write an illustrated and humorous essay about an unlucky knight. The proper metaphor for IGE in these schools is that of a machine that meters out "the right instructional method and content" to each student.[21] Efficiency was an illusion. *Technology's promise could not be kept. IGE became a routine in itself, an exercise in the use of a clear set of managerial means that let the cultural phantoms of school, living deep within the recesses of its belief system, creep forth amidst the busyness that so occupied the teachers and, unseen, decouple the managerial means from the educational ends. The teachers who set out to reform their schools ended up as technical captives to the reform itself, a captivity so complete that their intuitive doubts and concerns that surfaced occasionally along the way were never given expression in sustained conversation. Language and thought never had the chance to make these fleeting doubts solid or real, to bring them to the forum of discussion for thoughtful examination. The teachers became not only captives to the technology, they fell mute as well.*

The education offered in the IGE technical schools is robbed of its imaginative and liberating potential. It takes more faith than I can muster to believe that this kind of education is good for much, or that it might lead to anything good in the future. An education, I infer, that is imaginatively dead in its present life can offer nothing lively in the future life. When the practical is pursued too vigorously, the hand grasps but never holds.

Dewey's idea that any education to be good must be worthwhile in "its own immediate having" speaks to the impass in which the technical schools found themselves, but I wonder what new energies might have been released among the staffs of these schools if someone had stopped the busy activities for even one hour and asked the teachers to consider seriously a seminal idea. I offer one of Dewey's as a possible example. Dewey suggests that the strong desire for uniform procedures and for quick external results "are the chief foes which the open-minded attitude meets in school." The cause of our devotion to rigid methods, Dewey believes, "is that it seems to promise speedy, accurately measurable, correct results. The zeal for 'answers' is the explanation of much of the zeal for rigid and mechanical methods." Open-mindedness requires time for experience to accumulate, to ripen, and to sink in, if it is to develop. "Results (external answers . . .) may be hurried; processes may not be forced. . . . [It is] the quality of the mental processes, not the production of correct answers, [that] is the measure of educative growth. . . ." If more teachers (and administrators) understood this idea, Dewey continues, "a revolution in teaching would be worked."[22]

The qualitative field study by Popkewitz and his colleagues captures the feelings, the neglect of conversation and thought, and the unremarked contradictions between the promises made in the name of efficiency and more personal attention to students, better than any definition of the technological mindset could ever reach. Abstractions such as "technological mindset" or "intellectual and democratic" are often better described and shown in action than defined.

A Different Way of Learning: Individually Guided Education in a Progressive School

The teachers' beliefs about learning in the Kennedy School are suggested in the snapshots of teaching that follow. (The reader may notice that relatively extended accounts of student-teacher interactions are given for Kennedy while none was given for the three technical schools. This difference is accounted for, I believe, by the very different nature of student-teacher interactions in the two types of schools.)

Here is how a teacher at the Kennedy School approached an ordinary social studies lesson. The problem given to the students is how to make a graph that showed the oil exports or imports for countries such as the United States, Japan, and Germany. The children use a news article to get the number of barrels traded by the different countries. After several children have drawn graphs on the chalkboard based on the barrels of oil imported or exported by the countries, the teacher suggests another way of presenting the data, based on percentages. The students get busy converting barrels of oil into percentages. Three students indicate that they can make a percentage graph. After several false starts at the chalkboard, the students produce a graph that shows the percentage of oil imports by country. An observer reports what happened next.

> Once the graph is complete the students discuss the political implications [of their data.] The teacher asks: "What problems might develop between nations because of this sharp difference between who exports and who imports?" One student sees no problem. "We get their oil and they get our money" [a true classical economist in elementary school!]. The teacher suggests that maybe the exporting countries might get together to raise the price higher than we want to pay. This, she continued, can create a possible problem.[23]

Another example of relatively progressive learning and teaching is given by a teacher who brought to class an editorial from the local newspaper that was critical of advertising junk foods on children's television programs. The students wrote a response to the editorial, which involved creating ideas that either supported or did not support the position taken in the editorial. The children were expected to follow the rules of standard formal English in their responses.[24]

One final example will show how the teachers' ideas and values about learning and teaching influenced the quality of learning in their classes. All of the teachers and students on one teaching team turned the problem of an exploding chinchilla population into applied work in science, mathematics, and manual arts. The solution to the rapidly expanding chinchilla population was a new hexagonal cage, which the students planned and built. This required some knowledge of the environment needed by the animals, the ability to measure and to understand the concept "hexagonal," and, I assume, small group work, reading, and the use of oral language in a natural situation.[25]

There are several educationally worthy elements in these lessons, when viewed from a progressive perspective. First, content in the several subjects, as in social studies and mathematics in the lesson on graphs, comes together at times in a more integrated whole to solve a problem. Second, general concepts must be understood and used in the projects. Third, these activities are fun, which helps to develop a sense of purpose and social involvement.[26] Although the descriptions provided by Popkewitz and his colleagues of the learning activities at Kennedy are thin, and are little more than snapshots because no representative learning experience is presented over time to show its full development, it is reasonable to assume, given proper teacher guidance, that children at Kennedy had more opportunities than children in the technical IGE schools to exercise initiative, discipline, and responsibility in their work and to learn important social and language skills in more natural groupings that involved both individual and small group work, and that learning probably was seen as something "that made sense," which is one good motivator in learning.

The researchers make a very important educational distinction that relates to the democratic aspect of our criterion for fundamental reform when they say that the more problem-centered activities at Kennedy were typical of its way of learning and teaching and that these more demanding experiences were "available to all children . . . and were expected to add to everyone's learning ability. . . ."; whereas in the technical schools they were more like prizes given to able children and were, in any case, atypical of learning in these schools.[27] In a democracy, if the best is known, every student has a moral and social right to share in the very best that the society can offer.

It is difficult to know why the Kennedy School is different from the five other IGE schools. Kennedy serves a middle-class community of business and professional people very much like that served by Belair, a school that reflects a technical view of learning and teaching. Social class differences are not significant between the two schools. Perhaps the most important influence on the different education offered by Kennedy and Belair is to be found in their early histories. Kennedy was led in its first two years by an energetic principal who wanted to use its open-classroom architectural design to foster a more personal style of learning. Beginning in 1972, when

Kennedy was built, the principal recruited a teaching staff committed to IGE "that was willing to work hard on developing an individualized system. . . ."[28] The Belair School, in contrast, chose IGE because the superintendent saw IGE as a way to effective management and chose a principal who would produce "a more coherent and systematic program" to please the school's parents, who were unhappy with the former curriculum (which the current principal described as chaotic).[29] Things were not blissful at Kennedy: the creative principal left after two years of disputes with the superintendent about Kennedy's way of teaching. The superintendent still presses for "conformity and consistency" in the district, a stimulus that only the teachers at Kennedy, among all of the schools in the district, responded to by defending their professional responsibility to make judgments about the students' welfare in contrast to "bureaucrats" in the central office.[30] I will give more detail on this fundamental issue later, but I cannot resist a cheer for the courage and professionalism shown by the Kennedy teachers. Kennedy just might be "a kid's place" after all.

The early and formative years of the Kennedy School may have indelibly shaped its character. The observers imply that this conclusion may be true when they write that "Kennedy . . . appears to be running on the traditions and practices established in its early history."[31] Maybe schools have the social equivalent of biological genes, which, once activated in conception, exert a formative influence in their life even while the outside environment batters and assaults them in contrary ways. This observation seems to be true of great universities, which obstinately pursue a perspective imparted at "birth" that transcends famines and wars and even the press of time itself.

Although the prevailing beliefs among many educators and policymakers do not encourage learning activities that may have intrinsic worth or that may be, in themselves, educative and enjoyable removed from any consideration of measurable objectives, this attitude was held by many of the teachers at Kennedy and contributed to the school's intellectual and emotional environment. The teachers believed, the researchers write, that children have a right to enjoy life in school; that enjoyable activities elicit a strong and positive intellectual and social response from children that, in ways that may remain forever unknown, ripple out through the social waters of the classroom and school to engage children intellectually and emotionally in their studies; and that enjoyable and worthwhile activities create more situations that students may engage intellectually and socially.[32] Kennedy did not pursue "an enjoy curriculum" (as the learning activities that I summarized earlier indicate), which would be a romanticized perversion of what is truly educative. The teachers seemed to be saying, with great common sense, that all good activities do not have to be preplanned and linked to objectives because to do so deadens school life and reduces enthusiasm and spontaneity, which is important in living; and that the teachers were best situated to know what activities, from field trips to mathematics, could achieve the school's educational purpose. When some legislators today say that there is too much play in kindergarten, and press for a skills curriculum and testing all in hot pursuit of efficient school reform, we could do far worse than listen to the wise if softer concerns of the Kennedy teachers. These teachers know that school is not all about objectives any more than adult life is all about a paycheck or "getting ahead," important as these may be. "Important" does not imply "everything."

One bit of anecdotal evidence may show the value of the Kennedy philosophy. After several experiences were reported in which the Kennedy School resisted efforts by the superintendent to standardize procedures, such as requiring that all field trips be tied to specific and approved objectives, a teacher said: "I'm sure there are plenty of other teachers and schools in the district that teach kids to read just as well as we do. Maybe it's that good feeling that you have with kids that I'm really referring to. . . ." Comments by substitute teachers who go to other schools are positive when they talk about Kennedy's "discipline, the kind of kids we have, [and] their enthusiasm toward learning and toward school activities."[33] If the observations of the substitute teachers are true, does one need a research study to conclude that the kind of social and emotional energy shown by the students can be anything but good, whether we consider the necessarily restrained life of students in schools or in that larger, less restrained, and uncertain life that goes on in families, work places, and communities, of which life in school is but a tiny slice?

Given the happy and productive life that apparently marked this progressive school, we must consider the ways that IGE related to it.

How Does IGE Influence a Progressive School?

The short answer to this question is that the principal and teachers at Kennedy "sucked in" the basic technologies of IGE—somewhat in the manner of an organism ingesting food—*but once this IGE food was ingested, it was transformed by the metabolism of the teachers' philosophy to serve its own organic needs.* The meetings of the teaching teams, for example, were used for serious discussion of curriculum issues and children as well as procedural matters that so occupied the technical schools. Of great interest to me, given the isolation of teachers in schools and their general silence on important educational issues, is the way the teachers used the school-wide meetings attended by the principal, team leaders, and teachers to oppose the efforts of the superintendent to standardize teaching and the curriculum in the district. In IGE terms, this group is called the Instructional Improvement Committee. The opposition to field trips that were to be tied to objectives arose in this committee. This committee also provided a forum through which Kennedy teachers opposed the adoption of a basal reading series they felt was inflexible and did not permit the use of professional judgment in the choice of learning materials. A dramatic example of the invocation of teacher responsibility and the use of the Instructional Improvement Committee as a policy forum arose when the superintendent announced a policy of enforcing attendance at schools on the basis of neighborhood boundary lines, with less than two months remaining in the school year! The teachers again asserted their professional obligations and pointed out, among other objections, the harmful effect on students who would enroll in new schools near the end of the year. These discussions were often heated and reflected the teachers perception that the superintendent's policies "were 'eroding' the Kennedy traditions."[34]

In the accountability-managerial domain of student record keeping, the progressive school took a responsible but relaxed stance. Unlike the technical schools, there were no prominent displays of lists of objectives, charts of student progress, and record-keeping systems. The objectives and evaluative elements in IGE were subsidiary "rather than central in curriculum planning." Teachers at Kennedy did keep records on student achievement of the district's minimal objectives for each grade. Many of the students at Kennedy had achieved these minimal skills, which freed the teachers to deal with more complex and interesting subject matter. The Instructional Planning Model, which emphasizes a set-the-objective-teach-test sequence, was thought to limit what the teachers were trying to achieve and exerted only minimal influence on learning.[35]

We are left in the clouds of ambiguity if we try too directly to answer the question, How did IGE influence the intellectual and social character of the Kennedy school? I believe that the organizational restructuring of the school that created teaching teams and the school-wide instructional improvement committee were potent factors because this organizational seed fell upon a group of teachers who had a rather clear theory of learning and what schools should be about—and they had the conviction to act on this theory and the courage to resist persistent efforts by the superintendent to make Kennedy more like a technical school. The other pieces of IGE, such as behavioral objectives and criterion-referenced testing, as I have pointed out, were of little influence.

One important thing that IGE might have done for this progressive school, however, is to give its "radical philosophy" public credibility, not only because of its federal and university sponsorship and its reputation as a ground-breaking reform, but primarily because the technical language of IGE, which embraces a business-like planning process of clear objectives and frequent measurement, masks the softer, less publicly credible progressive language of thematic units, student initiative and responsibility, democratic process, and purpose and meaning in learning. All of this, if true, was fortuitous and, if one historical link can be found between the school and IGE, it is probably the decision of Kennedy's first principal to adopt IGE and to pursue it vigorously as an idea to achieve his own aims for the school.

Kennedy, in a word, became the kind of school it was because of the *ideas and values* about learning and teaching imparted to it by its first principal—ideas and values that were professionally and courageously pursued by most of its teachers in the following years. The pattern of the reported data supports this conclusion. The influence of the first principal is indicated by the teachers' belief that Kennedy is running "on the traditions and practices established in its early history."[36] The account is full of examples of the teachers speaking out for their beliefs, most often against the demands for bureaucratic standardization pushed by the superintendent. The data, then, support the conclusion that *the ideas and values held by the educators in Kennedy influenced their practical actions across a rather wide range of professional activity—including the remarkable opposition to the superintendent's policies.* I shall briefly support my belief that it is the ideas and values held by the Kennedy staff that was the singularly important influence on making Kennedy the kind of school it was.

I have come to believe, based on my experience teaching practitioners in graduate school and engaging principals and teachers in idea-based and democratic reform efforts, that the critical variable in school reform, whether we are dealing with urban schools or schools in the affluent suburbs, is the *ideas and values that teachers and principals hold about what is desirable and undesirable educational practice.* Education is, in other words, an intellectual and moral enterprise in which educators act *intentionally,* influenced by their system of beliefs, within a practical situation that offers both constraints and opportunities. I shall not offer more support here other than to say that this idea is consistent with Deweyan theory, among others, and to cite Jerome Bruner's book, *Acts of Meaning,* which supports this position from his perspective of a "new" cultural psychology in which individuals construct meaning within social situations, and which challenges the tenets of both behaviorism and cognitive psychology based on computer models and information processing theory.[37]

Consider the importance to reform of the ideas and values held by the principals of Belair and Kennedy. The principal at Belair, for example, was hired by the superintendent to "shape up" the chaotic conditions in the school.[38] There is every reason to believe that this principal's ideas were consistent with the beliefs of the technological mindset, which supports the more behavioristic elements in IGE. The first principal at Kennedy, however, based on the subsequent actions of the teachers and the principal who followed him, who was chosen from the Kennedy staff, had a belief system that could be described as "moderately progressive." She supported the more progressive elements of IGE. The data in the study reasonably support this conclusion. My analysis is given more force because the communities served by the two schools were similar in their social class orientation.

The same line of reasoning holds for the teachers in the technical schools. The teachers interpreted what was "desirable and undesirable" educational practice in accordance with their beliefs about education. They, too, emphasized or minimized elements in IGE in accordance with their technological beliefs. The data support this conclusion. The power of belief to affect actions is difficult to overlook with the teachers at Kennedy when they repeatedly stood up to the superintendent, actions which take a great deal of intellectual and emotional energy, and which can be taken as an *index of the power their beliefs exercised in their work.*

The Popkewitz study is helpful because it shows that a reform such as IGE is not a neutral, relatively inert and tangible creation, like a Ford car, that can be shipped from Madison, Wisconsin, to consumers around the country to be "driven" and "maintained" as its developers specify and, by doing so, to ensure that the contours and quality of "Fordness" will endure through the uses to which it is put by a diverse body of educator-drivers. A reform is not a commodity, although it is easy to think of it as such. IGE and, I believe, any reform, is reshaped and redesigned to fit the beliefs—the implicit theories—of the teachers and principals who "buy" it. In this way it is possible for a designer's "Porche 911" to become a humble "Honda Civic" in the minds and hands of its educator-drivers, or the other way around. This amazing transformation of one entity into another—a transformation accomplished without conscious intent, indeed a transformation accompanied with protestations of fidelity to the manufacturer's design throughout the long process of the reform's use—is a unique educational phenomenon. It is this idea of "immaculate transformation" that, to me, is the primary import of this study, although Popkewitz does not draw this significant inference from his research. *I believe fundamental reform must be seriously concerned with the ideas and values that all educators implicitly hold, and that reformers must make these beliefs explicit, open for discussion, so they can be retained or changed with knowledge and foresight and be more deliberately and intelligently used to achieve ends freely chosen. Only in this way can reform shift from its present mode where reform is unthoughtfully viewed as a commodity, to its functional mode where reform is viewed as an idea that is, in turn, shaped and reshaped by the ideas and values of the reformers who try to use it.* Dialogue, discussed in the next chapter, is one way to probe that which we take for granted and which, unseen, directs us from the shadows of our minds.

I hesitate to bring in another field study, however briefly, that describes the intellectual and emotional effects of IGE in a school that serves a middle-class community. The intellectual and emotional effects of schooling are often overlooked when measures of school quality are discussed in the public media and, strangely, in the journals, publications, and conferences of professional organizations to which superintendents and teachers attend, and in the more glittering reports of many national commissions and foundations. This second field study highlights the intellectual and emotional aspects of learning in one IGE school.

Flowing Brook—A School without Laughter

The children at Flowing Brook are clean, well dressed, and mannerly, often beaming a shy smile to the visiting team of three re-

searchers from the University of Utah. The building is designed on
the open-classroom plan of the 1970s (IGE seems to have an affinity
for schools that were built on the open-plan design). The school is
nongraded, organized by teaching teams, and has a schoolwide instructional improvement committee, made up of the teaching team
leaders and chaired by the principal, which gives teachers a voice in
curriculum decisions.[39]

Robert Bullough and his colleagues write that the students'
day is spent doing paper-and-pencil tasks from a workbook or work-
sheet. "The general pattern of the morning," the observers write,
"is one of the teachers explaining how to do assignments and cor-
recting completed work while students do the assignments and
have them checked off. It is a telling experience . . . [to] see every
student in almost every class doing the same thing: sitting, head
bent over desk, working. . . . Our impression is that much of the students' and teachers' day is spent this way."[40]

Laughter was virtually absent in this school. Little laughter
arose from interpersonal encounters among students or teachers
and students. Other feelings, such as anger or frustration, were only
seen occasionally. One case of genuine emotion arose when a
teacher, uncharacteristically, exploded with "If you don't knock
that off, I'm going to knock your head off!"[41]

If direct expressions of emotions through laughter or anger
rarely occurred, another form of expression filled the void: a pleasant but impersonal monotone in which the teachers addressed the
students. The teachers' voices held to this flat tone whether they
were praising, reprimanding, or explaining something to the students. It was the impersonal tone, Bullough reports, that we expect
"at the [checkout counter] or over the phone when we call about our
bank balance." Teaching at Flowing Brook was impersonal, more
like curriculum management. Emotions may get in the way of the
work: "Deadpan characterizes whatever is being said, whether
praise or warning."[42]

That teachers and children learned to play their school roles is
indicated by the change in feeling that occurred after school. After
school the voices regained their energy and their personal quality,
were more expressive, and there was laughter and friendly teasing
among students and teachers.[43] One might say that the emotional
flatness of Flowing Brook lay, in a strange way, within the dark cor-
ners of the school's routines when the children labored over their
worksheets and exercises.

The intellectual life of Flowing Brook had no after-school "saves." Facts were the common coin of intellectual currency. The shorter the time each "fact coin" was held and pondered, the faster it was spent in a short answer without elaboration or defense, the higher the Intellectual Gross Product in Flowing Brook rose. The "fact money" circulated widely in the school, but no one could purchase much of substance with it. Flowing Brook is very much like the one thousand classrooms John Goodlad studied in 1984.[44]

The following observation from one of the researchers suggests the texture that characterizes "fact bound" learning and teaching.

> [Teacher talking] "How many watch 'Mr. Merlin'?" [Hands go up]. "How many like it?" [Most]. "How many don't like it?" [None] . . . He has the kids read from their magazines. When they finish he goes through the questions in the manual—a,b,c,d. The kids raise their hands on what they think is the right answer. . . . Most of the questions get split responses—some of them get a near even split seeming to indicate the necessity of exploring differences. . . . [45]

No exchange of ideas or feelings marred the lesson. The questions are so routine and expected that the students raise their hands "well before the teacher has finished . . . the question."[46] Twelve years of this kind of Quiz Show mentality, in addition to thousands of hours of commercial television and other assorted chocolates of the commercial society, and the students will not be able to read *TV Guide* or recognize the proper channel number on their television set. (Imagine the possible. An American generation will sit mute before their darkened screens of mass forgetfulness, vaguely sensing that something went wrong, but they will be unable to communicate or think. They will live and die immobile and transfixed, having forgotten that conversation needs no screen and thought needs no plug.)

If we accept the picture of IGE snapped by the Brownie cameras of the researchers in seven IGE schools, six of which were considered to be exemplary IGE schools and to reflect a range of social classes, we see a bleak picture of American schools and of IGE. Six of the seven schools, Kennedy excepted, reflected an anti-intellectualism and an indifference to democratic values that have concerned reformers since the turn of the century. This is an issue that needs to be brought before the bar of probing discussion in education courses and in in-school teacher and administrator education sessions.

The developers of Individually Guided Education were more aware of the organizational and political dynamics of reform than were other innovators who launched their reforms in the heat of the 1960s. I shall sketch the interorganizational components of IGE before I turn to the final question: What is the educational worth of Individually Guided Education?

INTER-ORGANIZATIONAL SUPPORT SYSTEMS FOR INDIVIDUALLY GUIDED EDUCATION

The efforts of the University of Wisconsin staff to root Individually Guided Education in the existing state and local agencies legally responsible for public education, and to create partnerships among IGE schools and with teacher education institutions, suggests the political elements masked within the broad phrase that IGE was conceived as a "comprehensive educational reform." These linkages and partnerships have a contemporary ring with some reform efforts in the early nineties that have "reached out to touch someone" in ways more complex than a telephone call. I think, for example, of the several hundred schools tied into the Paideia reform; of the Coalition of Essential Schools that has political ties to state governors and chief state school officers through the Education Commission of the States, a reform sparked by James B. Conant in the mid-sixties; and partnerships of schools and universities led by John Goodlad and his colleagues at the Center for Educational Renewal at the University of Washington. The complex and intertwined networks created by IGE in the 1970s anticipated these developments.

The purpose of these complex organizational arrangements among the states and local school districts, the governmental structures of education, was clearly stated by Herbert J. Klausmeier and his associates in 1977: ". . . IGE as a comprehensive alternative form of schooling can function within the present governmental-educational structures of each state as an appropriate focus for mobilizing educational improvement and renewal efforts."[47] IGE was seen, then, as a springboard to reform efforts beyond itself. What could be more comprehensive in conception?

I sketch below many of the organizational links that were considered to be critical to the successful implementation of IGE and to educational renewal.

1. Legal agencies responsible for education are of great moment because "innovative organizations interact frequently with other

organizations in their environment." These agencies include the state education department, intermediate units such as county-based educational agencies, teacher education institutions, and local schools.

2. Links must be forged within the school district in which the IGE reform is adopted. Seven broad objectives are stated for the IGE school as it makes the changeover to reform, which include creating new structures within the district, joining forces with the state and other agencies listed above, and conducting continuing research on IGE as it unfolds. The new structures to be created within the district are the non-graded-team-teaching-organization, the school-wide Instructional Improvement Committee in which teachers have a strong voice, and the System-wide Program Committee, which includes the superintendent, representative principals, team leaders, teachers, and parents.

3. The last system of organizational links forged by the staff included two research and development agencies, four multi-state regional IGE institutes, and a national association of people involved in implementing IGE, which was called The Association for Individually Guided Education. In 1975 four regional institutes were set up in Connecticut, Florida, California, and at the already-established research and development center at the University of Wisconsin. The primary function of the institutes was to further the adoption of IGE in all states. The Association for Individually Guided Education was established in 1973 and represented educators from twelve states who were experienced with IGE. The purpose of the organization was to exchange information and successful practices among a nation-wide group of people who had adopted IGE. By 1976 this association was strong enough to employ a half-time executive secretary.[48]

One cannot but admire the energy and enthusiasm that attended the planning and execution of this single organizational component of IGE. This evidence alone is sufficient to attest to the seriousness and commitment to one comprehensive reform that was in full swing in the 1970s. Whether or not Individually Guided Education is considered a success or a failure, or is clothed in a more nuanced judgment less categorical, it is difficult to imagine a reform effort more complex, so long lived, or in which the changing tides of reform are so well documented.

I have drawn a picture of IGE in close to full dress, a picture that defines its foreground in the various forms IGE assumed when it was given life in schools, and the picture of IGE itself, which is seen against the background of the developers' hopes and intentions. I believe that the complexity of IGE, the care and money that went into its development, and the various documentations and research of IGE in schools over a span of at least fifteen years make IGE a rich source of ideals and actions that should not be neglected if reform is to be taken seriously. Reforms like IGE should never be put on the shelf because they are not "hot" in a given slice of a day's time. I believe the thrust of this book will show, for example, that while the body of reform is most often clothed in the fur of what is momentarily fashionable, the same old mechanical brain and heart live on in reform's Land of Oz, where the hapless Tin Man becomes reform's Wizard.

How Good is Individually Guided Education As a Reform?

Assessing the worth of Individually Guided Education is more difficult than assessing the worth of the other reforms I have discussed. IGE is more difficult because it has two conflicting theories of learning built into it: the behavioristic theory, with its behavioral objectives and sequence of skills; and another more intellectual and democratic theory, which tries to personalize teaching on bases other than criterion-referenced tests.

We saw the effects of the more progressive theory in its attempt to give teachers more decision-making power in teaching, curriculum, and school governance through structural reforms such as team teaching, vertical age grouping and, most critically, the schoolwide instructional planning committee whose purpose was to run the school. With this combination of "bads" and "goods," what kind of a fair judgment is warranted? I can suggest the quality of my judgment best through a metaphor.

Imagine that you are looking from some distance at a long valley. At first glance, you see this valley as arid, dry, without color, much like the desert country in Arizona. Having established yourself on this visual perch, you look more closely—and here we take a dreamlike leap—you see a high, white picket fence running the valley's length. In the middle of this fence is a huge gate, which is a mile wide and half-a-mile high. This gate has big black letters on it which read "IGE—University of Wisconsin—1965–1977." On the far side of this white fence and the Wisconsin gate, gardens grow and the land is lush with fruit and vegetation. On the near side of the fence, the land is arid and without life except for some cactus and a few scattered desert flowers which you know to be there but cannot see. You look at the scene again and realize that the IGE gate swings both ways, that it hangs ambivalently between the two forms of life in the valley.

If we take the intentions of IGE's developers into account, the gate opens most often into the lush garden; if we take the perspective of how schools used and interpreted IGE, the gate most often opens into a valley of few flowers. Both statements are empirically true, but they do not resolve the judgment-of-worth question. *Most writing on reform avoids the judgment-of-worth question.* Proponents of a reform generally assume its worth or argue for its worth indirectly by citing gains in test scores based on research. We saw this stance earlier in such reforms as mastery learning, Chapter 1 remedial programs, and the prescriptions for teaching based on the research for effective teaching. Much of the literature on IGE written by its developers assumes the worth of IGE. The assumption-of-worth position was also true of the new mathematics and science curriculums discussed in chapter 3. Another way to avoid the messy question of a reform's worth, and the invocation of an *educational* theory necessary to answer it, is to regard reform as a technically neutral problem in the change process. This is Michael Fullan's position, I believe, as he tries mightily to make more rational the process of educational change from the seemingly endless—and necessarily contradictory—findings of research on the process of reform. What this research does not and cannot address are the critical questions of what *ought* to be done and what is the *worth* of the alternatives proposed. One could take two contradictory educational theories or a loose set of beliefs, for example, and marshall a long list of supporting "findings" from Fullan's book to support each one.[49] This condition cannot be scientific, whatever else it may be, and it sinks ideas and values in a sea of disjointed empirical facts that makes me seasick as I try to make them cohere.

The developers of Individually Guided Education, too, made a critical error in underestimating the power a coherent set of ideas and values exerts on the development of a reform. The theoretical static within IGE was heard by some of its developers. Thomas A. Romberg concludes his implementation study of IGE with some important ideas for policymakers and academics who initiate and develop reforms for schools, and for practitioners who may adopt them. The importance of a coherent theory of learning and teaching, and of education itself, to the development of reforms that are intellectual and democratic in spirit must be stressed. Romberg suggests this idea when he says that IGE was developed "in an eclectic manner" and that no clear choice was ever made in favor of "one theory of learning." In its functional evolution IGE drew on "both the behavioral and constructivist [progressive] psychological traditions." The idea that students were to explore and discover to increase motivation and understanding was diluted by other ideas within IGE. Elements within the instructional planning model, perhaps the easiest component of IGE to interpret technologically, was one source of ambivalence. Romberg implies this when he says that organizing teaching through "task analysis [to be] assessed via tests related to behavioral objectives" and the use of classroom management procedures "based on systems analysis where the knowledge to be acquired is fixed" with the teacher free to choose appropriate methods to teach it, led to confusion about how students were to be taught in a way that met their unique intellectual needs and ways of learning.[50] This observation is supported, too, by the criticism the two teams of researchers who studied IGE's use in schools heaped on the systems-based instructional planning model.

If the ideas that shape a reform are critical in defining its educational characteristics at the University of Wisconsin, ideas are critical also in defining its educational characteristics when the reform is accepted by teachers and principals who try to put it into practice. The field studies that describe well how schools reshaped IGE support my statement about the importance of theory in school practice.

Recall how the teachers in the Clayburn Elementary School, which served a poor rural community, "developed" their reading objectives: they cut them out of a teacher's manual! Recall the teacher in the Belair School who said "the behavioral objectives are the concepts" to be taught in mathematics. Most often it was a dreary life in the technical schools witnessed by the field researchers. The technical schools accepted the technological elements of IGE at face value—such as behavioral objectives and criterion-referenced tests—and made them the center piece of their teaching. The Kennedy School, which I labeled progressive, de-emphasized these technical elements in IGE, and emphasized concepts, teaching through thematic units, and relating formal subject matter to the children's experience, e.g., the students' writing a response to the editorial on junk foods. We have one reform "on paper" and two very different versions of it in school practice.

We see again, as experience tells, that a reform is not a carefully machined steel ball that is put into one end of a steel pipe, austerely called the "change process," to roll with little friction through it and emerge unchanged at the other end where the reform is greeted with pronouncements of success and cheers for the machine-like perfection of the whole process. Reforms are more like clay that take the shape of whatever hand so lightly touches them. It would be exaggerating only a bit to say that there are as many "IGEs" as there are schools using it. Romberg, who was a key player in the three-year implementation study of IGE, concludes that the so-called reform-minded schools that adopted IGE did not understand that the *primary goal of IGE was to shift instructional planning from the group to the student, and that schools often made changes in response to short-term and pressing problems rather than IGE's comprehensive plan.* "Very often," Romberg continues, "the [IGE] label was used symbolically to justify . . . current practices (as in the technical schools), or to have a different administrative organization. . . . [T]he [school governance committee] was not devised as a new administrative arrangement to be used with conventional instructional goals. . . . We now believe that the impact of IGE was limited because most schools did not identify meeting individual student learning needs as their goal. . . ." Grouping was done annually, often on the basis of ability and not on intellectual need. The traditional classroom structure remained the same.[51]

When Romberg, one of IGE's developers, says that the adopting schools used IGE to sanction traditional practices, however unknowingly this conversion was done, we see the concrete effects of a way of *thinking* about learning and teaching. Something as intangible as "theory" is making a difference in the real world. When, for example, schools take something as potentially powerful as the school governance structure in IGE and convert it to a mechanism that fiddles with the routines of schooling and thus sanctions the very things that need to be reformed, we are seeing real-world effects of the teachers' and principals' implicit educational theory; this unexamined theory is the theory of the technological mindset. The tight grip of the technological mindset on the minds of IGE educators is suggested by its power in schools that serve both lower- and middle-class communities, and by its wide geographical spread among the three thousand schools that adopted IGE as a reform. This false intellectual *conversion* of a reform is one more bit of evidence that we cannot see the "objective" world "out there" as clearly as we see an old oak in a meadow, but that we see the world "inside our heads" as the stimuli from "out there" are given shape and meaning by the ideas and values that often live and do their work below the level of conscious awareness. Reforms usually come from "out there" to be snared like butterflies in the net of our perceptions only to become lifeless exhibits that, in a strange way, are to be understood as testimony to our reform-mindedness.

Fullan cites the conclusion by Paul Berman and Milbrey McLaughlin, in their study of change in federally funded programs, that the adaptations teachers made in a reform during the implementation phase took precedence over the reform's content. This adaptation of a reform by teachers, according to Berman and McLaughlin, is important if teachers are to work through and understand the precepts on which the reform is based.[52] This is helpful but is does not go far enough. What is overlooked is the *educational worth* of the adaptations that the teachers make and of the reform itself. To understand the precepts, for example, of a technological reform, and to adapt this reform in a manner consistent with its technological precepts, is not likely to encourage thinking in either teachers or students if the analysis I have given of technological reforms is even close to the truth. What is important is the unasked question: What drives the changes made by a teacher in a reform? I believe the adaptations are driven by what the teachers know and believe about learning and teaching, and their theories about what a good school is. What is important is that the adaptations made by teachers are truly *intellectual conversions* of the reform to conform with the teachers' implicit theories. (For ease of expression I use the term "teachers' theories," but I mean this term to include principals' and superintendents' theories as well.) Thus we must pay more attention to teachers' ideas in reform and learn to be less enamored with surface events in the reform process. The primacy of idea—of thought—in learning and teaching (and in reform) is supported by Deweyan theory, and this inference is consistent with the research of Popkewitz and Bullough. Individually Guided Education became "technical" in three schools, emotionally flat in Flowing Brook, and more intellectually and socially alive in Kennedy, because these schools reflect the teachers' and principals' ideas of what a school ought to be. The "adaptations" made to a reform follow a teacher's idea or theory as it works itself out in particular social situations. Reform puts theory to work for better or worse.

There is one essential lesson to be learned from this case study of a complex reform. The lesson is this: *nothing is more powerful in shaping the social and intellectual qualities of a reform, in both its development and life-in-school phases, than the coherence and power of the ideas and values from which the reform springs and through which it is given life in the schools. If it is the essence of reform we care to know—if we want to know what most influences the educational qualities of the reform itself and the quality of the reform when it comes to life in schools—it is the quality of the ideas, the quality of the theory, bred into it at conception and shaped further by the school environment in which it is nurtured.* Just as biological maturation cannot overcome severe structural limitations such as deafness, a reform's maturation in the hurly-burly that is life in schools is unlikely to create compensating structures to fill any intellectual and social-democratic voids left by building a reform on conflicting or substantively marred theory.

Although Individually Guided Education was a comprehensive reform in advance of its time for the reasons I have given, IGE embraced internal theoretical contradictions. *When the behavioristic elements in its instructional planning model met the technological mindset of teachers and principals, its fate was sealed: IGE became a mechanical model.* The intellectual and democratic elements in IGE, which extolled professional and democratic decision making by teachers, for example, could not be understood within the teachers' and principals' impoverished and implicit technological theories of learning and teaching. *These implicit theories limited their understanding of IGE and directed what they taught and how they taught it.* If more teachers had embraced the progressive theories of the teachers in the Kennedy School, the story of Individually Guided Education would have been a happier one.

If we think of the Wisconsin Center as a radio station, it was beaming too much technological static in its programs—a static that was amplified in the radios of receiving schools that were theoretically pretuned to hear the static as the message.

But my plea for the primacy of idea and thought in reform is, in some ways, an emotionally empty abstraction that misses the often gut-wrenching quality of a student's life in school, the environment in schools that punishes with a smile, the environment that punishes with true innocence. Books on education should be written by novelists to show the tragedy and the humor, the beauty and the pettiness, the pain and acid boredom we often inflict on students and ourselves. Education is art and can be only caught by art. Surely the pinched categories of "policy analysis" and much social science cannot capture the human and social qualities of education or the drama of true reform. Education, too, is probably beyond the grasp of even philosophy or history. Art might take us beyond the coves of academic discourse wherein we hide some truth, and in which many of us who profess and write hide much of ourselves as well. If a story lies in its details, as writers say, one cannot easily see the death of the imaginative and novel experience in the clunky phrase "technological mindset" or in the cool categories of educational research. Too few would see the Orwellian character in the Maplewood teacher's idea of what independent learning means. "Kids should be responsible for their own learning," she says. "They should follow instructions on the worksheets or books and proceed without having to be told." This is innocence.

Few would see the moral denial in the following incident reported by an observer:

> 1:13: The teacher says, "Everyone put their heads down. There's too much visiting. I don't want anyone to talk to his neighbor." Heads told to come up. Work went on.
>
> 1:20: Pupil says, "Bill is not carrying." [Lesson in arithmetic.] The teacher says, "That's his problem, Mark," (turns Mark's head around) "and not yours."[53]

This, too, is innocence. But after years of this kind of teaching we face an innocence that cripples the spirit. We face an innocence that kills.

A School of the 1960s:
The Everett A. McDonald, Jr. Comprehensive Elementary School Warminster, Pennsylvania

The McDonald school in the architect's model reflects the geometry of the space age rather than the rectilinear lines of the twentieth-century factory. The circular building at 12 o'clock is home to a wide range of special education students; the building on the left houses classrooms and the multi-media special experience room and planetarium; the third building includes a large library and classrooms. Photograph courtesy of the Centennial School District, Warminster, Pa.

INTRODUCTION

The Everett A. McDonald Elementary School built in 1968 reflects the optimism and creative spirit of the 1960s. In many ways the McDonald school is a child of the sixties: it has special classrooms for science and mathematics, for example, which is atypical of schools built for self-contained classrooms; art is honored in its very architecture and use of materials; and audio visual aids abound including perhaps the best and biggest one, the planetarium-special experience room to which the federal government contributed approximately $400,000 for the planetarium's projector and curriculum development under Title III of the Elementary and Secondary Education Act of 1965. The school has a large library and an Olympic-size swimming pool.

Superintendent McDonald's local vision and that of his staff and board is reflected in the near-equal composition of the student body drawn from special education (such as the trainable and physically handicapped), average, and academically talented. Some of the old is present, too. Regular classes are grouped by age and ability and the academically talented are in a separate track.

The McDonald school has forty classrooms to serve eight hundred children in grades kindergarten through six. The school's exterior walls of buff- and green-face brick offer a pleasing sight as one approaches the school seemingly secure on its thirty-acre site. It is easy to understand why this working- to middle-class community is proud of the McDonald school.

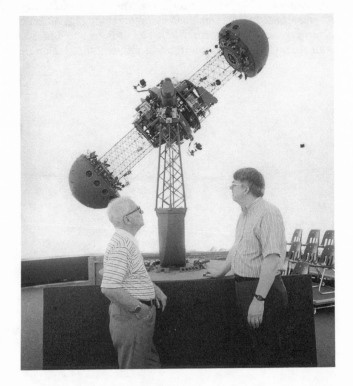

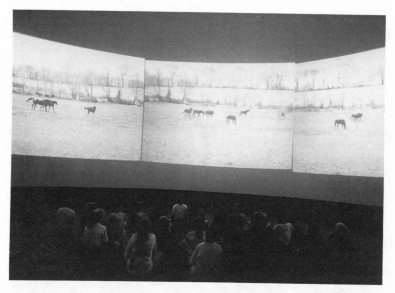

The special experience room and planetarium take students and teachers on life-like trips to the solar system, on a visit to a farm, inside a living cell, or to an African village. Here is a description of a "special experience" currently offered to fourth graders titled A Global View: "Using the dome of the SER as the inside of a giant earth globe, students will get an unusual 'worm's eye' view of the earth from which to study the concepts of latitude and longitude (35 minutes)." The special experience room is forty feet in diameter and permits images to be projected three hundred sixty degrees. Shown here is a single shot from a laser disk on the earth and its seasons; the planetarium projector with the room's designer, Henry Ray, and Donald Knapp, McDonald's multi-media director; and a picture to suggest what being in the special experience room is like. Photographs courtesy of Henry Ray.

This photograph shows students "wired" to the ever-present 1960s tape recorder. The presence of a tape recorder and ear phones (bought with federal
funds) is an almost certain way to date photographs of this period. Jim
Baldwin took this photograph in 1968. Photograph courtesy of the Centennial School District, Warminster, Pa.

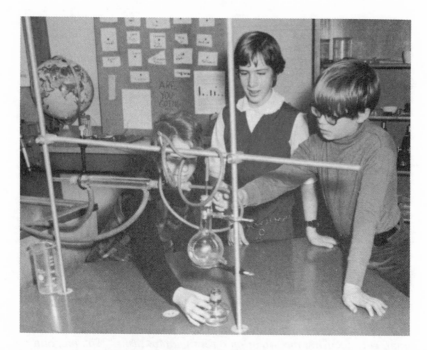

The text in the dedicatory booklet states that the science room is equipped with the junior high school science program in mind and that experimentation is essential in learning science. The influence of the federal "let's beat the Russians" policy and the more intellectual "structure of the disciplines approach" is evident. Only accelerated students are shown using this equipment. Patterning science on the junior high school program suggests the rush in the 1960s to correct our assumed gap in science and technology; and, finally, the emphasis on experimentation reflects the knowledge theory invoked by the major national science and mathematics curriculum projects that dominated thinking in the 1960s. Even creative local efforts may be adversely influenced by national policy and public anxiety. Photograph by Jim Baldwin. Photograph courtesy of the Centennial School District, Warminster, Pa.

Learning disabled students work in a cubicle that restricts the child's environment "focusing his attention on immediate tasks." The program includes "training in language experiences and intensive work in visual and auditory perception." Text is taken from the 1969 dedicatory booklet. Photograph by Jim Baldwin. Photograph courtesy of the Centennial School District, Warminster, Pa.

CHAPTER 6

LIKE A TREE PLANTED
BY WATER

He is like a tree planted by water,
that sends out its roots by the
stream,
and does not fear when heat comes,
for its leaves remain green,
and is not anxious in the year of
drought,
for it does not cease to bear
fruit.
—Jeremiah 17:8

Workers of the world, unite and fight. You
have nothing to lose but your chains, and a
world to win.[1]
1. These words are quoted here to mislead
those who will be misled by them. They
mean, not what the reader may care to think
they mean, but what they say. They are not
dealt with directly in this volume. . . . In view
of the average reader's tendency to label . . . it
may be well to make the explicit statement
that neither these words nor the authors are
the property of any political party, faith, or
faction.
—James Agee Let Us Now Praise Famous
Men, *1941*

Physical science has had its effect in changing
social conditions. But there has been no . . .

significant increase of intelligent understand-
ing. The application of... knowledge has
taken place in a technical way for the sake of
limited consequences.... Were we to define
science not in the usual technical way, but as
a knowledge that... deal[s] competently
with problems that present themselves, the
physician, engineer, artist, craftsman, lay
claim to scientific knowing.
—*John Dewey* The Quest for Certainty, *1929*

We have an educational system in decline that is not reforming itself, whose roots seek no water because it has forgotten that it needs water; we have leaders so bland, who question little, who often fail to speak for the good because they have not learned the good, who have forgotten the common interest, leaders in academia and the schools who would be embarrassed by the iconoclasm and moral courage of a James Agee writing about poor tenant farmers in Alabama; and we have a public and a profession whose conception of science is so stunted that they understand science to be a technical object, The Grand Wizard, without subtlety, devoid of social significance, rather than as a way of thinking about "problems that present themselves" in ordinary life. A "science," in short, that lacks its most essential capacity, intelligence *in* life.

The scene is bleak. I have drawn it as I see it in the preceding chapters, sometimes, I fear, with too much detail so there will be less doubt about what it is I see. I have tried to balance detail and perspective, but I have not always succeeded. My view is a minority view. I take no pleasure in that. I, too, would like to be in the mainstream, but I am not comfortable there when I know how much we could do for the children we have, whether they be able, average, or among those slowly sinking in poverty's waters.

I could stop here in this concluding chapter, recognizing that readers will do what they will and should do anyway: draw inferences for themselves. But to do so might seem abrupt and a needless violation of a convention in writing about Education. Convention is more uncaring of readers than even this. A critic is expected to have a remedy. So I must burden you further, however much readers not of my persuasion may find the "remedy" an even greater source of unease than my critique.

Permit me one compromise. I shall give the first of five inferences in the way all of the inferences should be rendered had I the nerve. All of the inferences that might be drawn from my discussion of reform can be thought of as rain from our past, a rain we are loath to recognize in the Sunny California of our minds, minds that see things not the way things are but in a way that discomfits us less, a way that interferes least with what we do everyday, which is to say the progress of our careers.

RAIN IN SUNNY CALIFORNIA

First, while principals improved the efficiency of high school scheduling with computers; while superintendents dealt with tax revolts and one-issue board members and some polished their image by snagging a reform or two on the run; while teachers taught with devotion and energy but with too little critical understanding; while deans and provosts in research-oriented universities chased grants and redemption in prestige, and ever more faculty published articles in refereed journals whose content more often than not was shorn up by the thin intellectual reeds of an empiricism disassociated from the gut-wrenching problems of practice, and the deans increased redemption's burden by shamefully neglecting the intellectual and professional quality of the education they offered to teachers and administrators, thus adding another decade to the four decades of neglect by those who preceded them; while foundation executives, educational snake oil salesmen, entertaining conference speakers, arrogant education governors and presidents, the mechanical men and women in many of our research and development centers of behaviorist belief, and researchers who put numbers on fragments of human behavior and correlated these numbers with other numbers derived from tests, thus putting their intelligence and those who followed them in cold storage—while all of this career-enhancing work was going on, education was slowly dying because no reform was taking place. While we were at the career party, the house was burglarized. We did not even know anything was stolen. Most of our education departments and their professors, flying at thirty thousand feet in a small Piper cub to which they had strapped the jet engines of a faltering social science, could not even see the house much less warn us of our loss.

What the burglars stole was reform. There has been no widespread intellectual and democratic reform in even 20 percent of our schools; and fewer than 20 percent of the reforms advanced in thirty years cultivated intellectual and democratic values. This is the face of reform today; it has been the face of reform since the death of the progressive education as an activist movement with the publication of the Progressive Education Association's Eight-Year Study in 1942 and the beginning of World War II a few years before.[1] The technological view of the human mind and learning dominates reform and educational practice. It puts most of what we do in its iron cage.

Second, reform is a by-product of good day-by-day educational practice. Reform is neither a commodity to be purchased nor a prize to be sought. Good practice is based on concepts and values that cultivate the intelligence and sensitivities of students, teachers, and principals. Theory suggests a way to do it. Good practice rests on a faith that any person within the broad normal range of capacities is capable of much learning. Further, this faith in the cultivation of intelligence and the development of human capacities within a democratic society is a moral belief; it is the subjective choosing of the good.

Third, the critical—and typically overlooked factor—in shaping the educational worth of a reform is the *quality of the ideas and values bred into it during its development, and the quality of ideas and values of the teachers and principals who adopt it.* Our theories shape the quality of reform. What is in the head and feelings count most. The ideas and values that guide practice are so powerful that they transcend social class divisions and geography. This is the singularly essential lesson I draw from the field studies on Individually Guided Education discussed in chapter 5. Theories do make a difference in the quality of a reform.

Without a theory, all directions point to Educational North. Theories suggest to us what is *most* important, what is *most* worthy, what direction we shall take. Theories sift the good from the clutter of everyday teaching or administering.

The thing to nurture in reform is the intellectual and practical transformation ideas and values make in the real-life use of a reform. Instead of worrying about effectiveness alone, or the change process, or the fidelity with which a blueprint for a reform is followed, we should encourage imaginative deviations from the developer's design. The more we encourage divergence, novel extrapolations, the more a broader range of possibilities can be realized in widely different practical situations. This is a way to encourage teacher and principal creativity if we must take our reforms from another. Since almost all teacher education and administrative programs offer training in routines, might not encouraging practitioners to make creative deviations in implementing a reform be one on-the-ground way to educate more professional teachers and principals?

Fourth, we do not learn from our past experience in education. We are not critical of present institutional practice in education. One reason for this is the neglect of history. The neglect of history lies deep in the psyche of the technological mindset: Descartes, for example, wanted passionately to invent a method that would "find the truth," that would rise above human entanglements and the terrible religious controversies of his day. He created the mathematical foundations for a new knowledge that was not kind to history. The germ of Descartes' assumption is still with us.

There is too little thoughtful criticism of education *within* either the academic or practitioner spheres of practice. Most of the tough criticism comes from outside, with more distortion than even those within the profession might achieve. Practitioners, for example, know deep down that education is complex and not easily "fixed," however much they may adopt superficial cures under public pressure. Academics too often have not learned this, awash as they are in either empirical data fragments or partial abstractions about policy, or teaching, or reform, or the change process, which are so removed from teachers and children that their ideas are of little use even when they might have something worthwhile to say. One example will make my point. Consider the appalling lack of broad academic criticism of the federally-funded Chapter 1 remedial programs. Is it unreasonable to expect academics to have scorched this program by now for its anti-intellectual and morally indifferent treatment of children from poor families; children who may be poor, but who are not poor in spirit? Most of the criticism we have is couched in the cool and supposedly neutral language of educational research and social science. How can a language and a perspective be neutral when it ignores such educationally and socially critical elements? It surely is not neutral. We have slipped once more into the blandishments of Descartes and of the technological mindset. Human and moral factors are ignored because science has no metric by which to assess such vital elements in life, science cannot not grasp them. Until educational research and educational social science spring from an educational theory that is comprehensive enough to entertain simultaneously fifty factors in its "head" instead of the usual two or three, we shall perpetuate more of the nonsense that deflects, demoralizes, and drains vital human intelligence and energy from our work and that deflates proper outrage at some of the things we have wrought. A weak science is not a substitute for good theory, nor is it a substitute for a novelist's sensitivity.

And fifth, one reason the technological mindset is so pervasive and smothers vital intellectual and moral energy is that it is more than an idea: it is a powerful idea to be sure, but it is an idea that sustains itself and is backed by a *technostructure of interlocking bureaucracies.* Thomas Hughes makes this fundamental point in a sympathetic account of technology in his book *American Genius.* Henry Ford's production system was much more than an assembly line. Behind the line was a system of banks, coal and steel supply systems, dealer networks, advertising agencies, and a complex system of human capital (a revealing phrase) disciplined by the organization.[2] Behind the "line" of the teacher and the school, we have an interlocking system of other structures such as unions, colleges and universities, foundations, government agencies, laws and regulations, research and development centers, professional associations, and so forth, which, in their historical and cumulative effect, embrace and advance the tenets of the technological mindset. As the technostructure behind Ford was unified by the explicit goal of profit, the interlocking educational technostructure is unified by the implicit philosophy that glorifies the machine. Surely the weight of the argument and detail in this book supports this conclusion. Teacher education is technique-bound, for example, because teachers are prepared for schools as they exist, which are also technique-bound; the schools look to research for guidance on teaching and reform, but the research also prizes technique over idea and feelings; reforms are advanced by research and development centers or by universities, and approximately 80 percent of these reforms value technique and small-step learning over ideas; teachers and principals go to conferences, peruse the publications of the National Diffusion Network, read journals, and go to inservice programs where, again, they are most often instructed in the techniques of mastery learning, thinking as skills removed from content, or packages of techniques on classroom management, discipline, or ways to teach; and principals enroll in graduate programs in administration, where the techniques and skills of management are yet again pursued. Congress passes a law to help poor kids to read, spends tens of billions of dollars to do so, and these programs value skill over idea and ignore the creation in students of a *desire* to read. Education governors hail reform and rain testing and accountability schemes on the heads of educators. The Carnegie Foundation believes that good teachers can be identified through a process of national assessment while a group of educators from research-oriented universities swear their faith in educational science and proclaim a "knowledge base" for teaching has at last been found. And more could be said. If all this does not attest to an interlocking technostructure of the material over the ideal, of blind faith in the techniques of science over common sense and the cumulative effect of thousands of past failures that have been rooted in the enfeebled idea of humankind as a watered down version of the physical universe, I am at a loss to know what evidence might arouse some doubt in those who propound this philosophy, or who feel that it does not touch them.

The problems that need to be solved are so entangled with the people and institutions from which the impetus for reform must come that we are caught in a chicken-and-egg perplexity. Who, or what force, for example, could initiate a simultaneous reform process among schools, colleges and universities, the research establishment, foundations, and federal and state agencies that might spark desirable reform? The smothering-blanket effect of a sprawling yet gridlocked educational system prevails, while the regenerative counter forces seem not to be able to rise above even the lower ridges of the status quo. Who asks whom to dance? And to what tune? Will islands of progressive reforms here and there do the job?

If I rolled all five of my major inferences into a general statement, I would say that, despite all of the talk and all of the money that has been spent since 1960, there has been no significant and widespread reform that enhances the intellectual and democratic quality of learning, teaching, or administering in American schools. The system of public education is deteriorating, not rebuilding itself. It is, in the blind eye of present practice, setting itself up to be blown over by the first hard wind that might blow from the social north of unfavorable economic or political events—the social equivalent of Sputnik in 1957, when policymakers went a little crazy with fear. And fear abounds today, fear about our declining standard of living and our ability to compete in the world market. The capitalist and efficient managers of corporations have not served America well. They, too, stopped rebuilding their enterprise and gloried in success with glittering but short-term achievements. The lack of significant intellectual and democratic reform in public education is caused by a nihilistic anti-intellectualism, a cool indifference to ideals, and the lack of a burning moral concern for children by academics and the profession at large that has had a reactionary effect on schools. Ideals, moral concerns, and some passion were not cool

in the seventies and the eighties. Further, an interlocking technostructure of educational institutions, themselves dominated by a
technological ideology, locks in the honored present and keeps ideas
and moral concerns from breaking out. Separately and collectively,
as we work within a veiled technostructure in schools and universities, publish journals, and do research, we think first of what
will advance our careers—what will fit in with present conditions,
not make waves, or offend the professional and political elites of
our constricted world. Prestige in research-oriented universities,
for example, is prized over doing good in the larger community.
We look decadence in the face and refuse to call it by its proper
name. All of this feeds and nourishes three hobbling attributes of
reform since 1960: we dishonor intelligent practice, the only true
source of solid reform, and look upon reform as a commodity to be
bought or a prize to be sought; we cannot see, because of our anti-
intellectualism and blind empiricism (on which the technological
mindset voraciously feeds), that the critically important attribute of
a proposed reform or a present practice is its educational worth,
which is, in turn, crucially dependent on the quality of the ideas
and values from which it springs in the mind of its developer, or in
the mind of the one who accepts it as a reform; and, last, both practitioners and academics taken in the whole are unable to render the
unremitting, fair, and informed criticism of practice and reform that
better education requires: we have accepted the most appalling and
humanly destructive reforms with little more than a whimper of
criticism; I cite the federally funded remedial programs under Chapter 1 as the prime exhibit that makes this case, although lesser examples abound (see chapter 4 and appendixes C and B).

I want to add a bit more to the third inference to prevent possible misunderstanding. In that statement I said that the quality of
the ideas bred into a reform by its developers and the quality of the
ideas of teachers and principals who adopted the reform were critical, and transcend social class lines and geography. I want to recall
some detail in support of the social class assertion. My point will be
that it is not only the poor who get an inferior education. The teachers' intellectual transformations of Individually Guided Education
breached the compartments of social class. Recall that two of the
schools that interpreted IGE in a technological manner served
middle- to upper-middle-class communities. Flowing Brook, the
school without laughter, meets this criterion, as does Belair. Maplewood School, which served a working-class community, was characterized by its emphasis on systems of elaborate record-keeping
that plotted student progress through countless tests. I believe it is

an index of the power of the technological mindset when the privileged and the less privileged alike suffer its ministrations. (It is still true, however, that the very poor get the most sterile version of this treatment, which, I suppose, develops a stoic character.)

Also in the third inference, I followed convention and assumed that a reform comes from outside the school although I believe that teachers should be encouraged to create high quality deviations from the reform "as delivered." This recognizes present realities, but it is better to encourage teachers and principals to develop their own reforms as a by-product of good practice, as I say in the second inference. Novel deviations are then moot. "Adaptation" becomes an intrinsic part of making one's own creation better. But should schools be encouraged to make their own reforms? I admit that given the pervasiveness of the technological mindset, the chances that thousands of schools will soon create intellectual and democratic reforms are slight. But consider this: if most of the reforms produced by the research community and government agencies, for example, are as bad as I say they are, can the schools do worse? Is there more harm in a locally produced inferior reform than in an establishment-sanctioned inferior reform? Is a reform any less harmful to kids, for example, because it was hatched at the University of Chicago than, say, at Bird In Hand, Pennsylvania? I would argue that an inferior reform produced by the University of Chicago is worse than an equally bad reform produced by Bird In Hand, Pennsylvania. If the University of Chicago produces it, the reform has all the clap-trap of science and prestige about it, and it is "disseminated" by the National Diffusion Network, journal articles, and conferences to the whole country. The educational pollution is spread. But if Bird In Hand produces it, the reform will get no farther than Blue Ball, Pennsylvania, or maybe Paradise, Pennsylvania. Should we not invoke the nonutilitarian principle that holds that harm to the smallest number is a good? And in time, might not Bird In Hand, Pennsylvania, learn to produce better reforms?

Reforms are usually seen as a prize to be sought outside of, and added to, practice. Of all the reforms I discuss, none was initiated by a local school or school district (except the Foxfire experience). Reforms came from England, from research and development centers, Congress and federal agencies, foundations, state government; reforms came from everywhere except the local, supposedly free and diverse all-American public school system.

The five inferences that flow from my discussion of reform suggest that intellectual and democratic reform will not come until we rediscover that education is an intellectual *and* a practical enterprise. The inferences suggest also that the obstacles to educational reform are pervasive and systemic. In the short run, these obstacles are probably insurmountable because I find little life within the system as a whole, or within parts of the system, or in society, that is capable of kindling the fire of significant and widespread renewal. The system is gridlocked and dying. Dewey may have spoken more truly than he knew when he said that we have not used science to increase our intelligent understanding of social events, and that we have used science only in a technical way "for the sake of limited consequences." Much of what I have written is little more than a documentation of the "limited consequences" that flow from a scientism unfeelingly applied to education.

I want to make one observation about an interesting detail before I describe the modest action we might take to advance reform within the limits that press upon us. Although school restructuring was a buzzword in the early 1990s, it was overt in several of the 1960 reforms. Individually Guided Education offered the most radical and thorough change in the way schools were organized and governed, with its vertical-age grouping and teaching teams and, most radical of all, its schoolwide committee of team leaders, parents, and the principal that made school policy decisions in areas beyond the purview of the teaching teams. J. Lloyd Trump also offered a change in high school organization with his flexible twenty minute schedule modules. Six hours each week were to be spent in small discussion groups with fewer than fifteen students. If teachers were to conduct these groups in anything close to a seminar-type discussion and lock their own tongues, I believe that this tactic alone would have raised the intellectual quality of the high school and increased student interest. Twelve hours each week were to be devoted to independent study, another potential boon to mind and interest. The nongraded school was another organizational and curriculum reform that would have enhanced student learning and made teaching more professional. But, of course, few of these reforms made it through the technological mindset of educators; or if the reforms were adopted, they were gutted of their substance and caricatured as they were reshaped into the iconic image of modern culture, the seductive Earth- and Community-Destroying Machine.

Some form of merit pay or "career ladders" was a part of both IGE and the Trump plans almost three decades ago, although I do not believe that these are fundamental reforms.

Team teaching pops in and out of several reforms. Team teaching could be a universal solvent that might erode some of the in-school barriers to reform. Imaginatively used and guided by progressive ideas, team teaching can be used to change the way a school is organized and governed, and can thereby influence curriculum, guidance, and inservice activities as well. The Marticville Middle School (discussed in chapter 3) is an example of using team teaching this way. Team teaching can be used with nongraded schools, the Trump high school, Paideia, IGE, and the reforms envisioned by the Coalition of Essential Schools. One could begin with team teaching, properly conceived, and move out to a number of reforms such as those I mentioned, as well as new forms to be invented.

I turn next to reform gridlock—what to do until the People demand schools that cultivate the intelligence of all who gather there, schools permeated by democratic values.

WHAT TO DO ABOUT REFORM GRIDLOCK

I have a partial solution to reform gridlock—a modest proposal that might let some reform traffic take a side street and arrive at more schools. Can something as ordinary as conversation make schools better? Can conversation between teachers and their principal informed by solid readings be a useful way to revitalize schools choking on busyness and routine? I believe there is great intellectual and practical power in a reform process that honors ideas, that respects practitioners' rich practical knowledge of education and their school, and which dignifies people in honest talk. But what is this conversation like? What is its content? I share below a bit of one conversation with eighteen high school teachers and their principal to suggest the content and flavor of this kind of informed dialogue. This excerpt is a condensed forty-minute segment from a three-hour session based on a verbatim transcript.

TEACHER: The readings say that one thing that changing the structure of a school means is more staff involvement. Now one thing that hit me in the readings is that teachers need more involvement, interaction with their students. So conceptually we are talking about the same idea for kids that we are talking about for teachers. The same idea works both ways, it seems to me.

TEACHER: But when we are dealing with teachers and administrators, we are dealing with adults about professional things. Dealing with kids is different.

TEACHER: I disagree. We stand up front and lecture. We do "top down." But I know why. It's what we are supposed to do—it's what teaching is to the students. They want me to learn it for them.

[*Discussion continued with neither teachers nor administrators willing to make an educated guess on the amount of teacher talk in the school.*]

MODERATOR: Let's take humanities. How much do teachers talk in these subjects?

TEACHER: Well it depends again. In honors sections, there is more discussion. The regular sections need more direction because of the materials and the students.

MODERATOR: But those are choices teachers make. There are other choices. Don't you have a gut feeling on teacher talk? Let's walk around ten minutes on each floor, and I'd bet we would know.

TEACHER: Okay. There are times when we all talk too much. But I find that to get students to talk takes more time, it's more work with all the other things. When I have more student talk, I run short on time. It is much easier to just tell the kids what's what. Days I talk too much, I feel bad about it.

MODERATOR: There are lots of influences on teacher talk.

TEACHER: That's what everybody ignores in these articles. The articles imply that teachers do it on purpose because they don't know better.

TEACHER: Isn't it because we want to be in control? There's lots of stuff wrapped up in this one.

TEACHER: Maybe, too, it's how others see the teacher. The community thinks that teachers should be in control (and they should be). But a teacher is demonstrably in control if she stands up there in front. Anyone can see she is in control. But if the teacher sits and the students are talking, she doesn't appear to be in control. We do not want to give up the idea of seeming to be in control.

TEACHER: Involving students takes more than time. It takes tremendous amounts of energy and imagination to do that day after day. We need other things, too. Collaboration time to share ideas with others. This is more than teachers can hope for now. Maybe in the future.

TEACHER: All of this takes more time than people imagine.

PRINCIPAL: But there must be more than time to it. My professors had time, but they lectured, and I imitated them when I began to teach.

[*Positive and negative contrasts between college and high school teaching were then discussed.*]

TEACHER: Back to my original point. You [the moderator] said in one of the sessions that change begins with an idea and that teachers need more interactions with adults and more intellectual stimulation. More involvement with principals. It seems to me that the same thing applies to how we interact with our students.[3]

I chose this segment because much was said that coheres well in print. This is not usually the case for so short a segment. The conversation dealt with important issues: a fast pace in teaching is likely to lower the quality of learning; too much teacher talk has its roots in the need to control a class; community and student expectations influence a teacher's style; the typical distinction that permits more discussion in honors sections than in the regular sections is made (this in one of the wealthiest high schools in Pennsylvania in which the achievement of students in the "regular sections" probably exceeds that of "honors sections" in many high schools); and most important of all, I believe, is the last comment by a teacher, which is a moral insight: if interaction between teachers and principals is good for us, the same principle applies to relationships between teachers and students. Teachers do know a lot. Too often their practical knowledge and insights are not allowed to surface when inservice programs are didactically taught by a consultant, and the teachers are passive absorbers of her message and method.

The moderator (myself in this instance) did not guide or structure the discussion to bring out the points I enumerated above. They "fell out" of the teachers' responses to some of the readings. At this point in the dialogue, the teachers had read Raymond Callahan's *Education and the Cult of Efficiency*, Theodore Sizer's *Horace's Compromise*, and chapters from John Goodlad's *A Place Called School*, in addition to articles that viewed teaching and testing from different points of view. Although the teachers and principal are expected to define a *significant* practical problem or problems in their school that will improve the intellectual quality of students' learning, in the first half or so of the dialogue the expectation is relaxed and discussion focuses around the general question, How can we cultivate the intelligence and sensitivities of teachers, administrators, and students in this school? I know this sounds ever so goody-goody, but is it not the fundamental problem reform should address? In no case is the dialogue put on a timeline with certain products to be delivered by set dates, nor is the outcome itself specifically set in ad-

vance, other than what might be inferred from the general question
I have stated above and by the expectation that serious practical
problems will ultimately be defined and addressed.

You might think that this dialogue group turned out to be a
smashing success. Not so. The teachers were unable to coalesce
around a significant problem that might be addressed in the next
several years. They splintered and fizzled out. The principal had
formed a number of teacher committees the previous year that the
teachers thought could be used as a vehicle for change. For good or
ill this was their judgment. The principal was an active and supportive member of the dialogue group, but the superintendent at
that time was lukewarm toward it. This exerted a negative influence, but the teachers, in my opinion, never "got with it." One early
indication was their desultory treatment of *Horace's Compromise*.
They could not come to terms with the issues raised there and could
not, or would not, make the imaginative connections between some
of the issues in the book and their good but traditional high school
(Scantron scoring machines worked overtime, for example). I remember, too, the vice principal pressing for a skill-based inservice
program. "What good is all of this talk," he said, "if we don't *give*
people *specific skills* to do things?" (Ah! That mindset again.) The
teachers were a joy to work with; they were bright and responsive in
many ways, but they were unable to grasp the school in a comprehensive way, to see it as a whole organism. The need to reform did
not burn within them. The school is no different today than it was
before the dialogue. The promise implied in the fourth session, from
which this excerpt came, was not fulfilled by the tenth and final session. The teachers did not elect to continue the dialogue in the following year.

I do not want to get into a full assessment of the dialogue's
"success rate"—this would require a chapter in itself—but I will
briefly address it. Since 1983 the dialogue has been tried in nine
schools, seven high schools, one elementary school, and in one
whole school district in 1993–94.[4] In five schools where data have
been systematically collected, we have had one rather strong
district-wide diffusion of the dialogue as the primary vehicle for reform, two moderate successes, one success with a group of urban elementary teachers who markedly improved students' achievement
and interest in social studies,[5] and the failure I described earlier.
There was also a glorious failure in a high school in which no data
were collected. The principal, who was hired after the dialogue had
begun, very effectively undermined it despite the wishes of the
teachers and the central administration to continue it. The princi-

pal's idea of reform was to require standard teacher-made examinations in all subjects, the questions of which were written on Bloom's taxonomy of cognitive levels. The principal's educational mind was narrow, his cunning deep. Anyone who says principals have no power is thinking of principals who choose not to exercise their power.

By "moderate success" I mean a school in which the principal actively supports fundamental reform and where serious reform work is underway although the teaching, curriculum, and organizational components still fall well short of full reformation. The William Tennent High School, Warminster, Pennsylvania, is a good example. William Tennent held the first in a series of dialogues in 1983–84. Its profile of reform reveals a series of sharp upward spurts followed by plateaus until about 1988, when progress was less sharp but more steady. In 1992 all ninety teachers were engaged in reform-oriented discussion groups of their own choosing on such topics as tracking, student evaluation, and curriculum; a school governance structure has been instituted that gives teachers real power in deciding school policy; and, at the district level, many of the inservice programs are led by teachers without reliance on outside consultants. All of these developments are a result of the dialogues in the high school that "spread" by word-of-mouth among teachers and administrators, and because of the constant pressure for reform exerted by Kenneth Kastle, the high school principal. William Tennent High School joined Theodore Sizer's Re:Learning project and has two teaching teams functioning based on the Coalition's principles. As Kastle says, "Reform is a constant struggle, but it's worth it although we still have a long way to go before we can say our school is as good as it can be."[6]

It is important to mention that in all of the dialogue groups, teacher morale increases markedly; important and often "hot issues" get on the table for discussion between the principal and teachers, which leads to more honest and direct communication (one factor, I assume, that increases teacher morale); teachers learn good things about colleagues they never knew; and, in the case of William Tennent High School and the Marticville Middle School, most of the teachers voluntarily modified their teaching style in a progressive direction. This conclusion is based on data obtained from pre- and post-dialogue classroom observations, review of tests given, and teacher interviews.[7]

I learned much from my experience in these schools. I learned, for example, that good ideas are important to reform, but good ideas will not do the whole job—although they are reform's critical starting point—given our history since 1960. I relearned my respect for the complexities of "doing education" compared with writing about it, important as writing is. I wish that more politicians and many academics who write so fluently about reform would get out there in a few schools and try it: a subdued and salutary silence would settle over this land that would be good for everybody.

I believe that informed conversation (dialogue) is a reform intervention worth trying. It links conceptual knowledge to practical knowledge; it dignifies practice and practitioners by trusting them to think through and to invent their own reforms. The destructive dependency on outsiders with their load of usually technological reforms might thus be avoided or deflected. But how does one set up this kind of dialogue? What are its aims? What are its logistics? I shall try to answer some of these questions based on my experience and that of others who have tried informed conversation as a modest reform intervention.

The Structure of the Dialogue

The dialogue is energized and disciplined by the elements that interact to create its structure.

1. *Participation*—Principals and teachers volunteer for the dialogue. Volunteerism is valued on the principle that one person cannot make another do anything worth doing. Personal choice and commitment are important because a renewal process that uses dialogue involves the risk of failure and exposure to an open process that demands both individual initiative and thought.

2. *Group size*—High school groups range in size from fifteen to twenty people. Groups may start with twenty or more because a few people usually drop out without prejudice. Elementary schools are different. If a school's total faculty volunteers, for example, the moderator must judiciously use small-group work along with total-group discussion in a way that increases interaction through the small groups without breaking the continuity that total-group work provides.

3. *Moderator*—The moderator is a "teacher" in a facilitative role. The moderator's primary function is to help the group find its strength in efforts to realize the aims of the dialogue. The moderator helps the group reach *independence* within the structure of the dialogue. The moderator is not responsible for the group's success or failure. The group makes the decisions along the way with whatever knowledge or advice it chooses or does not choose to use. A good moderator has her ego under control, has a deep respect for

the complexities of practice, has a sound knowledge of education, and wants to use ideas to transform practice in ways that are intellectual and democratic, which means in ways that are truly professional and open.

4. *Time*—Time is a critical variable. The minimum length of time required for the dialogue is three successive semesters. Fifteen months to two years is about right. The dialogue usually takes place on school time, although the dialogues in the Owen J. Roberts district are held on Mondays after school. Teachers are paid to attend these sessions and earn credit toward a higher step on the salary schedule. Regular inservice days are also used. Substitutes free teachers to participate. Forty-five hours should be scheduled in fifteen months. This time block reduces to about twelve three-hour sessions or so, with some full-day sessions in the middle and toward the end of the fifteen-month period as work demands.

5. *School-based*—The dialogue takes place in a school that we are trying to renew and whose history and character are known to the participants from their perspective as players on its stage. When a school is offered as a theater in which renewal is to be staged, it becomes a place in which mountains of academic words and reams of administrative paper can be re-energized and put to the test of practical action.

6. *Books*—Books and selections from books provide the depth and many of the ideas that are necessary to examine critically the participants' present practice. Articles are used early in the dialogue to introduce the importance of reading or to provide close-ups on a topic that might open the door to a more fundamental idea. An article on effective-teaching research might be critically discussed as a current issue and to raise important issues about teaching.

The readings must be used with several cautions in mind. The sequence of readings is not set out in advance, to be read in the manner of a college course. The readings are, rather, "salted" into the dialogue as the responses of the participants dictate—responses that cannot be known with certainty before the session occurs. The moderator selects the readings in advance of each session, but she decides how much time to spend on each one, or even when to suspend the readings for awhile, based on the *responses of the teachers.* She is guided in these decisions by her knowledge of the content itself and by the theory on which the dialogue is based. The readings are used to enhance and to enrich the quality of the dialogue as it unfolds; they are *subordinate* to the dialogue itself. The reading and talk use an interactive process.

Books and chapter-length excerpts are used to "frame" the conversation and to provide a conceptual structure from which to criticize and to sanction present practice as the particulars of a given discussion warrant. Teachers are often relieved, for example, to learn *why* something that they were doing is good. Until the reading and discussion had taken place, they were uncertain. Books also provide a stimulus for conjectures and ideas about ways to move to something better.

The logic of the book selection is suggested by three questions. How did schools and teaching become the way they are? The historical perspective. What is going on in schools today? The present perspective. What might be done to make things better? The future perspective. These questions provide a framework in which the readings are introduced.

Raymond Callahan's classic, *Education and the Cult of Efficiency*, is well-received by teachers. It shows how schools became models of managerial efficiency that blunted the intellectual qualities in teaching and administration. John Goodlad's *A Place Called School* and Theodore Sizer's *Horace's Compromise* document typical school practices that are partially rooted in the quest for efficiency and technological solutions. The future perspective is best developed by John Dewey's *Democracy and Education*, supplemented with some of his less difficult but relevant work. Dewey's book is critical because he sees education comprehensively. He does not let important pieces dominate the whole. He views teachers and principals, for example, as thinkers and doers. Teaching technique and management are enriched and subsumed within this larger whole. Science is seen as intelligent practical inquiry, as a way of thinking, not as a list of atomistic research findings removed from their social contexts.

Although the amount of reading and the specific books and articles read varies from group to group, most participants read about fifteen hundred pages of materials in fifteen months. Our research shows, too, that most of the participants enjoy the intellectual stimulation of the reading and the talk.

7. *Aims*—The primary aims of the dialogue are to empower teachers and administrators; to improve teaching and administrative practice in ways that cultivate the intelligence and feelings of students, teachers, and administrators; and to change the organizational structure of schools as needed to support the first two aims.

8. *Ideas*—The dialogue must include a body of solid ideas that both inform and criticize the ideas and values learned implicitly

through years of practice. Talk uninformed by serious reading, or talk that follows a prepackaged formulation, or talk restricted to the participants' experience, is rejected because such talk is limited on its face. *Schools cannot become intellectual and democratic through means that are themselves nonintellectual and undemocratic.*

9. *Spanning the hierarchy* —The dialogue involves participants who must come from at least two levels in the school-system hierarchy. In no case are people at the same level of the hierarchy talking only with each other: teachers to teachers or principals to principals. In one high school that used the dialogue, *spanning the hierarchy* meant that the participants came from the structural layers labeled principal, department chair, and teacher. In another site that involved two secondary schools, the participants came from the levels between the superintendent and teacher.

10. *Fundamental problem focus*—The initial problem focus stated by the moderator is general yet fundamental. The important condition is not to state a narrow problem that preselects a solution, for example, Which of three thinking-skills packages should we adopt this year? This unthoughtful and ultimately impractical question implicitly contains answers to hidden questions: Is thinking primarily skills? Will the package hinder or encourage thinking by the *teacher*? I use a general initial problem statement that is capable of more specific redefinition (or rejection) as the dialogue process matures: How can we improve the intellectual and emotional quality of learning for teachers, students, and administrators in this school?

11. *Rigor with flexibility*—The essential structure of the dialogue as an intervention strategy is created by the synergy of two dimensions that appear to be different or conflicting if one thinks of them superficially—rigor and flexibility. The dialogue is both rigorous and flexible; it is both tight and open. Rigor comes from five major sources: the educationally significant and complex nature of the initial problem focus; the expectation that something both practical and fundamental will be accomplished within the constraints of the known school situation; the readings; the participants' practical knowledge; and the provision of adequate time reasonably to accomplish some things that are educationally difficult. Flexibility comes from four major sources: the dialogue is democratic and open; the agenda can be made and remade across the sessions by the participants within the general aims and structure of the dialogue; the initial problem focus is more specifically and thoughtfully redefined over time as experience warrants; and no topic or concern is

arbitrarily ruled out because its discussion may be unsettling to someone or some group or because it questions the value or purpose of the dialogue process itself. These interactive structural dimensions may generate a reconstructive social power in ordinary schools.

Informed conversation in schools may reduce teachers' isolation from each other and from their principals; conversation uses language to foster thinking to make schools more stimulating places in which to learn and to teach; and conversation may be a practical way to renew schools in educationally fundamental ways.[8]

This structure suggests how seemingly contradictory elements complement each other within the dialogue. Practical experience is honored in the dialogue, for example, but this practical knowledge is "played off" the conceptual knowledge that comes from serious reading; the teachers are given a legitimate and powerful voice in the dialogue but not to the exclusion of the principal's voice; the dialogue is explicitly rooted in Deweyan theory that prizes both the intellect and the democratic process, but the ultimate ends of the process demand that *fundamental* practical actions be taken to renew the school; and, last, the dialogue is "free" and "open," but this openness occurs within an explicit structure that prevents the conversation from degenerating into idle theory, at one extreme, or endless anecdotes and complaints at the other.

School reform efforts that rely on the play of powerful social dynamics exact a cost. This cost is paid for in hard physical, emotional, and intellectual dollars. The value of these dollars is created by the participants' willingness to deal with uncertainty within a dialogue process that demands both thought and practical action. These are tough demands, but any serious reform, whatever its mode of intervention, will require that this payment be made. Our seriousness about reform and our maturity as a profession will be determined by our willingness to undertake this work and make the payment.

THE DIALOGUE'S DYNAMIC QUALITIES: GLADWYNE ELEMENTARY SCHOOL

I want to share the excitement and struggle masked by the abstract words above—to show how this payment was made by the teachers and principal in one elementary school. Twenty-five teachers and the principal from the Gladwyne Elementary School, Ard-

A teacher and a principal combine talents to solve a mathematics problem within the dialogue process. This task gave teachers and administrators a concrete experience in learning a bit of mathematics in a new way. When this exercise was completed, for example, participants were encouraged to talk not only about how they thought about the problem, but they spoke about their concurrent feelings as well. Thinking and feeling are not separated in life. Photograph by Richard A. Gibboney. Photograph courtesy of the Owen J. Roberts School District.

more, Pennsylvania, made up the dialogue group. The conversation was held in 1987–88. This condensed account of the first four sessions shows the rough and tumble of the dialogue as it began a downward spiral toward failure that was reversed by a confrontational strategy that required the teachers to either face the implications of their actions in the dialogue or evade them. The session summaries are based on a verbatim transcript that is a part of a case study research design coupled to pre- and post-dialogue assessments on certain dimensions of the conversation, some of which will be mentioned in this account.[9]

The October Session—Everyone is Happy

The first session in October was characterized by easy talk and optimism. The dialogue process was described and a few questions about its aims and process were answered. The teachers said that they volunteered for the dialogue because they looked forward to talking with colleagues and that they hoped to improve their teaching. "I want to be more effective with my colleagues as well as with children," one teacher said. "I have learned more from other teachers than I ever did in my college courses." The openness of the dialogue process appealed to some of the teachers, but this openness also induced some anxiety. "I think I will like to talk about the readings, but I am anxious about today's session . . . I don't know what to expect."

The reading for this session was Elliot Eisner's article, "The Art and Craft of Teaching." The craft person, Eisner says, follows rules for teaching set by another without questioning either the rules or the consequences of acting on the rules. Bored students are not seen, for example, by rule-following teachers. The artist teacher, on the other hand, invents new ways of teaching based on the responses of the students and her reflection on what is happening. The teachers liked the article. Teaching is presented as the creative act it is. Some of the teachers' comments were incisive. "Teachers might try to be creative, to be good. But the atmosphere around schools, the excessive testing and all of that, says 'Be standard, be conservative. To be a craftsman is to be safe and good. But to be creative is to be sort of dangerous.' It has always been that way."

I noticed, however, from the moderator's line of sight, that teachers did not savor the article. They liked it, yes, but their discussion was hurried. Their talk clothed the feeling that we-will-not-find-anything-important-here. They were moving through beautiful educational scenery on a fast train. They were content with the blur taken in by a quick glance out the window.

The November Session—Resistance Surfaces

The teachers' discussion of the first two of four articles assigned for this session is revealing. The theme of the first article, "Are Teachers Ready to Teach Pupils to Think?" is that teachers will not be able to teach students how to think until they learn to approach their own teaching in a conceptual and critical way. The second article, "Can Educational Research Inform Educational Practice?" by Eisner, questions the validity of the research on teaching that ignores the intellectual and contextual complexity of teaching in its mistaken desire to derive easy-to-follow rules for teaching. These articles do not view teachers as good peasants who obediently till the fields of the educational manor.

But teachers see these issues very differently in the early stages of the dialogue. One teacher's irritation with the articles seeped through his voice as he said, "You know what's wrong with these articles? There's no refreshing point of view. There is no higher-order thinking coming out of them (laughter from the group). I already know what they're talking about. What do they tell me about my reality? I want someone to say, look, here is a new way of looking at your profession."

The laughter confirmed his point. I decided to make the confirmation explicit. "How many of you reacted negatively to the articles?" I asked. All but five hands went up. Par for the course.

I defended the articles in a light-hearted way. I pointed out, for example, that Pennsylvania's induction plan for new teachers was heavily based on the kind of research that Eisner criticized—that this plan required new teachers to learn the research-based techniques of "what works." The teachers could not make the connection between the ideas in the article and the state policy that disempowers them.

The tone of the session was labored. The teachers' responses were understandable and mirrored what the teachers had learned about themselves and their profession. The articles were not getting us on new ground. I assigned parts of Dewey's *How We Think* for the next session. I wanted to see if an indepth reading might tap something more positive. I knew, too, that Dewey's approach to thinking could be applied to the practical issues of teaching.

How could I get the teachers to see that their unthoughtful responses to the readings undermined the foundation on which any claim to professional autonomy or reform must rest?

The December Session—A Look in the Mirror

I saw the possibility of failure with the Gladwyne teachers after the events in November. I thought about the teacher's comment that brought laughter from the group. His request "to speak to my reality" meant give us "universal" practical techniques; it meant that to follow the demonstrate-prompt-practice format to learn teaching skills removed from generative ideas on teaching would be fine with him.

The tone of the group was defensive and wary. Half of the teachers said nothing. I knew from a few random telephone calls to teachers that I make between sessions to help me get a feel for a new group, that some of them saw this defensiveness, too. Good. And I knew that the early sessions in a dialogue almost always precipitate a crisis of some kind.

The week before the December meeting I decided, with a feeling of great uncertainty, to use a high-risk confrontational strategy. My reasons to try this strategy were based on three conclusions.

1. Teacher resistance to the reading is a surface problem.
2. The fundamental problem is that the teachers *assume* that they can think clearly about educational issues, that "they already know this stuff" as they said. The teachers make this assumption because neither in their formal education nor in practice have they been taught to use *ideas as tools* to reach practical ends.
3. My teaching problem, therefore, required that I construct an exercise in which the teachers' false assumptions would be objectively apparent to them and one they could not rationally deny. I would let them see their present "operational theory" through the exercise and to decide what, if anything, they wanted to do about it. The exercise would mirror themselves to themselves.

The frame for the mirror was fortuitously provided by a teacher's suggestion that I ask the group to read an article that appeared in a newspaper published by their union.

The Mirror

The article reported on an interview between a teacher who was president of the state teachers association and the state secretary of education in which they gave their views on reform issues such as testing, teacher education, and teacher autonomy. When I read the article, I saw a revealing contradiction beneath the rhetoric of reform: both the teacher and the secretary of education viewed teachers as technicians! Here, I thought, was a vivid example of teachers being accessories to their own entrapment, as well as confirmation of the pervasive view that education is just another technology of the twentieth century along with planetary probes and VCRs.

I mailed the article to the teachers and asked them to come to the meeting prepared to *analyze* it and to draw *inferences* from the article on teaching as a profession. The day of the meeting I divided them into six groups of four, restated the problem they were to work on, and turned them loose.

We reassembled and each group reported on its work. Condensed excerpts from the group reports suggest the teachers' approach to the problem. "The problem that we addressed was how we felt about the article . . . we spent too much time talking about testing basic skills. Some ideas were brought out about teacher education. It is still like it was in the 1960s. We think teachers need more courses on teaching reading and critical thinking." Another group said that the article stimulated "discussion about some of the issues. We would go off on that. One member tried to bring us back to critiquing the article."

The reports made it clear that the problem I gave them to solve was not addressed. There was no systematic analysis of the views of the two educators relative to teaching as a profession.

I did not evaluate any of the group reports. After the group reports were finished, I asked for their charity and said that I would give my critique of the article. (This was the confrontational phase of the session.)

I pointed out, for example, that when the secretary of education extols "systematic approaches to pedagogy" and gives mastery learning and DISTAR as examples, he is defining teachers as technicians. Mastery learning often reduces teachers to clerks who manage a programmed curriculum and who dutifully record the students' endless scores on skill tests. DISTAR programs the teacher directly by giving her a script to follow. The president of the teachers' association never challenges these restrictive views of teaching. He agrees and states that with the changing student population (a practical concern, I suppose) teachers must be "armed" with this kind of pedagogy. How "armed" will teachers be, I asked, with a mechanical pedagogy based on the narrow stimulus-response psychology in the tradition of E. L. Thorndike and B. F. Skinner?

I concluded by saying that they did not do too well on a thinking task with professional content, despite their claims in November. It was clear, too, I observed, that they did not recognize a nonintellectual pedagogy dressed up in the finery of psychology because they would judge as "irrelevant" any analysis of the unstated assumptions that underlie behavioristic approaches to learning and teaching.

Emotions were high and interest was intense when I finished my analysis of the article. The contrast between their analysis and mine was too sharp to ignore. We argued, criticized, and reasoned for an hour about the meaning of the exercise. The typescript reveals a complex interplay of defensive statements (I had set up a sloppy exercise) leavened by more helpful ones (Let's do another problem. I was never asked to think this way about education). The teachers were willing to look into the mirror.

The January Session—A New Image

The lessons of the exercise seeped into the teachers' thinking in the weeks preceding the January meeting. This account of one group who reported on the implications of the December meeting is typical of the other group reports. "Let's face it. We didn't solve the problem last time. We tended to blame the moderator. [Today] we got on to another problem: a consultant's suggestion that we align the curriculum with the test. We agreed that the faculty sluffed over the implications of this policy when the principal asked us to react to it last year. There is a difference between reaction and analysis."

The group's reference to curriculum alignment is significant. This is the first evidence in the dialogue that the teachers were making conceptual connections between their teaching role and larger policies that affect them as professionals—policies that they had previously viewed as removed from their concern. This is a step toward reform, toward more intellectual and democratic schools. It is from such unglamorous and hard-earned changes in teachers' thinking, I believe, that fundamental changes in schools will come—if they do come.

The teachers' growth in conceptual power continued through May, when the first year of the dialogue ended. The teachers' increased sophistication in problem definition illustrates one strand in their ability to think more clearly about their work. In October, as part of the research design, the teachers were asked to list the significant problems of the school. They produced a diffuse list of over fifty problems. Discussion of the list in February revealed its practical limitations. This discussion led to a consideration of criteria that might separate a significant problem from a trivial one. Four criteria by which the significance of a problem might be judged were developed over several months and formally stated. The new reading during this phase was four chapters from Dewey's *Democracy and Education* on thinking related to experience and to subject matter and teaching methods. In May the teachers were again asked to list the significant problems of the school. No direct reference to the criteria was made. This effort produced a more coherent list of about ten problems. Problems on the October list, such as running in the hallways, did not appear on the May list. The qualitative improvement in the second list is evidence that the teachers' ability to define more significant educational problems had improved. Reasoned problem definition is a critical and neglected part of most school reform efforts and inservice programs.

The teachers and the principal unanimously voted to continue the dialogue for a second year on their own. Reading and discussion of material that reflects a conceptual view of education continued. The teachers' responses in interviews supported a second year of the dialogue because they found it to be intellectually stimulating and useful. Other assessments favored the teachers' growth in conceptual knowledge over a comparison group that received another kind of inservice program during the year. The principal agreed with the teacher evaluations. She felt, however, that the primary outcome of the dialogue was a more cohesive and a more productive faculty. Perhaps the only "new" thing that educators need discover and that researchers and local policymakers should be more concerned about is the practical power of human intelligence when it is free to probe within a democratic process. There is not truly much else that is as "effective" or as "efficient"—or as fundamental.

THE DOXOLOGY

But we need not fear that the idleness of thought and conversation will spill over American schools to confound routine and dull effectiveness. Most superintendents and principals will not answer the knock of dialogue on their door. Teachers will never know that a choice was denied to them. Any reform or inservice program that links a *comprehensive* educational theory to a critical examination of present practice at the grassroots level will be rejected as being "impractical" by 90 percent of our schools. Ideas, the values of democracy, and an honest exchange of views have come to be feared and avoided rather than sought. I know that there never was a Golden Age when these values were supreme, but there must be a deep fissure of contempt in our society and profession when the qualities of mind itself are rejected by those who should be its stewards. This turning against the essence of education—the cultivation of intelligence and a social sensitivity as John Dewey might phrase it—is as if the eagle refused to fly and the fox to hunt. Is not the present bankruptcy of mind and moral concern clear to anyone who has eyes to see? When educators do not educate themselves, whom can they educate?

I say now what I have said privately: school administrators who reject any effort at reform may be the wise ones. They may instinctively see what those of us removed from the social particulars of schools do not see: reform on any fundamental and district-wide basis is impossible to achieve in most of our school systems. Why get everyone stirred up for nothing? All I can honestly claim for those reforms I believe are good is that they may keep the idea of reform alive for a decade or two—one hundred years?—until the society at large, for reasons of its own, yearns to make schools more humane and more truly the cultivators of the mind and the democratic spirit. The gridlocked educational technostructure may then follow its lead and begin to jettison mechanical notions of mind and learning, the better to survive if for no better reason. *Widespread and fundamental school reform will only come when the larger society demands and forces it.* And, too, by trying fundamental reform in hundreds of schools across this land, infinitesimal as this will be in the national scene, we may learn new things about reform that will be useful in the better era I trust is coming. Theories about reform or the "change process" that come from the kinds of technocratic reforms I have criticized in this book, and which support the anti-intellectual values of the present system, teach us little worth knowing. We can no more build a theory of reform on the blind empiricism of these atheoretical research studies than an aeronautical engineer can build an airplane on a false theory of gravity.

Reform has an even stranger characteristic than its devilish complexity and near impossibility. Reform is a social phenomenon that those of us in universities have a difficult time telling the truth about. I recall a discussion in a divisional faculty meeting at the University of Pennsylvania a few years ago. We were discussing school leadership and what "school leaders" should do about reform. The discussion slipped into pessimism about reform, whether the individual perspective taken was filtered through the lenses of social science, history, or educational practice and theory. Then, in one of those unflagged transitions conversations sometimes take in response to the unease of the speakers, we all agreed, nonetheless, that we "had to offer our students some hope." There was no duplicity here. "Offering some hope" seemed to be the right thing to do. I still get a visceral kind of breath-stopping-guilty reaction when I write that widespread reform is virtually impossible. No one wants to be the bearer of bad news, however much he may believe that reality should be unflinchingly faced.

Seymour Sarason bit off a piece of this apple in print, which makes it a little easier for me to do so. He tells of a conversation with a former student who is actively engaged in urban school reform. At one point his friend asks him, "You think it is hopeless, don't you?" Sarason was surprised to hear himself saying "yes" because it was the first time he had ever given that answer to anyone. Sarason attributes his reticence to say what he had long believed because it engendered a sense of "intellectual loneliness" and because it may sound to others as if he was "kin to those who proclaim that the end of the world is near."[10] The desire to belong to the educational Rotary club is a strong and legitimate desire in all of us who, out of the pain we feel, are driven to criticize what we truly admire and devoutly want to endure—our system of public education open to all.

Sarason goes on to make an even more important and disturbing point. Trying to work through the reasons for his pessimism about reform, Sarason talked to people in the schools and in universities who were working in the public schools. From these conversations he writes, ". . . what many of these people were saying in a private, face-to-face interchange was different from what they were saying publicly."[11] What an amazing statement! Here were informed people, presumably of reputation, who could not say what they believed about reform: that past and present efforts were and would be failures. Some of them had spent several decades leading reform efforts. Surely we have all lost something from their silence, however much we understand it. But this statement, and Sarason's decision to write what he believed about reform, was reassuring to me although I was well into writing this book when I read it. His statement was reassuring because it helped to answer this question I had posed many times to myself: if there had been no fundamental reform since 1960, and there is virtually none now, as I believed, why were not more people saying something about it? There is no sustained and critical stream in the literature that speaks to this condition. What was too often there was the irrelevant happy talk of policy studies, or the forced tapestries made by those who stitched together patches of little studies on the change process, or the bold pronouncements of those selling one reform nostrum or another, be it mastery learning, cooperative learning, or programmed instruction. Maybe we are on the threshold of a new candor about education and reform that opens the door to what we sorely need—a constructive directness in criticism that will eliminate our self-imposed censorship and our desire to be too much in step with our peers. Surely we cannot ask our colleagues in the schools to be critical of their practice, as I do, if those of us in the safe haven of the university are afraid to speak our minds. Of what are we so afraid? I suspect it has much to do with maintaining a shiny career image.

We need not only to see, but we must have the courage to say what we see.

The seemingly small thing—being open to an idea, or questioning something we have long assumed, or engaging in ordinary conversation—may offer us a narrow ledge on which to keep the idea of reform alive while we are stranded on the rock face that is today's hostility to fundamental reform. Let us take advantage of the relative quiet and stability a no-reform condition brings, and pay attention to those "little things" in ordinary experience that have the power to shape us. Tolstoy tells the story of a painter who corrected a student's work. "Why, you only touched it a tiny bit," the student exclaimed, "but it is quite a different thing." The teacher replied: "Art begins where the tiny bit begins." Tolstoy then draws his moral in honor of the prosaic experience in life. "One may say that true life begins where the tiny bit begins—where what seem to us minute and infinitely small alterations take place. True life is not lived where great external changes take place—where people move about, clash, fight, and slay one another—it is lived only where these tiny, tiny, infinitesimally small changes occur."[12]

Let us, then, pay attention to those "tiny alterations" in our individual and social selves from which great good or great evil may come. Evil comes quietly in the night with no grand design; it seeps into ourselves and our institutions with stealth, in our neglect of the little things of ordinary experience. The good, as Tolstoy and Dewey believed, requires constant attention to the mundane particulars of our ordinary experience because it is through these particulars that we make and remake ourselves. If we cannot will or think our way to a culture that supports intellectual and democratic reforms, a culture that is outraged at the intellectual and moral neglect that infuses the present system, some of us can keep the small fires of vision and hope alive on the ledges of our classrooms and schools as we take our ordinary experience for what it truly is—the material from which to create a better self and a better school. In this way, although it be a time of great drought, our trees will remain green and in time will bear much fruit when the fresh spring of social change at last arrives.

Appendix A

Toward a More Thoughtful School: Some Ideas to Build On[1]

The twenty-one criteria below offer a platform from which to re-examine the things we too often take for granted about what schools do for (or to) students. The criteria are ports of departure for the difficult journey of problem definition, the development of and the trying-out of possible solutions within the life of a *particular* school.

The twenty-one criteria are cumulatively listed under four categories which account for much of what we need to know to improve the quality of learning and teaching:

> Thinking and Experience
> Seven criteria
> Teaching Objectives
> Five criteria
> Subject Matter
> Three criteria
> Teaching Method
> Six criteria

Thinking and Experience

The criteria in this section are intended to help educators explore the understanding of thinking and experience that underlies thoughtful and democratic teaching.

In a thoughtful and democratic school—

1. Teachers and principals believe that the cultivation of thinking in a decent and humane environment is the primary goal of teaching.
2. Teachers and principals value and encourage student perplexity.
3. Teachers and principals understand (and want students to understand) that meaning comes from seeing continuities and connections within one's experience.
4. Teachers and principals know they cannot afford to underestimate what is involved in "knowing something."
5. Teachers and principals know that learning results when we do something with foresight, with a purpose in mind, and then reflect on the consequences that follow.
6. Teachers and principals understand that thinking is not separated from an activity leading to a desired end; that mind is *in activity*, not outside it.
7. Teachers and principals understand that intellectual effort—both the teacher's and the learner's—is necessarily an emotional effort, too.

TEACHING OBJECTIVES

The criteria below apply to the goals for student learning set by administrators, teachers, and students.

In a thoughtful and democratic school—

8. The objectives suggest the kind of *environment* needed to increase the capacities of the learner.
9. The objectives value both *what* is to be learned and *how* it is to be learned. Objectives reflect the understanding that the *quality* of learning is critically dependent on *how* that learning is achieved.
10. Objectives are stated tentatively and may be modified—by the teacher and students—as the learning–teaching process unfolds.
11. The immediate classroom objectives are made with larger, overarching aims in mind, and they free the student to go toward the larger aims. For instance, the objective that overarches "learning to read" is "*wanting* to read and to read *widely*."

12. Most of the objectives are likely to make sense to the learner at the time of learning; that is, the gap between past learning and present learning is challenging but bridgeable. The objectives do not depend for their apparent usefulness on exhortations to the effect that "it will all become clear later."

SUBJECT MATTER

The following criteria pertain to the content—the subject matter—considered apart from method.

In a thoughtful and democratic school—

13. Essential content is considered that content most widely shared in society—that is, knowledge of general social significance. Technical knowledge related to specialized groups is given less emphasis, e.g., science for engineers or physicians, statistics for psychologists.
14. Content is related to the needs of present community life (local and regional). Content should improve the quality of future living—both social and individual. As such, content throws light on significant social issues, e.g., technology and the quality of life, war and peace, the possibilities of finding satisfying work, and so forth.
15. Content does not consist, necessarily, in information easily made available by technology (computer retrieval, printed materials, films, etc.). Rather, good content is subject matter used to assist learners in their inquiry, their attempt to create personal meaning—whether that inquiry concerns long-term problem-solving or a more immediate task, e.g., preparing an oral report/presentation.

TEACHING METHOD

The criteria in this section encourage teachers and principals to consider some generic indicators of quality for professional and thoughtful teaching.

In a thoughtful and democratic school—

16. Good method is understood by administrators and teachers to mean the creation of a total school-classroom environment for

learning that cultivates the intelligence and sensitivities of learners, teachers, and administrators.

17. Educators recognize that direct attention to results for their own sake (that is, the short-circuiting of meaningful experience through rote or conventional learning) closes down the growth of intelligence. Neither ends nor means can be hurried if one wishes to provoke thoughtful learning.

18. Teachers select problems for the purpose of thoughtful and meaningful analysis so that they are (a) within the experience of the learner at the start of the learning, (b) related to the problems of ordinary life, and (c) require thought, i.e., reflection about the consequences of actions taken to solve the problem.

19. Teachers allow students to try ideas out in their present experience because without this "trying out," ideas are likely to remain abstract and, therefore, inert. Such ideas are unable to influence experience and action.

20. Since democracy requires that individuals have an opportunity to consider and shape group ends, learning activities support educative group work, shared experience, and conversation, as well as individual work.

21. The teacher, the one who best understands where a series of lessons is heading, sees the logical order of the content and tries to relate that content to the learner's more fluid, partial view of it.

The spirit of the preceding criteria is reflected in the following "We Believe" statements that guided learning and teaching in two progressive public elementary schools built in the early fifties. These schools served the children of workers in the auto plants of Detroit. The "We Believe" statements were first developed by the parents in the Andrew Jackson school community with the help of Superintendent Roy E. Robinson. The parents of the Jackson and Paul Best school communities never wavered in their support of these principles. When a conservative group captured the board of education in 1959 and forced report cards on the two schools in addition to the successful parent teacher conferences, for example, parents stood fast but eventually lost to citizen and teacher opposition in other sections of the district who feared "progressive contamination" in their schools. I can testify as a teacher at the Jackson school that these statements of educational principle captured my imagination and were a major influence on all of us who chose to teach in schools with a clear theoretical view.

THE ANDREW JACKSON SCHOOL COMMUNITY'S "WE BELIEVE" STATEMENT

Ferndale, Michigan
May 1950

1. WE BELIEVE that children should learn the tool subjects (3 Rs) by the best available methods, utilizing their interests whenever possible.
2. WE BELIEVE the children's learning experiences should be related to their physical, mental, social, and emotional development.
3. WE BELIEVE there should be a close relationship between home and school so each can reinforce the learnings fostered by the other.
4. WE BELIEVE maximum use should be made of new-type learning aids and materials—radio, movies, etc.
5. WE BELIEVE the school should provide many opportunities for creative expression.
6. WE BELIEVE the school should provide for the continuing development of pupil self-direction and self-control.
7. WE BELIEVE that more attention should be given toward establishing better human relations.
8. WE BELIEVE the school should seek ways to foster in each child a feeling of security, satisfaction, and a sense of belonging in the group.
9. WE BELIEVE there should be freedom in program planning on the part of the teacher and class group.
10. WE RECOMMEND that the teacher-parent conference method of reporting be used for at least one year, with a re-evaluation of this method at the end of such period.
11. WE RECOMMEND that the teacher and the children work together for at least a year, and as much more as the school staff may decide is necessary, to gain a long time view of the children's growth and development.
12. WE BELIEVE parents can help in the school program and activities through teacher-parent conferences, PTA, and room meetings; and by helping with trips, hobby groups, child organizations, and the like.
13. WE RECOMMEND a twelve-months program—ten months regular school, and two months supervised recreation.
14. WE BELIEVE that the school should be a community center.

15. WE BELIEVE that these, and other characteristics the board and school staff will think of, will, if achieved, make the Andrew Jackson School a good school for our children.

Appendix B

1. "In This Land of Dolts. . ." Competency-Based Education
2. Individually Prescribed Instruction in Reading and Arithmetic
3. Thinking Skills—CoRT and Instrumental Enrichment

Comment

Competency-based education is the most important reform discussed in appendix B. Competency-based education is important because state and local efforts to make educators more accountable in the 1980s most often used competency-based systems. In my discussion of competency-based education I weave from diverse strands in this still-contemporary movement: an eye-catching newspaper story by George Will; Jerome Bruner's battles with the behavioristic psychologists who tried to equate "meaning" with "information processing"; how one district used mastery learning and Madeline Hunter's teaching method to set up a competency-based system; and the use of competency-based education in thirty-six states in 1979, which has deep roots in systems analysis. Competency-based education is very much like a technological octopus whose tentacles grow from seemingly unrelated technological developments of reform but are brought together and powerfully coordinated in this single policy. One can see in this reform the real-world effects of a technological educational theory.

Individually Prescribed Instruction is dead and is important today as evidence of the educationally limiting reforms that too often fly out of our federally funded research and development centers and regional laboratories. Thinking skills is an almost innocuous reform compared to the first two, but the CoRT and Instrumental Enrichment programs have intellectual and social deficiencies uniquely their own.

"IN THIS LAND OF DOLTS. . ." IS COMPETENCY-BASED EDUCATION WHAT WE NEED?

The headline over syndicated-columnist George F. Will's article reads, "In this land of dolts, a national test might wake up the education establishment." Drawing his ideas from Chester Finn of Vanderbilt University, voiced in Finn's book *We Must Take Charge*, Will writes that testing is necessary for accountability. Testing leads to a result-oriented system of education, according to Will, a system that would make the public look at something other than the money spent. Testing will change America from a culture of lassitude to a culture of achievement. Warming to his discovery of testing, Will continues

> When it comes to consumer information about outcomes, the American educational system has been engaged in a massive cover-up. If the Securities and Exchange Commission allowed publicly traded corporations to conceal this much data about their profits and losses, we'd have a crisis of investor confidence—and a lot of ruinous investments.[1]

In a fit of optimism uncharacteristic of critics, Will attains epiphany as he envisions national testing "leveraging" and "measuring"—and revitalizing—everything from curriculum to thinking to merit pay for teachers to teacher education (which is as difficult to reform as it would be to bring peace to the Middle East). In light of the current multibillion-dollar scandals in the savings and loan industry and the trading in "junk bonds," Will (or Finn) might have chosen icons from a field other than finance on which educators are to model "full disclosure." But I might be quibbling. What is important about Will's column is that it reflects the emotions of many state and federal legislators about what education must do (or, better, what must be done *to* education) if it is to be reformed. And testing is the heart of competency-based education, whether we are concerned with children learning the 3 Rs or with teacher education.

Competency-based education and testing is not in itself so much a curriculum or a method of teaching as it is an intention: let us make money-devouring educators show us in numbers the results that our tax dollars are paying for. Accountability policies and the supposedly objective data they generate will be the energizing force to reform the moribund educational establishment. The article by George Will forcefully expresses this intention. Accountability and competency-based education have a commonsense ring that appeals to many property-tax-paying citizens as they see taxes rising, taxes that may often amount to most of the month's net pay for many middle class workers. And, too, these citizens have been "conditioned" to believe that almost any problem will yield a solution if it is hammered by the scientific method—they live, after all, in an age of moon shots, an age of "smart bombs" with their precision guidance systems built on mathematical and scientific principles, an age where the complexities of economics can be stated mathematically in terms of a Gross National Product. On what grounds can educators reasonably expect tax-paying citizens not to believe that education, too, can be reduced to numbers? Does not mathematics "tell the truth"? The implicit cultural curriculum of our age has taught its citizens lessons that lie deep within the interstitial spaces of their psyche and feelings to form a materialistic way of "looking at things" that is beyond conscious knowledge and recall and hence is almost impervious to rational persuasion.

The intention of accountability—which is to show what students are learning—slips into curriculums and teaching methods when educators act on this intention. And waiting there on the educational shelf are the curriculums that purport to demonstrate competency and mastery of the basic skills: Individually Guided Education as the technical schools acted it out, the research on effective teaching and the allied Hunter teaching and supervisory approach, the skill-based remedial programs funded under Chapter 1 of the Elementary and Secondary Education Act of 1965, mastery learning, Individually Prescribed Instruction in reading and arithmetic, and some of the programs that try to reach the mind through "thinking skills." Skill-based curriculums with criterion-referenced tests based on the idea of "mastery" and "continuous progress" are made to order to meet the cry for accountability. This confluence between the curriculums that the psychologists had developed and many educators eagerly adopted and the two-decade movement for accountability is ironic. Many local policymakers and administrative leaders often adopted mastery-learning-type programs to make teachers accountable for what they taught and to make the curriculum "uniform" across schools in a district. Now, as the states (and very likely the federal government) impose accountability tests of various kinds on unwilling educators, often with school-by-school test scores published in the local papers, these local policymakers who themselves imposed accountability on teachers become restive and wary. This response is wise. But I cannot but question the superficial kind of thinking and the morality of a position that says, "This X is good for teachers and children, but the same X applied to us is hurtful." Educational positions that are unthoughtfully taken to meet short-term problems, and that offer the seeming simplicity of tightly sequenced skills tied to a high-sounding creation like "criterion-referenced tests" to achieve competency, may return to hobble the lord as well as the peasant.

While practicing educators are swimming like spooked fish in an ocean of political opinion that pushes ever-more stringent accountability measures, the students of the psychologists of behavioristic belief, who created the "individualized" and "mastery" systems in the 1960s on which their educator cousins are now skewered, are busy cooking up new mechanistic schemes. The computer is the model for a mind in these reforms, and information processing and short-term memory shunt aside more useful ideas about learning and teaching, such as purpose, meaning, and active involvement. These computer-influenced categories will repeat the anti-intellectual work that reinforcement, small-step learning, and feedback did in the 1970s and the 1980s. And once more, the aura of legitimate science will be invoked to sanction them. Once more there will be many educator buyers, and when this "new" scheme fails, as it will, the educators will be again skewered while the neobehaviorists slip away unscathed to concoct yet another machine-form that is to pass as a scientific rendering of learning or thinking. If this indictment is offensive to readers who believe that there is (or can be a science of education by, say, 2050), I can only say that I have presented the story of education and behavioristic psychology for most of this century. But even within psychology the plot is the same. Jerome Bruner's book, *Acts of Meaning*, is a reasoned yet passionate indictment of the technical way that behavioristic psychology muddled mind. Bruner's thesis (as is Dewey's) is that cognitive psychology must be about *meaning* and that meaning is socially constructed. The old individualistic psychology cut humans from their social (cultural) roots. The flavor of Bruner's ideas about computers and information processing is suggested by the following quotations although they are not intended to summarize his argument. Writing about the cognitive revolution that he and others were seeking in the late 1950s, Bruner writes:

> Very early on . . . the emphasis [in the cognitive revolution] began shifting from 'meaning' to 'information,' from the *construction* of meaning to the *processing* of information. These are profoundly different matters. The key factor in the shift was the introduction of computability as a necessary criterion of a good theoretical model. Information is indifferent with respect to meaning. . . .
>
> [I]nformation processing cannot deal with anything beyond well-defined and arbitrary entries that . . . are strictly governed by a set of elementary operations. Such a system cannot cope with vagueness, polysemy, with metaphoric or connotative connections. . . . Information processing needs advanced planning and precise rules. . . .

Bruner then shows how even traditional behaviorists with their methodologically driven tenets of learning could come into the fold of the cognitive revolution under the "new reductionism" offered by the computer and information processing model. This model was so permissive

> that even the old S-R [stimulus-response] learning theorist and associationist student of memory could come right back into the fold of the cognitive revolution so long as they wrapped their old concepts in the new terms of information processing. One did not have to truck with 'mental' processes or with meaning at all. In place of stimuli and responses, there was input and output, . . . reinforcement [was] converted into a control element that fed information about the outcome of an operation back into the system. So long as there was a computable program, there was 'mind.'[2]

If the heirs of E. L. Thorndike, Clark Hull of Yale University with his T-maze animal learning experiments, and B. F. Skinner were sneaking into Bruner's cognitive revolution shielded by the glamour of the computer and the catchy phrase "information processing," "straight behaviorists" needed no cover for their stimulus-response and reinforcement learning theories to enter the educational arena of competency-based curriculums, effective teaching, and mastery learning, which promise success to virtually all students. Many educators welcomed these 1930 ideas, believing them to be not only efficient but new. And they fitted nicely with the accountability movement of the 1970s and 1980s.

But educational life is rarely conducted with conscious attention to the several ways of viewing what knowledge is worth teaching and how one learns. The superintendent of the Sparta Unit District No. 140, Sparta, Illinois, implicitly conveys this message in his account of how one reform—outcome-based education—was adopted. This reform came to life in Sparta from a swamp of serious problems: two teacher strikes, severe financial problems, low morale, teacher layoffs, and below-average test scores. Teachers, board members, and administrators "recognized that the fundamental educational delivery system in Sparta schools had to be improved," writes the superintendent.[3]

Outcome-based education was mandated by the Illinois State Board of Education in 1984 because, I am sure, it fits well with the perceived need for accountability. Outcome-based education (OBE) rests on a simple idea: state what you want students to achieve and ensure that the curriculum and the school routines support these outcomes. Practitioners of OBE "start by determining the knowledge, competencies, and qualities they want students . . . to demonstrate when they finish high school. . . ." according to William Spady who was one of the developers of OBE at the Far West Laboratory for Educational Research and Development in San Francisco. These "exit outcomes" will be demonstrated by *all* students. In Spady's view, OBE expects students to succeed through "intensive engagement" with the curriculum and through diagnostic assessments and frequent feedback. Wary that OBE might be criticized for falling into the narrow-skills, behavioral-objectives syndrome, Spady cites one district whose outcomes include creative expression, tolerance, "skills in adapting to and creating personal and social change," and sustaining self-esteem through emotional, intellectual, and physical well-being.[4] I return to Sparta, with which Spady worked as a consultant according to the superintendent.

Educators in Sparta planned a "holistic school improvement program" that reflected three basic tenets of OBE: success for all students, success breeds success, and schools control the conditions for success. And what means to reform did these educators take? After the staff had been trained in OBE principles, the superintendent reports that

> we selected four strategies for improvement: (1) adoption of an instructional strategy for all staff (we chose the Hunter [teaching] model); (2) adoption of Mastery Learning as a supplemental instructional strategy; (3) adoption of a uniform discipline program (Can-

ter's Assertive Discipline); and (4) development of outcomes at each grade level.[5]

Are the reforms in Sparta, so proudly recounted by a concerned superintendent, worthy reforms? I can only look on the Sparta reforms with a heavy heart. I think of the normal, bouncy, children of Sparta who will face, in all innocence and faith in their elders, the mind-numbing routines I have earlier described that are inherent in the Hunter model and mastery learning. Imagine how many children, bored and restive with nothing more to do than filling in blanks on skillsheets and taking tiny tests on bits of subject matter, will deny their normal responses and blame themselves for their feelings and their intuitive sense that learning should offer more than this. But their reasonable faith that the adults who set school policy must know more than they about such matters will only confuse and pull their feelings in yet another conflicting direction. And assertive discipline appears to make students overly docile. It is interesting that Lee Canter describes assertive discipline as a competency-based approach.[6] Although the fourth element in Sparta's competency-based reform is content neutral on its face, requiring that grade-level outcomes be stated, it is virtually certain that the outcomes *achieved* (regardless of what outcomes are *written*) can have no more quality than that which is inherent in the means used to "get to" the outcomes; and the means are technological when the Hunter-effective-teaching-research and mastery learning approaches are used with the consequent diminishment of mind, language, and democratic processes. I will put it another way: is it likely that educators who have chosen three of the most restrictive approaches to learning and teaching and discipline would write outcomes much different from outcomes that are only obtainable from the means chosen? If I chose to jump over a high hurdle, would I wear shoes with soles of lead?

In fairness I must cite the superintendent's conclusion that in 1988 "50 percent or more of our kids scored above average on a nationally normed test in all grade levels, kindergarten to grade 12, whereas in 1984 no grade level had scores this high."[7] But the use of test scores to show that a reform worked is strewn with technical problems. The superintendent gives no detail on the data or analysis to support his conclusion. There is no way to know if his analysis was properly done. Even professional researchers sometimes use questionable or invalid designs. Recall, for example, how some researchers used very short three-day "experiments" to assess the efficacy of mastery learning, and another introduced eighty-three quasi-longitudinal studies that he said supported the claims of mastery learning—a claim that is not scientifically true because other factors, such as higher promotion standards, widely used by schools at the time these studies were done, would also inflate test scores. No study judged to be valid by competent researchers has shown significant student gains in reading and arithmetic for the Hunter approach, which is Sparta's model for teaching (see the discussion of mastery learning and the Hunter approach in chapter 4). Even if we grant Sparta its claimed rise in test scores, there are reasonable grounds to believe that the narrow technical means it has chosen will not lead to fundamental educational achievement. In the Belair Elementary School, one of the three schools that interpreted Individually Guided Education in a technical manner, the students consistently scored at the 90th percentile in reading and arithmetic. But observations of learning and teaching in these technical schools, as I have pointed out, reveal a dreary managerial style of teaching in which skills and worksheets pushed out conceptual and creative learning. Making meaning—thoughtful learning—was not important in the high-scoring (and middle-class) Belair School (see chapter 5). I doubt if Sparta's "instructional delivery system" will have much worth delivering.

But it was at the state level where accountability through competencies took hold. The state superintendent in Michigan, for example, writing in 1972, approvingly quotes Leon M. Lessinger, former associate commissioner for elementary and secondary education in the U.S. Office of Education, that accountability is a powerful catalyst for reform because "accountability requires fundamental changes." George Will echoed these sentiments two decades later in his "land of dolts" article with which I began this discussion. The state superintendent states that quality in education is less a function of input and "more a function of output or results—observable changes in the learner's performance." Michigan's accountability model involves six basic steps that stress performance objectives, assessment, "the analysis of delivery systems," and program evaluation. The superintendent caps his description of accountability in images that would evoke pleasant feelings in Frederick Taylor or Franklin Bobbitt, turn-of-the-century practitioners of a scientific approach to human affairs, when he writes that, in the terminology of industry, we are saying "that this model will permit us to apply realistic quality control at all educational levels . . . to ensure a product . . . [that will] become a contributing member of our society rather than a reluctant welfare recipient."[8] I have never seen "a product" on welfare so I assume that this goal will have been met.

Oregon mandated minimum competencies for high school graduation in 1972. The effort became bogged down in a maze of proliferating competencies. In 1976 the state board of education limited the competencies to be tested to those that related to practical activities such as using reference materials, completing the short form of the federal income tax report, and computing the interest on time payments when items are bought on credit. This "life-functions" approach solved the logistical problems associated with the first try at competency-based testing, which resulted in "extremely long lists of . . . skill and recall items that . . . required too much teacher time in verification and record keeping." In Oregon the competencies to be tested are selected by the local board of education, which the local community can support as acceptable evidence that the schools have "provided students with the minimum abilities needed to function in the six life roles identified by the State Board of Education."[9]

Minimum competency testing had been adopted in thirty-six states by 1979. This political movement is based on a very simple idea, according to Chris Pipho, who is associated with the Education Commission of the States: the public wants to know "Is my son or daughter performing up to grade level? . . . Why can't students read and write when they receive a high school diploma?" Pipho believes that policymakers want competency testing to be used throughout the school system and not only at the last step of the twelve-year process when a student graduates.[10] His belief is probably correct and helps to account for the popularity of "individualized" and mastery-learning-type reforms in the 1970s and 1980s that reduce a subject to a series of discrete and easily tested skills. If a policymaker believes that education can be specified into competencies and that these competencies can be tested, why hold such a good thing off for eleven years and waste it on the graduating class?

Pipho believes that competency testing is desirable and that educators should be quiet and bow to the public will. A few others, reflecting the values of the loyal opposition, believe that competency testing will not improve education. In the years since thirty-six states embraced competency-based education, its proponents would be hard pressed to show that education has improved. Arthur Wise argues that competency-based education and testing will not improve education and that it is a fad—it overly rationalizes and reduces to simple elements (competencies and tests) a process that is far too complex to yield to a simplistic analysis. If there is any doubt that competency-based education is technological in substance and spirit, I will list some of the chips off the same technological block—systems analysis—that Wise gives as examples of reforms that one or more states had adopted beginning about 1970: accountability; program planning and budgeting systems; management by objectives; operations analysis; program evaluation and review technique (PERT); systems engineering; and zero-based budgeting.[11]

Systems analysis is used by the Defense Department to orchestrate complex systems relating to the design, development, scheduling, and financing of new weapons. It is also widely used in industry and business. Systems analysis views entities as a collection of interdependent parts within a hierarchy that may contain subsystems. The process of analyzing or synthesizing these elements is called "systems analysis." One problem with systems analysis in education is that it breaks down when important elements cannot be validly quantified. Removed from the complexities and richness of human interactions, and the chance factors associated with any social situation, education "becomes mechanistic and artificial" when the techniques of system analysis are applied.[12]

Given the parentage of competency-based education in engineering and defense with roots in systems analysis, the short discussion given here, and considering whether or not the competencies assessed are minimal or more general, the odds are very high that a random sample of competency programs would revel that almost all of them would be technological: they would employ behavioral objectives, would emphasize skills more than conceptual knowledge, would neglect the student's interest in the content being tested, would use criterion-referenced tests on small chunks of content, would tightly sequence content within a hierarchy, and would employ the teacher as a manager of a curriculum system that she cannot substantively change. Keeping detailed records of students' progress would depend on the age group being "competicized" as well as the particular curriculum or testing program used.

Let us not conclude competency-based education and testing on this technical note. I do not want to leave George Will hanging with only the support of his article on testing to prop his dangling feet. A few days after Will wrote that column, he wrote another on literature and adult reading. This article is about small, low-volume bookstores, such as those run by the Border brothers of Ann Arbor, Michigan, that do a good business catering to good taste. Will brings up some interesting points on who reads, what they read, and the intrusion of electronic images on the mind. He properly laments that eighth graders spend almost three hours watching television for each hour they spend reading for pleasure. "The rising generation is characterized by 'alliteracy': It can read but it doesn't. It prefers less demanding . . . activities. . .", Will writes. But then, only 12 percent of the adult population are serious readers. Tellingly Will adds: "Small wonder that SAT scores measuring verbal skills . . . have declined."

Will makes some incisive—and too little known—comparisons between the mental process involved in watching visual images and in reading. Visual images, electronic ways of learning things, are passive, noisy, whose meanings are immediately known. Reading is inward, silent, active, where logic and coherence are essential. Television, for example, is less suited than reading for developing intellectual maturity—"the complexity needed for governance of self, and for self-government in society," Will believes. A civic interest is served, Will concludes, whether by a school or a bookstore, "that stimulates the wholesome addiction to printed words."

This does not sound like the man who, a few days earlier, believed that *tests* will change America from a "culture of lassitude to a culture of achievement." But Will is a better educator writing about literature than he is when he writes about education. I would be tempted to honor a competency test that could assess "a wholesome addiction to printed words" and a "mature intelligence necessary for self-governance." But Will's formal educational ideas, like those of many policymakers and educators, that endorse an almost punitive policy of testing, embrace a "culture of lassitude" while denying a true "culture of achievement" and a love of ideas and the printed word.[13]

INDIVIDUALLY PRESCRIBED INSTRUCTION IN READING AND ARITHMETIC

Individually Prescribed Instruction in reading and arithmetic was an important reform in the 1960s and mid-1970s—and the major rival to Individually Guided Education for federal largesse and favor of school districts. Although Individually Prescribed Instruction died when federal funds for dissemination were abruptly stopped in the mid-seventies, my discussion introduces a revealing quotation from B. F. Skinner that is a blunt statement of the behaviorists' view of the mind and understanding.

Robert G. Scanlon, head of Research for Better Schools, a federally funded regional laboratory in Philadelphia, Pennsylvania, disseminated Individually Prescribed Instruction (IPI) to the nation's schools until 1976. Scanlon ties IPI to diagnostic-prescriptive instruction and to programmed instruction. He cites the work of Carleton Washburne, the energetic superintendent of schools in Winnetka, Illinois, who led the development of self-instructional and self-corrective materials for students, which, Scanlon says, "pioneered programmed instruction. . . ."[14] Washburne's work was done in the 1920s. After the socially privileged children in Winnetka worked through their self-teaching materials, they took a self-administered test and, later, a check-test that was given by the teacher. This approach was used only in the "tool subjects" of reading and arithmetic. "Class assignments and recitations were abolished," according to Tanner and Tanner.[15] The Winnetka Plan varied the rate of learning in a well-intentioned effort to "individualize" instruction in a way that reflects the spirit of today's mastery learning and "continuous progress" curriculums.

A second major influence on Individually Prescribed Instruction was the work of Robert Glaser in 1961 at the Learning Research and Development Center of the University of Pittsburgh. Some way had to be found, according to Scanlon, to break up the organization of the intact classroom if individualized learning, defined as the flexible progression of individual students through the curriculum, were to be achieved. Glaser did this. Programmed instructional materials arose from his work. "Out of this experience," Scanlon continues, "grew Individually Prescribed Instruction . . . an instructional system based on a set of behavioral objectives correlated with diagnostic instruments, curriculum materials, and teaching techniques."[16]

"Individualization," conceived as behavioristic psychologists see it, isolate students in "independent work" and thus remove the social environment from learning that Dewey, for example, saw as an essential element in learning. Behavioristic views of knowledge and learning (their epistemology) also sever the natural use of language from learning when the social environment is educationally constricted for what amounts to isolated seatwork—performing dance drills with few opportunities to dance. If reading involves thinking and reasoning, "children need the opportunity to think and reason together; to challenge and to be challenged by others after having read a story, poem, or a section of a social studies text," according to A. S. Artley, an expert in reading.[17] Technological approaches to the desirable aim of "individualizing learning" is missed in the systems metaphor, which cannot grasp what is subtle, intangible, fragile, and what is, indeed, the essence of what the "system" should be about.

Based on the ideas from behavioristic psychology that ground IPI, and on the examination of the instructional materials themselves, or on examples given in curriculum texts,[18] IPI is a technological curriculum. Tamar Ariav used criteria that I had developed from a progressive perspective to analyze the IPI arithmetic curriculum (see appendix A).[19] I repeat in summary form three of her findings about IPI and the related criteria.

Criterion: Method recognizes that intellectual effort is always accompanied by emotional and moral elements. One cannot isolate the mind from emotional and moral functions.

Analysis: The [student's] mind responds to narrow stimuli. The process is repetitive. Boredom is likely to be felt by many students (a conclusion supported by other evaluation studies). The moral element of discipline is present insofar as the student completes the tasks. But this discipline is based on unnecessarily restricted and predetermined social and intellectual stimuli.

Criterion: The teacher, as the mature orchestrator of the classroom environment, sees the logical order of the content and tries to relate this content to the learner's more fluid, partial view of it.

Analysis: IPI assumes that proper pretest placement and pacing are sufficient adaptation to the learner. IPI is presented as a preset logical system with little effort to relate its context to the learner's present experience and more partial view. The teacher's role is primarily that of a clerk to the system. The teacher's opportunities to enrich the system or to relate math learning to other subjects are minimal.

Criterion: The cultivation of thought is the primary goal of instruction.

Analysis: Problem-solving, use of insight, experience in dealing with unordered data, etc., are not in this system. The cognitive level is low—working through computational exercises in the booklets. Limited processes are used to achieve results (mastery); these processes (means) short-circuit richer processes and limit thought.

Ariav's analysis, based on Deweyan criteria, consistently revealed the anti-intellectual stance of IPI arithmetic. But this view of mind should not surprise us because the theory that energizes programmed-type curriculums, with their emphasis on frequent reinforcement in small-step content sequences, clearly eschews the development of understanding. In support of this statement I offer a short quotation from B. F. Skinner from a speech given at the

University of Pittsburgh in 1954 and approvingly cited by Robert Glaser. Glaser says that Skinner's address reflects the "force, spirit, and tactics of Skinner's translation of work done on the programming of animal behavior into the educational application of programmed instruction. . . ." Skinner's speech anticipates the objections that will be made to the use of teaching machines [programmed curriculums] in schools: the child is being treated as a mere animal and that the human intellectual achievement in mathematics is being analyzed in unduly mechanistic terms. After saying that mathematical behavior is usually regarded as the product of reason rather than as a repertoire of responses involving numbers and numerical operations, Skinner says: "It is true that the techniques that are emerging from the experimental study of learning are not designed to 'develop the mind' or to further some vague 'understanding' of mathematical relationships. They are designed . . . to establish the very behaviors which are taken to be the evidences of such mental states and processes."[20] Indeed, the "experimental study of learning" is not designed to "develop the mind," which is a consistent failing of each of the technological programs that I have discussed. Individually Prescribed Instruction faithfully reflects Skinner's philosophy of learning.

THINKING SKILLS: CoRT AND INSTRUMENTAL ENRICHMENT

Schools in the 1980s sought not only to improve the learning of basic skills in reading and arithmetic by adopting some form of mastery learning or by pursuing programs such as Individually Guided Education that promised to "individualize learning"; many tried to face the problem of mind directly by adopting prepackaged thinking skills programs. Two widely known thinking skills programs in this period were developed by Edward deBono in England and Reuven Feuerstein, an Israeli psychologist. Edward deBono's program is known as CoRT, which teaches sixty thinking skills through a series of "stories" or situations to which the learner responds. Reuven Feuerstein's approach is called Instrumental Enrichment which requires students to manipulate geometric figures through a series of puzzle-like exercises. These exercises teach twenty-one cognitive functions such as systematic exploration and categorization.[21]

I shall give more detail on the CoRT program to suggest its flavor. CoRT is designed to be simple and practical, to be independent of the learner's prior knowledge, to transfer the thinking skills learned to life experiences, and to be used over a wide range of ages—age six to adult. It will be easier to see how CoRT tries to achieve its aims by walking through an abbreviated lesson on "Consequences and Sequel," one of CoRT's sixty thinking skills. The first step in the lesson explains why the skill, consequences and sequel, is important. A seven-line introduction explains that if the pollution consequences of the internal combustion had been foreseen, electric or steam engines might have been used for cars. The last two lines of this introduction assert that inventions, rules, and decisions have consequences that need always to be considered. The second step gives an example which I give in full below.

Example

A man introduced rabbits to Australia to provide sport for his friends who had nothing to shoot at. The immediate consequences were good because his friends had plenty to shoot at. The short term consequences were also good because the rabbit provided an alternative source of meat. The medium term consequences were bad because the rabbit multiplied so much that it became a pest. The long term consequences were very bad because the rabbit was now such a pest all over Australia that it did a great deal of damage to crops.

The third step, practice, poses five situations to which the student is asked to anticipate consequences. One situation suggests that a new device has been invented which makes it possible to tell if someone is lying; another situation poses the problem of "so many colored people [moving] into a district" that equal numbers of colored and white people live there. The student is asked to imagine the immediate and short term consequences of this situation ("short term" had been defined in the introduction as one to five years). Under process, the fourth step, a discussion is to be held in small, heterogeneous groups around such questions as "If it is not easy to see the consequences should you bother with them?" and "Do long term consequences matter?" The last step lists five principles related to this skill, some of which state that other people may better see the consequences of a person's action than the person taking the action, and that consequences should be viewed as affecting the one who acts as well as other people. The teacher is told to read each principle twice to the class for emphasis.[22]

CoRT is organized into six units, each of which contains ten thinking skills. Breadth includes, for example, the skills of planning objectives, consequences and planning; organization involves the skills of analyzing and finding alternatives; the unit on interaction includes the skills of examining an idea for its effects and for making judgments including the use of values. The remaining units deal with creativity, information and feeling, and action.

CoRT attempts to place great responsibility on the teacher's creativity and vigor. The manual that comes with CoRT is an outline and the teacher is not given the correct answers to the questions posed. The major emphasis in CoRT is to develop what de Bono calls "lateral thinking which is the ability to see things differently and creatively. . . . It is up to the teacher to move the students toward that goal."[23]

Allan Thrush, whose study I have been citing, used Deweyan-based criteria to evaluate the CoRT and Instrumental Enrichment curriculums. His major finding with both thinking skills programs was that whatever the students learned in these programs about thinking was unlikely to be transferred to academic content in the regular school curriculum. Both developers say that teachers should make this transfer but *they offer no way within their programs to effect this essential transfer* other than to say that transfer should be done. Nor can the developers assist in the transfer of what was learned to the curriculum because the content in the case of Instrumental Enrichment is a series of abstract geometric exercises; with CoRT the content is a series of unrelated "stories" about situations. "When children use IE or CoRT," Thrush concludes, "they are led to think in a restrictive context and do not learn much about thinking in general nor do they gain experience in approaching other [content] more thoughtfully."[24] The isolation of the "content" in these thinking skill curriculums from the content in regular school subjects is similar to the isolation of the content in the Chicago mastery learning program from the "real content" in reading; the mastery learning exercises were mastered, but reading was not.

The pattern revealed by applying Deweyan criteria to the CoRT and Instrumental Enrichment thinking skill programs suggests that the content in these programs is unrelated to the content in the sciences and the humanities—content that thousands of years of cultural history says is worth knowing—and is thus unable to improve thinking when school subjects are studied.

Thrush found the content and teaching methods used in CoRT and Instrumental Enrichment to be artificial and that the objectives and prescribed routines controlled the way in which the teachers might use the materials. The learning environment was thus intellectually and socially restrictive.

Another View on Thinking Skills

My analysis of the CoRT and Instrumental Enrichment thinking skills programs has been from a conceptual and qualitative perspective: what knowledge is to be taught, and how worthy are these critical dimensions in learning and teaching when they are critiqued from the line of sight offered by a theory of education that embraces intelligence and democratic values? Does a more traditional assessment made from the perspective of empirical research significantly change my conclusions? The answer is "No" for Instrumental Enrichment, according to one research review (no studies were reported for CoRT).

The lead author of this review, Robert J. Sternberg, a psychologist from Yale University who is a proponent of thinking skills instruction, and his co-author comment on the highly abstract, nonverbal nature of the IE materials—that the content is similar to that in a nonverbal IQ test. They sum up their review of thirty-eight studies that were done in many countries and reflected a diverse range of student characteristics, saying: "We see no evidence of gains in insightful, creative, or synthetic thinking abilities, and a content analysis of the course materials lead[s] us to believe that such gains were not likely to be attained . . . because they are not built into the . . . program." The authors believe, however, that IE might increase scores on standard IQ measures in abstract reasoning and spatial visualization if the teaching were done by "carefully trained, intelligent, motivated, and conscientious instructors. . . ."[25]

Since the use and appreciation of language is much of the game in education, I cannot resist mentioning the reviewers' comments on Philosophy for Children, which tries to develop thinking through the reading and discussion of six novels in which the characters use philosophical thinking to work out problems in their lives. The content in Philosophy for Children is educationally important, in my opinion, and very unlike the trivial examples in CoRT or trying to see geometric forms in clouds of dots that is so prized in Instrumental Enrichment. The studies done on Philosophy for Children are technically sketchy and, I infer from their review, not worth too much, but Sternberg and Bhana offer the opinion that this highly verbal program seems to produce gains on verbal tests of critical thinking, is interesting to children, and carries over to learning in other subjects.[26]

Be all this as it may, I reiterate the notion that thinking, like language, must permeate every subject taught in school and drip from the school's social environment or we will have lost the educational Olympics. If isolated programs in thinking skills, detached from the permeating environment of the classroom, are to become the primary way of feeding the mind, the mind, it is certain, will slowly die of starvation.

Appendix C

1. Performance Contracting: The Psychological-Industrial Complex
2. The Enfeebled Research-Development-Diffusion Model
3. The Effective Schools Research
4. Assertive Discipline
5. Accountability and State Testing Programs
6. Aligning the Curriculum to the Test

Comment

Two of the accounts given here should arouse even the most complacent policymaker or educator who believes that "garden-variety psychology" can reform education. When performance contracting crashed and burned in 1972—in what should have been a public and academic display of the severe limitations of capitalist efficiency ideology and psychological behaviorism—one would think that the profession might have begun a pained examination of its practical theories. Not so. Ellis Page, a psychologist of behaviorist persuasion, must have been one of ten people in 1972 who drew the conclusion that behaviorist doctrines lacked the power to teach the most rudimentary skills to poverty's children. Rather than think—and put much of the academic research and policy establishment in jeopardy—we enshrined these failed doctrines in Chapter 1 remedial programs for poor kids under the Elementary and Secondary Education Act of 1965, and have spent billions of dollars turning these kids off to reading (documented in chapter 4).

But remember that behaviorism and systems analysis were built into the mind of the U.S. Office of Education as early as 1966 in the person of Richard Loomis Bright, the new assistant commissioner for research at USOE. Bright was a systems engineer for the Westinghouse corporation before coming to the Office of Education. Bright put life into the research-development-diffusion mode of reform. He launched the system of research centers and regional laboratories we still have. Despite serious limitations in the top-down, linear model of research and development extolled by Bright, its deep flaw lay in Bright's limited understanding of what is the proper subject matter of education. When he said in the *Kappan* interview that basic research in the "biophysics and biochemistry of learning and memory" might be the focus of basic research in education, the educational cat jumped out of the research and development bag.

As if all this were not enough, we have the effective schools people, whose correlations among vague variables are believed to lead to effective schools. These correlations will tell us how not only to increase achievement, but how to enhance "school climates" as well. If mere correlations had this power, I would be among the first to jettison not only my theories but my life experience and become a missionary in the service of this simple gospel.

PERFORMANCE CONTRACTING: THE PSYCHOLOGICAL-INDUSTRIAL COMPLEX

It might relax harried educators, threatened by vouchers, school choice, and privatization reforms, to learn a bit about the excitement aroused in the early 1970s when private companies agreed to teach urban children for pay. The amount to be paid was based on a predetermined improvement in test scores. Performance contracting was an unusual mix of capitalism's "can do" spirit and the technological mindset. And it failed miserably, despite the commendable intentions of the federal government to help children struggling in poverty. A full description and critique needs to be written about this failed reform.

The Texarkana Dropout Prevention Program, marred by scandal and "teaching to the test," was the first performance contract ever awarded. This contract, and later ones, were based on the idea that a "private contractor will have greater freedom to innovate and thus be more successful in motivating students" than the regular school system has been, Leon Lessinger, former associate commissioner in the U.S. Office of Education, wrote in 1970. Lessinger was a strong advocate to bring "engineering accountability" to education. In 1970 private companies had contracted to teach—raise test scores—in Gary, Indiana; Providence, Rhode Island; Philadelphia, Pennsylvania; and Flint, Michigan.[1] But the real action was with the well-designed experiment in eighteen school districts that contracted with six companies to put the claimed successes of performance contracting to the test. This study was conducted by the Office of Economic Opportunity (OEO) and completed in 1972.

The OEO study included a diverse range of low-achieving ethnic groups from urban Anglos to Alaskan Eskimos in grades one to three and seven to nine. The performance of the twenty-five thousand students (and the companies) was to be assessed on the basis of achievement gains in reading and arithmetic. Companies were to be paid on the basis of each student who gained one year between the fall and spring tests.[2]

The results of this study were shocking. "The pupils fell far short of the year's gain required by [the] contract; the contractors were . . . in deep financial danger. . . ." and the OEO was embarrassed. What is important about this experiment with companies teaching the 3 Rs is not that it failed, regrettable as this failure may be if one thinks of the students living in poverty, but that the ideas and values of learning and teaching on which it was based failed. Ellis Page, a psychological behaviorist whose account I am citing, says that performance contracting was based on "our behaviorist doctrine of the past several decades. . . ." and included programmed instruction, reinforcement and incentives, and behavior modification. But Page is a behaviorist with an open mind. After recounting the poor results of the OEO study, he says that they dealt a "severe blow to certain of our professional illusions." Page recounts these illusions when he says that applied psychology has certain powerful skills which he enumerates.

> We understand task analysis; input repertory; stimulus shaping . . . the provision of reinforcement; the arrangement of repetition, sequencing, looping; concept formation; the practice of transfer. . . . [We believe that] as a profession . . . we can make incalculable improvements in education.
> This belief has been one cornerstone of our faith in ourselves.[3]

The OEO experiment, Page writes, has offered what may be the first solid test of our theories—whether garden-variety applied psychology can contribute to learning in schools. We cannot be so casual about our statements in the future, Page asserts "because our skills in training do *not* seem [to be] the immediate solution to our problems in education."[4]

Page's candor and his lament were not heard by those of behaviorist persuasion in the two decades of reform that followed his critique. If anything, the belief in technical rationality has increased and the technological mindset sails free on the pond of reform.

The experience of reformers at the federal level, such as Leon Lessinger and officials in the Office of Economic Opportunity, who believed that the rationality of engineering combined with the profit incentives of capitalism could help poor children achieve in reading and arithmetic was a clear and unfortunate failure. It is a harsh lesson that mainstream researchers, officers in the U.S. Office of Education, and public school educators refuse to acknowledge, much less learn. But Page does not say only that performance contracting failed, he generalizes this *management* failure to the core of the *learning-teaching* process: the most sacred tenets of behaviorism such as task analysis, reinforcement, sequencing, and programmed instruction failed. *The theory failed.* Yet this confirmed failure of behaviorism did not deter the development and dissemination of curriculums, teaching methods, and inservice programs to the children and teachers of this country—some of which I have critiqued in this book. Behaviorism rolls on like a juggernaut because it offers simplicities where profundity is needed, and it is fed by the larger cultural dominance of the technological mindset to which it is both son and father. Behaviorism is a destructive philosophy, but it feeds a lot of professors, research grants, book publishers, and a huge testing industry. We should be worried about this psychological-industrial complex.

THE ENFEEBLED RESEARCH-DEVELOPMENT-DIFFUSION MODEL

The basic idea behind the research-development-diffusion model is clear: researchers uncover knowledge, which is, in turn, developed into programs or strategies for use by schools, and these "development packages" are made known to educators in the schools through systematic diffusion efforts. Diffusion is ideally accompanied by expert assistance to adopting schools that may be provided by the regional laboratories, universities, or others. We earlier saw this process at work in the development and dissemination of Individually Guided Education by the University of Wisconsin Center for Education Research, which did the basic research on which IGE is based (see chapter 5). The Center initiated complex diffusion efforts with state agencies, and regional laboratories, conducted research on the quality of IGE's implementation, and arranged for third-party evaluations of the innovation's worth. The discussion of IGE provides a concrete example and a context for this brief discussion of research and development.

The core assumption on which the research-development-diffusion model rests is that knowledge is objective and finite and that it can be diffused to that swarm of bees that is educators in practice. The views of Richard Bright, who was assistant commissioner for research in the U.S. Office of Education, suggest the flavor of the ideas behind the research and development model in the early days when federally funded research centers and regional laboratories were established. Bright was a systems engineer with Westinghouse before entering government. I give below excerpts from an interview conducted by the *Phi Delta Kappan* in 1966.

Bright believes that basic research should be concerned with cognitive studies and that work in learning and memory could be supported. A regional laboratory, in Bright's view, "will identify what it believes to be are one or two major educational problems in a region and mount a program to solve the problems" and will use research, demonstrations in schools, and dissemination activities to further the spread of innovations. The research centers, on the other hand, will pursue problems in depth, take a longer range view and "will have much less responsibility for dissemination."[5]

The supreme position in reform of the research expert and research-based knowledge is clear when Bright speaks about how the best use can be made of Title I and Title III funds (which were earmarked to promote innovations in schools) under the Elementary and Secondary Education Act of 1965. Competent researchers from the regional laboratories and local and state officials will decide on the innovations to be supported. "I agree completely . . . ," Bright continues, "that if we spend our Title I and Title III money without the guidance of competent researchers, the great majority of these funds will be utterly wasted."[6]

This account is not a full treatment of Bright's views, nor does it reflect the many permutations and policy changes that marked the federal push for education research and development. But I cannot escape the belief, based on practical experience with reform and research, that Bright and his followers today are expressing a *faith* dressed up in the language of systems analysis and research. Is the knowledge we need to reform education, for example, knowable through scientific methods and, if this knowledge can be known, can it be disseminated through technically rational means alone? Might there not be other ways of knowing, such as thinking through the problematics of everyday experience, that are useful and that the scientific materialism of the research-to-practice *philosophy* ignores? Are not a will to take action, the nerve to take risks, and a moral commitment in which will and nerve are grounded, critical dimensions in reform? How does an objective science deal with such things? I know of two principals, for example, part of a small local group of schools that are a part of a national effort to reform high schools who *admit that they are deliberately making superficial accommodations to the reform* and who, further, inquire wonderingly of those who are trying to make fundamental changes! How can research knowledge, or knowledge of any kind, be "disseminated" to people who have neither the will nor the moral commitment to receive it? Is this not a prior and overlooked problem that must be addressed in any "model" that purports to reform schools? Can the science of education alone provide what is needed? Might not "reverse will" be a problem in reform that should be addressed? A philosophy of materialism that comes out of scientism cannot develop the knowledge education needs. The complexities of dissemination, not to mention reform, are beyond its thought range. It is common knowledge in academia that most of the work of the research and development centers is of low quality. I am sure a fair sample of their "products" would reveal that the technological mindset guides much of their work.

THE EFFECTIVE SCHOOLS RESEARCH

Wilbur Brookover has done research on effective schools—schools that this research claims will produce high achievement gains with students in inner-city schools—and he is an advocate of this research. Since I have been discussing reforms from the perspective of learning and teaching, I shall summarize some of the characteristics of effective schools that Brookover says mark their "instructional practices": mastery of clearly stated objectives in the basic skills; structured, direct instruction that is incorporated within a mastery learning program; a high percentage of time spent on learning tasks; effective use of reinforcement; diagnosis and regular feedback to pupils; and accurate records kept of all objectives mastered by the students.[7] Brookover spells out what these criteria mean in some detail in his book, along with two other components that include the beliefs and attitudes of the school staff and the way the school is organized.

At this point we know that the research on effective schools is a technological reform based on our earlier analysis of reforms such as mastery learning, Chapter 1 compensatory programs, and the Hunter-effective-teaching-research way of teaching. The focus on basic skills, reinforcement, and the mastery of "clearly stated objectives," for example, echoes the essence of these reforms and the failures of performance contracting.

What is interesting, too, given the ready acceptance of research findings by practitioners and the general lack of a critical review of these findings within the research community itself, is that another and, I believe, more critical researcher on effective schools offers evidence that contradicts the research of Brookover and others. Lawrence Stedman and Brookover debated these issues in a journal exchange that is enlightening.[8] Some of Stedman's criticisms of this research and its implicit theory of learning and teaching are pertinent to the thesis I am advancing. Stedman cites convincing evidence from multiple sources to show that the research on effective schools overemphasizes reading and arithmetic skills and testing. Schools that adopted the effective schools formula often restricted children's learning to lower-order skills (which is what the technical schools did when they adopted Individually Guided Education). This orientation to drill and practice has "hurt higher-order skills and brought down the test scores of higher-achieving students," Stedman claims. In his exchange with Brookover, Stedman mentions other groups that have begun to question the traditional schools formula and says that such factors as basic skills and time-on-task do not stand up under critical analysis. Based on a close analysis of several dozen case studies, a review of the literature on school effectiveness, and his technically sophisticated analysis of four years of data on more than eight hundred Pennsylvania schools, "the effective schools formula is seriously flawed. An alternative approach that values an academically rich curriculum, personal attention to students, cultural pluralism, and shared governance with teachers and parents should be considered," Stedman believes.[9] The debate between Stedman and Brookover is worth reading not only for the solid issues that it raises and explores from the vantage points of two different philosophies of education, but for the question embedded within it: can research ever settle anything because it alone cannot penetrate very deeply into the beliefs we all bring to educational matters however heavy the shield of objectivity we put on in honor of the ceremony?

ASSERTIVE DISCIPLINE

Assertive Discipline, developed and marketed by Lee Canter and Associates, Inc., is characterized as a "take-charge approach for today's educator."[10] The advertising literature from Canter and Associates published in 1989 claims that more than five hundred thousand teachers have been trained in Assertive Discipline.[11] Even if we reduce Canter's claim by 30 percent, it is possible that Assertive Discipline has affected the lives of approximately one million children. Any reform that may affect the lives of one million young Americans is worth comment.

I shall touch on one aspect of Canter's method, in which he instructs teachers how to deal with parents because this focus will reveal the essential characteristics of his approach. I believe, too, that procedures for dealing with parents are less subject to the feelings that a prescribed way of dealing with children may arouse. The problem faced by the teacher in Canter's example is that Fred, her student, is not completing his work in class. Canter gives an edited transcript of a conference between the teacher and the parent to show how the teacher is being properly assertive, which I shall summarize. In this conference the teacher follows a systematic plan that documents the problem (the teacher shows the parent examples of uncompleted work and the parent exclaims, "None of these are [sic] even half finished!") The teacher asserts her goal for the conference in response to the parent's comment by saying, in effect, "Now you see my problem with Fred." The parent says that she cannot believe Fred is a problem in school because he has never been a problem at home. The teacher proceeds to the third step and gives her rationale by saying that Fred needs to know that they are working together and that his disruptive nonworking behavior will not be tolerated. When the parent expresses feelings of disbelief over Fred's behavior, the teacher says that Fred is not a bad child and moves to the next step in which she states her objectives: she will send a note home every day, which will say whether or not Fred has done his work. If the work has not been completed the parents are to see that it is. If the work has been completed the parents are to show pleasure and "maybe provide him with some special treat." The parent raises the objection that she and her husband work and that it will be difficult to find the time. The teacher responds that Fred is a year behind in reading and arithmetic and if his behavior continues his achievement will continue to fall. The parent says, "It's really that bad, isn't it?" The teacher moves to the conclusion (what Canter calls the "active sending of a message") and asks the parent to repeat what the teacher has said.

> PARENT: "Well, I'll have to sit down with my husband. I hear what you are saying—we need to do something."
> TEACHER: "Could you tell me what you heard me say?"
> PARENT: "We have to get on Fred." [Parent repeats the teacher's plan of daily notes and so forth] and concludes with "Well, I guess he's just not going to be watching T.V. for awhile."
> TEACHER: "What do you mean?"
> PARENT: "If Fred doesn't do his work, he's not going to watch T.V. until he finishes it at home."
> TEACHER: "How do you plan to let him know that you like it when he gets a good note?"
> PARENT: "Ice cream, what else? He loves ice cream."
> TEACHER: "It sounds excellent. I really appreciate your cooperation. . . ."[12]

What can be so bad about this seemingly routine conference between a teacher and a parent? The teacher is concerned, she has expended a great deal of energy in conducting the conference, the parent is cooperative, and there is nothing punitive or mean in the assertive approach that the teacher deliberately uses. And maybe the teacher's plan is exactly what Fred needs. This "smooth surface feature" of Assertive Discipline is appealing and this is what many teachers and principals see when they use it. But there is a darker side to this method, too. *Everything good hinges on the teacher's plan being correct. There is no two-way talk, no sharing of ideas and observations between the teacher and the parent.* The parent is being manipulated by the teacher in a closed, linear plan that was conceived before the parent arrived. This controlling feature marks the techniques teachers are to use with children also. There is nothing in the teacher's plan, for example, to show that the teacher critically examined *her* learning and teaching procedures. Maybe Fred is fed up with workbook drills, sitting still, and working alone among twenty-five other students. Fred's refusing to "cooperate" with a dull teacher may indicate intelligence and potential leadership abilities. None of these contextual issues is explored in Assertive Discipline. Assertive Discipline takes *existing* school procedures and, like the Madeline Hunter model or the mechanical exercises in Chapter 1 compensatory programs, freezes them into an efficient, technologically refined system of behavior control. Has Big Brother come to school? Assertive Discipline runs counter to the intellectual and democratic values that should mark any fundamental reform. (I do believe that Assertive Discipline may be one way among many that might be used as a *short-term* approach with students who have *serious* problems in acting normally in a group setting.)

Accountability and State Testing Programs

The technological thrust of competency-based education covers the essential qualities inherent in accountability and state testing programs (appendix B). Each of the three is a variation on one theme: the objective testing of students will reform education. I feel justified in calling this idea the George Will syndrome, which I discussed earlier, to reduce the burden I have placed on behavioristic psychologists and educators. The fallacy in the testing-will-reform-education approach is that while all of the testers are packed around the downhill end of the pipe testing the water quality, too few are up in the hills trying to remove the pollution in the spring from which the water comes.

Aligning the Curriculum to the Test

Aligning a curriculum to a test is more of a survival technique than it is a reform. But its understandably wide use makes it worth listing. Aligning a curriculum to a test reflects the pressure policymakers put on teachers and administrators. Curriculum alignment merely fudges the numbers higher on the testing instrument and leaves everything else that is important unchanged. A "test" should reflect what is judged worthy to be taught, but this is a very different idea from aligning a curriculum to a test. This technique cannot break the technological qualities inherent in objective testing. The ultimate logic of curriculum alignment would lead one to dispense with the curriculum and only teach the test. This condition attains perfect alignment between the "curriculum" and the test.

NOTES

CHAPTER 1

1. Harold Hodgkinson, "Reform Versus Reality," *Phi Delta Kappan* 73 (September 1991): 10, 11, 12.

2. Michael W. Apple, *Ideology and the Curriculum*, 2nd ed., (New York: Routledge, 1990), pp. 158, 40–41. See also Lois Weis's *Working Class Without Work: High School Students in a De-industrializing Economy* (New York: Routledge, 1990). Weis's groundbreaking work moves beyond the static arguments of class to show how white adolescent males define themselves and others in a life with few jobs. One outcome among this group is a political movement toward the Right.

Although my intellectual and practical orientation is unapologetically liberal-progressive, I endorse the critique of education made by many critical theorists. See for example Peter McLaren's *Life in Schools: An Introduction to Critical Pedagogy in the Foundations of Education* (New York: Longman, Inc., 1989) or Ira Shor's *Empowering Education: Critical Teaching for Social Change* (Chicago: The University of Chicago Press, 1992). My criticism of the critical theorists as a broad group is that, while they have a good critique of education, they are surprisingly indifferent to the theoretical and practical need for a *comprehensive*, constructive theory of *education* (not society, but education). Critical theorists are very much like the progressives Dewey criticizes in *Experience and Education:* it is not enough to be against traditional education, he said; one must *construct* a positive intellectual view and work *concretely* to carry it out. Too many critical theorists (along with most isolated academics) are content to "so-

259

cially reproduce themselves" within the career culture of today's research university that pays well for writing and less well for doing.

3. William A. Galston, "Home Alone," *The New Republic* 205 (December 2, 1991): 42. William Julius Wilson, in *The Truly Disadvantaged: The Inner City, the Underclass, and Public Policy* (Chicago: The University of Chicago Press, 1987), says that compensatory education cannot address the joblessness of black youth without attacking the economic factors that underlie these conditions.

4. *USA Today*, "Student Skills 'Not Good Enough'," 1 October 1991, pp. 1, 4D.

5. *USA Today*, "Workers Are the Key, Top Firms Find," 1 October 1991, pp. 1B, 2B.

6. *USA Today*, "Workers Are the Key," p. 2B.

7. *USA Today*, "Nation's Education Goals: A Progress Report," 1 October 1991, p. 11A. Governor Roy Romer, a former chairman of the National Education Goals Panel, made the statement.

8. For one example of this approach, see two books by Mary Walton on the quality control methods that W. Edwards Deming is credited with introducing to Japan after World War II: *The Deming Management Method*, with a foreword by W. Edwards Deming, (New York: The Putnam Publishing Group, Perigee Books, 1986), and *Deming Management at Work* (New York: The Putnam Publishing Group, Perigee Books, 1990).

9. My inference that education reform typically neglects the human and context-specific factors in particular classrooms and schools is consistent with either the data presented or the positions taken by Richard F. Elmore and Milbrey W. McLaughlin in *Steady Work: Policy, Practice, and the Reform of American Education* (Santa Monica, California: The Rand Corporation, 1988); William A. Firestone, Susan H. Fuhrman, and Michael W. Kirst, *The Progress of Reform: An Appraisal of State Education Initiatives* (New Brunswick, New Jersey: Center for Policy Research in Education, Rutgers University, October 1989); Seymour B. Sarason, *The Predictable Failure of Educational Reform: Can We Change Course Before It's Too Late?* (San Francisco: Jossey-Bass Publishers, 1990); Thomas Toch, *In the Name of Excellence* (New York: Oxford University Press, 1991); Chris Pipho, "States Move Reform Closer to Reality," Kappan Special Report, *Phi Delta Kappan* 63 (December 1986): 1–8.

Another important dimension of the low and life-endangering quality of the reforms imposed on the public schools is that the schools can expect little help from schools of education in research-oriented universities. These schools are often so prestige-deprived that they ape the focus and procedures of the academic disciplines and shun their true mission, which is professional education: educating teachers and administrators and learning how to improve students' learning in the complex circumstances within which educators work. In the elegant statement of Geraldine Clifford and James Guthrie, schools of education should "work with practitioners in ways that enrich their wisdom," *Ed School: A Brief for Professional Education* (Chicago: The University of Chicago Press, 1988), pp. 352, 348–54.

10. John Goodlad, *Teachers for Our Nation's Schools* (San Francisco: Jossey-Bass Publishers, 1990).

11. Goodlad, *Teachers for Our Nation's Schools*, p. 214.

12. Goodlad, *Teachers for Our Nation's Schools*, pp. 203–204.

13. Gary B. Campbell, "Staff Development through Dialogue: A Case Study in Educational Problem Solving," (Doctoral dissertation, University of Pennsylvania, 1989), pp. 90–117.

14. Campbell's reform effort was based on an approach I have used in secondary schools that links educators' practical knowledge to conceptual knowledge within a democratic process. See Richard A. Gibboney, "Just Words: Talking Your Way Past Reform to Educational Renewal," *Journal of Curriculum and Supervision* 4 (Spring 1989): 230–45, which gives a practical structure for dialogue and reports the outcomes in one senior high school with teachers and their principal over a three-year period.

15. Ann Lieberman, ed., *Building a Professional Culture in Schools* (New York: Teachers College Press, Columbia University, 1988), and Ann Lieberman and Lynne Miller, *Teachers, Their World, and Their Work: Implications for School Improvement* (Alexandria, Virginia: Association for Supervision and Curriculum Development, 1984).

16. *The Philadelphia Inquirer,* "Video Courses for Teachers: Districts Raise Concern over Practice," 9 October 1991, pp. 1, 10A.

17. Diane Ravitch, *The Troubled Crusade: American Education 1945–1980,* (New York: Basic Books, Inc., 1983), p. 168. Although I doubt if Ravitch is a progressive of whatever stripe, her account of the mindless child-centered practices in the 1960s which characterized too many "reformed schools" has more than a germ of truth (pp. 228–66). Teachers or principals who try to be "progressive" without some knowledge of educational history, and some understanding of John Dewey's comprehensive philosophy which values mind as well as experiential learning, are almost certain to invent another poor school—as did their 1930s predecessors.

18. James Agee and Walker Evans, with an introduction to the new edition by John Hersey, *Let Us Now Praise Famous Men* (Boston: Houghton Mifflin Company, 1939), p. 13. This classic was reissued in 1960.

CHAPTER 2

1. By a "Deweyan-progressive perspective" I want to suggest a perspective that reflects John Dewey's philosophy and to suggest also that this philosophy influenced some of the qualities in the broad and variegated "progressive movement" in education and politics. I intend to disassociate Dewey from the romantic child-centered wing of progressive education (which is inconsistent with the permeating intellectual component in his educational philosophy), from the social reconstructionist wing of progressive education advocated by writers such as Theodore Brameld and George S. Counts, from the administrative progressives of whom David Tyack writes, and from the "social policy experts" Walter Lippman endorsed, who reflect a lack of faith in the ability of citizens to govern themselves.

I do not want to do more here than to correct some of the common misunderstandings of John Dewey's philosophy and to point out some of the diverse currents within progressive education. I am thinking of those students of mine who are in their thirties and forties and who, forgive me Lord, have no idea of educational history. Their images of things past are wildly imaginative. And I do not want to engage in an academic game of definitions, interesting as this might be. On politics and Dewey's radical social views see Robert B. Westbrook, *John Dewey and American Democracy* (Ithaca, New York: Cornell University Press, 1991); Dewey's debate with Lippman is discussed on pp. 293–306. That Dewey held liberal and more-than-compromising views toward capitalism is discussed in chapter 12 by Westbrook. Of greater significance is that a scholarly and fair reading of Dewey's major works would show that his views are radical if "radical" means to question those things in the present capitalist system that deny to many citizens the benefits of education, a decent job, and health care, which *restrict* citizens' ability to participate fully in the fruits and responsibilities of a democratic society and to realize their capacities as human beings. Dewey's beliefs (and many of his actions but not all of his actions) support the conclusion that he was deeply concerned with the lives of the dispossessed in our society, that he was more than a spongy liberal—a conclusion denied by many neo-Marxists. For an unscholarly and distorted reading of Dewey from the neo-Marxist position see Clarence J. Karier, "Liberal Ideology and the Quest for Orderly Change," in Clarence J. Karier, Paul C. Violas, and Joel Spring, *Roots of Crisis: American Education in the Twentieth Century* (Chicago: Rand McNally College Publishing Company, 1973). I believe that a broader reading and understanding of Dewey's philosophy is impeded by a lack of first-rate criticism. We need a criticism of Dewey's philosophy that matches Westbrook's sympathetic criticism in its quality and sweep, but from a more critical position. Such a work would also be a contribution to knowledge and practice.

2. The best single source to understand the deeper meaning of the intellectual and democratic criterion is John Dewey's *Democracy and Edu-*

cation: An Introduction to the Philosophy of Education (New York: Macmillan Publishing Company, Free Press, 1966; first published in 1916). No work in educational theory published in this century approaches *Democracy and Education* in its intellectual and social power. This book is the only statement we have of a *comprehensive* theory of education whose aim is to develop a new education consistent with the demands of a democratic society. It would be good for all of us if we had a comprehensive competitive theory, but this work awaits genius. While Dewey's work in aesthetics, ethics, and politics influenced my thinking about education, these works addressed issues that were not as congruent with my professional experiences and the two questions I was struggling with: Why are schools the way they are? and How can they become better? At least two other treatises by Dewey were helpful as I tried to make sense of what I saw in schools, in state education departments , and in my school of education. Slowly I came to the conclusion, too, that the *body* of literature I had read in educational research and in social science approaches to educational problems was intellectually incoherent because it rested on no fundamental educational theory or explanatory theory in the social sciences and thus was of little practical value nor aesthetically satisfying in its own right. All of these influences pushed me to philosophy and history. Dewey's *Human Nature and Conduct: An Introduction to Social Psychology* clarified some of my concerns. Dewey made the case for the neglected idea that learning is a social phenomenon: learning is a result of the individual's impulses interacting with people and customs in a social environment. This learning Dewey calls "habit." The social medium (culture) can increase the range of human responses or narrow them. If the intrinsic human impulses are too long thwarted, they will try to "liberate themselves and to make over social institutions. . ." (p. vii). This is one energy source for reform. Dewey relates the individual *and* the society in this work. We learn through association with others. We are shaped by social institutions as, in turn, we may shape them. Since there are a number of native impulses which are organized into ways of responding to particular situations, "the *meaning* of [these impulses] is not native" but acquired. Their meaning depends "upon interaction with a matured social medium" (p. 90). By showing that learning is an *interaction* between individual characteristics and a social medium, Dewey displaced the older behavioristic stimulus-response psychology of the *individual* with a more realistic and humane social psychology. The educational implications of this social psychology are that teachers should think less of lesson plans and more about creating social environments in their classrooms that are educative. It is clear from the theory that these environments should provide many opportunities for students to use language and to interact in purposeful and educative ways. To use language, to interact with others in pursuit of a shared goal, is the essence of the social. The isolation of the student within an aggregation of other students in which she pursues fragmented tasks in seatwork—a static environment encouraged by behaviorist psychology—is thus challenged. [*Human Nature and Conduct: An Introduction to Social Psychology,* with a foreword by John Dewey (1929), (New York: The Modern Library, Henry Holt and Company, 1922).]

The Quest for Certainty is an intellectual history of grand sweep that offers an alternative to the old physics of Isaac Newton and the mechanical view of a universe of immutable physical laws which separated the subjective experience of everyday life and knowing from mathematically expressed scientific laws. This book opened my eyes to the limitations of science, which I had more intuitively and emotionally felt as I reviewed much of what passed as "new knowledge" conveyed in the frequently used expression "What does the latest research say?" (not too much I came slowly and reluctantly to believe). As criticism, *Quest for Certainty* directs us to examine a major source of one limited view of knowledge—physical science. Dewey resolves (or attempts to resolve) the subjective-objective dualism in a manner we could predict from the major themes in his philosophy. He says the findings of physical science tell a part of the truth. But we do experience the qualities of things—scents, colors, feelings, sounds in everyday life—however much science may properly exclude these subjective experiences for its purposes. It is a mistake, Dewey held, to deny our direct experience because one way of knowing (science) excludes it. One possible solution is to give *practical intelligence* full play in ordinary affairs as science gives detached reason full play in its affairs. The intellectual class, Dewey continues, has usually depreciated practical activity. This view condemns the use of intelligence in ordinary experience to impotency (p. 214). How could we ever get better schools, I wondered, if the "intellectual class" sees only mind in the disciplines, books, and libraries? Dewey's next statement should serve as a rallying cry for every cowed practitioner and professor of education everywhere: "All materials of experience are equally real; . . . all are existential; each has a right to be dealt with in terms of its own special characteristics and its own problems" (p. 216). In this one idea we have a basis for the grounding of education in itself: education does not have to be transmuted (and often distorted) into subject matter it is not such as psychology or social science (although these and other studies may assist along the way). As he does in *Democracy and Education,* Dewey put intelligence in ordinary experience and asks us to think, to make decisions, and to judge the worth or the "truth" of these decisions by their consequences in the real world. This idea provides an in-this-world and intellectual way to judge the worth of our decisions and actions in schools by their results: what consequences (effects) do we see in teachers, students, and principals as a result of our actions? Do they act more intelligently? Can they think? Do they care about others? Do they feel some responsibility for their own life and the larger social life going on within and about them? Do they have a desire to learn and to grow? We have no certainty. We have contingent situations in which we act, guided by intelligence. These actions generate consequences by which the worth and goodness of our actions shall be judged. [*The Quest for Certainty: A Study of the Relation of Knowledge and Action* (New York: G. P. Putnam's Sons, Capricorn Books, 1929).]

A theory unsituated in a social and intellectual context lacks an essential dimension. A theory nests with a complex range of competing ideas, events, and practical actions in the society and its schools. These things we should try to know. I shall cite without comment some of the histories and commentaries which, in their varying perspectives, add a complementary dimension to Deweyan theory which I have found instructive: Michael W. Apple, *Ideology and the Curriculum* (London: Routledge & Kegan Paul, 1979); Raymond E. Callahan, *Education and the Cult of Efficiency* (Chicago: The University of Chicago Press, 1962); Lawrence A. Cremin, *The Transformation of the School: Progressivism in Education 1876–1957* (New York: Random House, Vintage Books, 1961); idem, *American Education: The Metropolitan Experience 1876–1980* (New York: Harper & Row, Publishers, 1988); Herbert M. Kliebard, *The Struggle for the American School Curriculum 1893–1958* (Boston: Routledge & Kegan Paul, 1986); William J. Reese, *Power and the Promise of School Reform: Grassroots Movements During the Progressive Era* (Boston: Routledge & Kegan Paul, 1986); William H. Schubert, *Curriculum: Perspective, Paradigm, and Possibility* (New York: Macmillan Publishing Company, 1986); Daniel Tanner and Laurel N. Tanner, *Curriculum Development: Theory into Practice* (New York: Macmillan Publishing Company, 1980); and David B. Tyack, *The One Best System: A History of American Urban Education* (Cambridge, Massachusetts: Harvard University Press, 1974).

3. Dewey, *Democracy and Education*, pp. 87–88.

4. Dewey, *Democracy and Education*, pp. 159–60.

5. Ira Shor, *Empowering Education: Critical Teaching for Social Change* (Chicago: The University of Chicago Press, 1992), pp. 79–85.

6. Maggie Cox, "Foxfire: The Democratic Process," *Hands On: A Journal for Teachers* 37/38 (Fall/Winter 1990): 19–25. Eliot Wigginton tells how Foxfire evolved from the perplexities of a high school English teacher in *Sometimes a Shining Moment: The Foxfire Experience* (Garden City, New York: Doubleday & Company, Inc., Anchor Books, 1985). John Puckett gives the history and critical appraisal of Foxfire as cultural journalism in *Foxfire Reconsidered: A Twenty-year Experiment in Progressive Education* (Urbana and Chicago: University of Illinois Press, 1989).

7. Derek Bok, "The Challenge to Schools of Education," *Harvard Magazine*, May/June, 1987; Russell Jacoby, *The Last Intellectuals: American Culture in the Age of Academe* (New York: Basic Books, Inc., Publishers, 1987); Page Smith, *Killing the Spirit: Higher Education in America* (New York: Viking Press, 1990); Bruce Wilshire, *The Moral Collapse of the University: Professionalism, Purity, and Alienation* (Albany, New York: State University of New York Press, 1990). It is difficult to overestimate the harm that is being done in education and social science because of narrow specialization and a mechanistic view of knowledge. Bok reports, for exam-

ple, that education journals are filled with shoddily researched and poorly reasoned articles. One panel review found that more than 80 percent of the published articles were deficient (p. 52). Jacoby found that the professionalized disciplines filter out dissenters so views and analyses that depart from orthodoxy will rarely be expressed (p. 200). When a Nobel Prize winner in economics decries his profession's cult of mathematized formula building, it is time to notice what is going on in academia. Jacoby cites Wassily Leontief's criticism that mathematical models do little more than find algebraic "fits" between old data and the models. Leontief concluded that model building will continue as long as senior economists control the training, promotion, and research activities of their younger members (pp. 159–60).

8. The educationally worthy thing to do is to develop a first-rate curriculum based on a comprehensive educational theory and societal needs, and evaluate it by using real-life examples of students' work, results of teacher-made tests and observations, and student and teacher evaluations of the course over time—then see if the standardized test is a valid measure of the curriculum-as-taught. The odds are that the test will be invalid.

9. Geraldine M. Joncich, ed., *Psychology and the Science of Education: Selected Writings of Edward L. Thorndike* (New York: Teachers College, Columbia University, 1962), pp. 101, 104.

10. Robert V. Bullough, Jr., Stanley L. Goldstein, and Ladd Holt, *Human Interests in the Curriculum: Teaching and Learning in a Technological Society* (New York: Teachers College Press, 1984), pp. 6, 7.

11. Alfred North Whitehead, *Science and the Modern World* (New York: Macmillan Publishing Company, 1925), pp. vii, 17.

12. William Barrett, *Death of the Soul: From Descartes to the Computer* (New York: Doubleday, Anchor Books, 1986).

13. Stephen Toulmin, *Cosmopolis: The Hidden Agenda of Modernity* (New York: Macmillan Publishing Company, Free Press, 1990), p. 184.

14. Whitehead, *Science and the Modern World*, pp. vii, 17.

15. Floyd W. Matson, *The Broken Image: Man, Science and Society* (Garden City: New York: Doubleday & Company, Inc., 1964), p. 138.

16. William Barrett, *The Illusion of Technique: A Search for Meaning in a Technological Civilization* (Garden City, New York: Doubleday & Company, Inc., 1979), pp. 22–23.

17. Lewis Mumford, *The Myth of the Machine* (New York: Harcourt Brace Jovanovich, Inc., 1970), pp. 86–87.

18. Barrett, *The Illusion of Technique*, p. 22.

19. Puckett, *Foxfire Reconsidered* and Wigginton, *Sometimes a Shining Moment.*

20. Mary Jean LeTendre, "Improving Chapter 1 Programs: We Can Do Better," *Phi Delta Kappan* 72 (April 1991): 578.

21. Arthur Wise, "Why Minimum Competency Testing Will Not Improve Education," *Educational Leadership* 36 (May 1979): 548, 546; idem, *Legislated Learning: The Bureaucratization of the American Classroom* (Berkeley: University of California Press, 1979), p. 12.

22. William A. Firestone, Susan H. Fuhrman, and Michael W. Kirst, *The Progress of Reform: An Appraisal of State Education Initiatives* (New Brunswick, New Jersey: Center for Policy Research in Education, Rutgers University, October 1989).

23. Kliebard, *The Struggle for the American School Curriculum 1893–1958*, p. 256. Kliebard's insight that Dewey's ideas were not fully reflected by any of the diverse interest groups that participated in progressive reform is true. Kliebard sees Dewey as "hovering over the struggle rather than as belonging to any particular side" (p. xii).

24. Charles E. Silberman, *Crisis in the Classroom: The Remaking of American Education* (New York: Random House, 1970), pp. 169–70.

25. James B. Conant, *The American High School Today: A First Report to Interested Citizens* (New York: McGraw-Hill Book Company, 1959), pp. 50–51.

26. National Commission on Excellence in Education, *A Nation at Risk: The Imperative for Educational Reform* (Washington, D.C.: Government Printing Office, 1983).

27. Conant, *High School*, quotation on back cover.

CHAPTER 3

1. John I. Goodlad, *School Curriculum Reform in the United States* (New York: The Fund for the Advancement of Education, 1964), pp. 14–15.

2. Goodlad, *Curriculum Reform*, pp. 14–15. Goodlad reports that the University of Illinois project began in 1951; Charles E. Silberman gives the date as 1952 in *Crisis in the Classroom: The Remaking of American Education* (New York: Random House, 1970), p. 169.

3. Goodlad, *Curriculum Reform*, p. 14.

4. Goodlad, *Curriculum Reform*, pp. 16–18.

5. Goodlad, *Curriculum Reform*, pp. 22–23; Leslie W. Trowbridge and Roger W. Bybee, *Becoming a Secondary School Science Teacher*, 5th ed. (Columbus, Ohio: Merrill Publishing Company, 1990), p. 287.

6. Goodlad, *Curriculum Reform*, pp. 29–30.

7. Trowbridge and Bybee, *Science Teacher*, pp. 289–90.

8. Goodlad, *Curriculum Reform*, pp. 25–26.

9. Trowbridge and Bybee, *Science Teacher*, p. 290.

10. Trowbridge and Bybee, *Science Teacher*, pp. 290–91.

11. Goodlad, *Curriculum Reform*, pp. 13–42; Diane Ravitch, *The Troubled Crusade: American Education 1945–1980* (New York: Basic Books, 1983), pp. 231–32; Daniel Tanner and Laurel N. Tanner, *Curriculum Development: Theory into Practice*, 2nd ed. (New York: Macmillan Publishing Company, 1980), pp. 519, 535.

12. Jerome Bruner, *The Process of Education* (Cambridge, Massachusetts: Harvard University Press, 1961).

13. Goodlad, *Curriculum Reform*, pp. 60, 69–70; Ravitch, *Troubled Crusade*, p. 265; Tanner and Tanner, *Curriculum Development*, pp. 548–49.

14. Tanner and Tanner, *Curriculum Development*, pp. 518–67.

15. John Dewey, *Democracy and Education: An Introduction to the Philosophy of Education* (New York: Macmillan Publishing Company, Free Press, 1966. First published in 1916), pp. 228–29.

16. Dewey, *Democracy and Education*, p. 230.

17. Dewey, *Democracy and Education*, pp. 223–25.

18. John Dewey, *Experience and Education* (New York: Macmillan Company, 1938), p. 97.

19. Dewey, *Experience and Education*, p. 87.

20. Dewey, *Experience and Education*, p. 103.

21. J. Lloyd Trump and Dorsey Baynham, *Guide to Better Schools: Focus on Change* (Chicago: Rand McNally and Company, 1961), p. 1. This book reports the recommendations of the Commission on the Experimental Study of the Utilization of the Staff in the Secondary School appointed by The National Association of Secondary School Principals and funded by the Fund for the Advancement of Education and the Ford Foundation.

22. Trump and Baynham, *Guide to Better Schools*, pp. 5, 6.

23. Trump and Baynham, *Guide to Better Schools*, p. 24.

24. Trump and Baynham, *Guide to Better Schools*, p. 43.

25. Trump and Baynham, *Guide to Better Schools*, p. 20.

26. Trump and Baynham, *Guide to Better Schools*, pp. 47–48.

27. Trump and Baynham, *Guide to Better Schools*, p. 115.

28. Arthur Zilversmit, *Changing Schools: Progressive Education Theory and Practice, 1930–1960* (Chicago: The University of Chicago Press, 1993), pp. 154–57.

29. Zilversmit, *Changing Schools*, p. 156.

30. Trump and Baynham, *Guide to Better Schools*, p. 125.

31. Vito Perrone, *Working Papers: Reflections on Teachers, Schools, and Communities* (New York: Teachers College Press, Teachers College, Columbia University, 1989), p. 53.

32. Silberman, *Crisis in the Classroom*, p. 208.

33. United Kingdom, Department of Education and Science, *Children and Their Primary Schools: A Report of the Central Advisory for Education (England)*, vol. 1 (London: Her Majesty's Stationery Office, 1967), p. 2.

34. Roland Barth, *Open Education and the American School*, with a foreword by Joseph Featherstone (New York: Agathon Press, Inc., 1972).

35. Barth, *Open Education*, p. 204.

36. To cite one example, Dewey criticizes progressive schools for ignoring history and for neglecting to relate solid content to student experience (*Experience and Education*, pp. 91–96); see also Ravitch, *The Troubled Crusade*, pp. 248–56, for valid criticisms of open classrooms as a movement (and, I would add, as a reform untied to the balance and discipline that a comprehensive theory of education affords).

37. Allan A. Glatthorn, *Alternatives in Education: Schools and Programs* (New York: Dodd, Mead & Company, 1975), p. xiv.

38. Silberman, *Crisis in the Classroom*, pp. 349–69.

39. James Voigt, Public Information Division, Portland, Oregon Public Schools, telephone interview by author.

40. George Dennison, *The Lives of Children: The Story of the First Street School* (New York: Random House, 1969), pp. 12–14

41. Joel Spring, *The American School 1642–1985* (New York: Longman, 1986), p. 134.

42. Quoted in Spring, *The American School*, p. 135. The account of the Quincy school is drawn from Spring pp. 132–36.

43. John I. Goodlad and Robert H. Anderson, *The Nongraded School* (New York: Harcourt, Brace & Company, 1959), pp. 79–112.

44. Trump and Baynham, *Guide to Better Schools*, p. 83.

45. Trump and Baynham, *Guide to Better Schools*, p. 84.

46. Trump and Baynham, *Guide to Better Schools*, p. 84.

47. Gary Campbell and Ellen Griffis, Marticville Middle School, Penn Manor School District, Millersville, Pennsylvania. Interview by author.

48. Quoted in Silberman, *Crisis in the Classroom*, pp. 167–68.

49. Trowbridge and Bybee, *Science Teacher*, pp. 291–92. See Tanner and Tanner, *Curriculum Development*, chapter 12, for a comprehensive analysis of the 1960 curriculum reforms that illuminates the intellectual and social issues that are implicit in any curriculum reform effort.

50. Theodore Sizer, *Horace's Compromise: The Dilemma of the American High School* (Boston: Houghton Mifflin Company, 1984), pp. 9, 20.

51. "Inside Re:Learning," published by the Coalition of Essential Schools and the Education Commission of the States, Providence, Rhode Island, No. 1/November 1992, p.2.

52. Lisa Lasky, Manager of Communications, Coalition of Essential Schools, Brown University, telephone interview by author April 1993.

53. Theodore Sizer, "Diverse Practice, Shared Ideas: The Essential School" in *Organizing for Learning: Toward the 21st Century*, (Reston, Virginia: The National Association of Secondary School Principals, 1989), pp. 1–8.

54. Sizer, "Diverse Practice," p. 2.

55. *Horace* 6 (March 1990). *Horace* is published five times yearly by the Coalition of Essential Schools, Brown University, Providence, Rhode Island.

56. Crefeld School, Chestnut Hill, Pennsylvania, mimeographed, no date.

57. *Horace* 4 (April/May 1988); *Prospectus,* Coalition of Essential Schools, Brown University, Providence, Rhode Island, 4 pp.

58. *U.S. News and World Report* (February 26 1990), pp. 50–55.

59. Lisa Lasky, Manager of Communications, Coalition of Essential Schools, Brown University, telephone interview by author April 1993. Calls to several of the schools suggested by Lasky did not result in any claims for whole-school reforms. I did not call one school, Thayer High School, Winchester, New Hampshire, because it is atypical of rural schools. The charismatic leadership of its principal, among other considerations, make it atypical of rural high schools. Two schools do appear to be well down the road to whole-school reform. Walbrook High School, Baltimore, Maryland, has 95 percent of its teachers involved in some aspect of the reform, according to Marian Finney, Coordinator. Every graduating student has given an exhibition to show he has learned. Most students also keep portfolios of their work as part of Walbrook's assessment policy. Twenty of Walbrook's 80 teachers are on five teacher teams, which meet 125 students everyday. Woodward High School, Cincinnati, Ohio, involves 900 of its 1400 students in its efforts to become a neighborhood school. Thirty of its 100 teachers are engaged in six teacher teams. "This was a whole-school project from Day One," reports Diana Porter, Woodward Coordinator. Commendable as these reform efforts are, most teachers in these schools remain outside the team teaching structure. If we link the experience of the Coalition to the inability of public education to mount fundamental reforms in even 20 percent of its schools since 1960, we see the virtual impossibility of fundamental reform under today's social and educational conditions. Our experience since 1960 also suggests that Deweyan-progressive reforms themselves cannot overcome the sea of indifference to reform among most administrators, teachers, and school board members. The good side to all of this is that we are at last learning what some of the problems are when serious intellectual and democratic reforms are tried. My conclusion that not one school reformed itself in a comprehensive way is based, in part, on the ethnographic studies of eight schools that were early members of the Coalition. These studies were made by Donna E. Muncey and Patrick J. McQuillan (see below). Muncey and McQuillan wanted to find out how teachers and principals interpreted and implemented the Coalition's nine principles. This research is not a formal evaluation of the eight schools according to Muncey and McQuillan. The conclusions I draw here are my own. See Donna E. Muncey and Patrick J. McQuillan, "Sustaining School Change: Case Studies from the Coalition of Essential Schools," unpublished manuscript (Providence, Rhode Island: Brown University, October 1992), and idem, "Teachers Talk about Coalition Reforms at their Schools," Working Paper #7, unpublished manuscript (Providence, Rhode Island: Brown University, October 1992). I chose five schools from the eight schools studied that I believed were typical of public schools: Elliston High School, Evans

Hill High School, Lewis High School, Russell High School, and Silas Ridge High School.

60. R. Freeman Butts and Lawrence A. Cremin, *A History of Education in American Culture* (New York: Henry Holt and Company, 1953), p. 494.

61. Dewey, *Experience and Education*, pp. 114–16.

62. *Horace* 3 (January 1988).

63. Letter from Kenneth Kastle, Principal, William Tennent High School, Centennial School District, Warminster, Pennsylvania, October 15, 1990.

64. Mortimer, J. Adler, *The Paideia Proposal: An Educational Manifesto* (New York: Macmillan Publishing Company, 1982), p. 61.

65. Adler, *Paideia*, p. 23.

66. Adler, *Paideia*, p. 78.

67. For a more critical view of Paideia with respect to its treatment of auxiliary studies such as health, work, and citizenship, see D. G. Mulchay, "Is the Nation at Risk from the Paideia Proposal?," *Educational Theory* 35 (Spring, 1985): 209–22.

68. Carnegie Forum on Education and the Economy, Task Force on Teaching as a Profession; *A Nation Prepared: Teachers for the 21st Century* (New York: Carnegie Corporation, 1986).

69. *A Nation Prepared*, p. 3.

70. *A Nation Prepared*, pp. 66–67.

71. *A Nation Prepared*, p. 76.

72. *The Universal Almanac*, John W. Wright, ed. (Kansas City, Missouri: Universal Press Syndicate Company, 1990), p. 206. Data used are from the National Center for Education Statistics.

CHAPTER 4

1. Lawrence A. Cremin, *The Transformation of the School: Progressivism in American Education 1876–1957* (New York: Random House, Vintage Books, 1961), pp. 114–15.

2. The Holmes Group, *Tomorrow's Teachers* (East Lansing, Michigan: The Holmes Group, 1986), p. 52.

3. Raymond E. Callahan, *Education and the Cult of Efficiency: A Study of the Social Forces that Have Shaped the Administration of the Public Schools* (Chicago: The University of Chicago Press, 1962), p. 221.

4. Lynn Olsen, "Proponents of Mastery Learning Defend Method After Its Rejection by Chicago," *Education Week,* August 28 1985, pp. 1, 30.

5. Callahan, *Education and the Cult of Efficiency,* p. 30.

6. Callahan, *Education and the Cult of Efficiency,* p. 33.

7. Callahan, *Education and the Cult of Efficiency,* p. 23.

8. Callahan, *Education and the Cult of Efficiency,* p. 36.

9. Kenneth D. Kastle, "Madeline Hunter and the 'Science' of Education, "course paper in Ed. 545C "Twentieth Century American Educational Reform," December 15, 1988, pp. 21, 32, 42; Joseph O. Milner, "Suppositional Style and Teacher Evaluation," *Phi Delta Kappan* 72 (February 1991): 464–67; and David Holkzkom, "Teacher Performance Appraisal in North Carolina: Preferences and Practices," *Phi Delta Kappan* 72 (June 1991): 782–85.

10. David G. Savage, "Why Chapter 1 Hasn't Made a Difference," *Phi Delta Kappan* 68 (April 1987): 581.

11. Mary Jean LeTendre, "Improving Chapter 1 Programs: We Can Do Better," *Phi Delta Kappan* 72 (April 1991): 578; and Thomas W. Fagan and Camilla A. Heid, "Chapter 1 Program Improvement: Opportunity and Practice," *Phi Delta Kappan* 72 (April 1991): 582.

12. Fagan and Heid, "Chapter 1 Program Improvement," p. 583.

13. Fagan and Heid, "Chapter 1 Program Improvement," p. 583.

14. Fagan and Heid, "Chapter 1 Program Improvement," p. 583.

15. Fagan and Heid, "Chapter 1 Program Improvement," p. 585.

16. Robert E. Slavin, "Making Chapter 1 Make a Difference," *Phi Delta Kappan* 69 (October 1987): 110.

17. Launor F. Carter, "The Sustaining Effects Study of Compensatory and Elementary Education," *Educational Researcher* 13 (August/September 1984): 7.

18. Lorin W. Anderson and Leonard O. Pellicer, "Synthesis of Research on Compensatory and Remedial Education," *Educational Leadership* 48 (September 1990): 15.

19. Anderson and Pellicer, "Synthesis of Research," pp. 13, 15.

20. Anderson and Pellicer, "Synthesis of Research," pp. 12–13.

21. Frank Smith, *Insult to Intelligence: The Bureaucratic Invasion of Our Classrooms* (Portsmouth, New Hampshire: Heinmann Educational Books, Inc., 1986), p. 98.

22. Smith, *Insult to Intelligence*, p. 4.

23. Smith, *Insult to Intelligence*, p. 5.

24. Richard C. Anderson, Elfrieda H. Heibert, Judith A. Scott, and Ian A. G. Wilkinson, *Becoming a Nation of Readers: The Report of the Commission on Reading* (Washington, D.C.: National Institute of Education, 1985), p. 97.

25. Robert E. Slavin, "Chapter 1: A Vision for the Next Quarter Century," *Phi Delta Kappan* 72 (April 1991): 589.

26. Slavin, "Making Chapter 1 Make a Difference," p. 116.

27. National Diffusion Network, *Educational Programs That Work*, 16th edition (Longmont, Colorado: Sopris West Inc., 1990), p. G-13.

28. National Diffusion Network, *Educational Programs That Work*, 1990, p. G-13.

29 Slavin, "Making Chapter 1 Make a Difference," p. 118.

30. National Diffusion Network, *Educational Programs That Work*, 1990, p. J-12.

31. National Diffusion Network, *Educational Programs That Work*, 1990, p. J-12.

32. National Diffusion Network, *Educational Programs That Work*, 1990, p. J-12.

33. National Diffusion Network, *Educational Programs That Work*, 1990, pp. J-3, J-7, J-14, and J-22.

34. Slavin, "Making Chapter 1 Make a Difference," pp. 116–19. The fifteen drill- and skill-based curriculums from the twenty Slavin cites are listed below. All of these programs are atomistic and reflect a mechanical view of learning and teaching. I use the categories and program titles that Slavin used in his article. *Continuous-Progress Programs:* DISTAR; U-SAIL (Utah Systems Approach to Individual Learning); PEGASUS-PACE (Personalized Education Growth and Selective Utilization of Staff—Personalized Approach to Continuous Education); ECRI (Exemplary Center for Reading Instruction); Project INSTRUCT; GEMS (Goal-based Educational Management System); and The Early Childhood Preventive Curriculum. All four of the continuous progress curriculums are technological. *Cooperative Learn-*

ing Programs: Team Accelerated Instruction (from two listed). *Preventive Tutoring Programs:* Programmed Tutorial Reading and Prevention of Learning Disabilities—New York (from four listed). *Remedial Tutoring Programs:* SCORE (Success Controlled Optimal Reading Experience) from a list of three programs of which two used standard tutoring approaches. *Computer-Assisted Instruction Programs:* Computer Curriculum Corporation Study 1; Computer Curriculum Corporation Study 2; Computer Curriculum Corporation Study 3 (Merrimack Education Center); and Basic Literacy Through Microcomputers. All four of the computer-assisted programs were technological in their approach to learning and teaching. Descriptions of the content and teaching procedures for the twenty programs Slavin listed on which I based my judgment were drawn from Slavin's descriptions and from two publications of the National Diffusion Network, *Educational Programs that Work,* 8th edition (San Francisco: Far West Laboratory for Educational Research and Development, 1981) and the 16th edition (Longmont, Colorado: Sopris West Inc., 1990).

35. Paul Berman, "Aztecs and Iraqis," *The New Republic* 201 (21) (May 27 1991): 17.

36. Berman, "Aztecs and Iraqis," pp. 16–18.

37. Nancy A. Madden, Robert E. Slavin, Nancy L. Karweit, Lawrence Dolan, and Barbara A. Wasiik, "Success for All," *Phi Delta Kappan* 72 (April 1991): 593–99.

38. Lawrence J. Schweinhart and David P. Weikart, "Education for Young Children Living in Poverty: Child-initiated Learning or Teacher-directed Instruction?" *The Elementary School Journal* 89 (November 1988): 214–25. The authors report that various curriculum models achieved their objectives. Children in the child-initiated program, for example, had lower school absence rates and scored higher on a test of nonverbal reasoning and problem solving; children in the teacher-directed program had better reading and mathematics scores. See also the longitudinal study of three preschool models in Lawrence J. Schweinhart, David P. Weikart, and Mary B. Larner, *A Report of the High/Scope Preschool Curriculum Comparison Study: Consequences of Three Preschool Curriculum Models Through Age 15* (Ypsilanti, Michigan: High/Scope Educational Research Foundation, 1988).

39. Benjamin S. Bloom, *Human Characteristics and School Learning* (New York: McGraw-Hill Book Company, 1976), p. 5.

40. Bloom, *Human Characteristics,* p. 4.

41. Benjamin S. Bloom, *All Our Children Learning: A Primer for Parents, Teachers, and Other Educators* (New York: McGraw-Hill Book Com-

pany, 1981) from Lorin W. Anderson's "Introduction to Instruction and Curriculum Development," in *All Our Children Learning*, p. 126.

42. Bloom, *All Our Children Learning*, Anderson's Introduction, p. 127.

43. Bloom, *All Our Children Learning*, Anderson's Introduction, p. 128.

44. Bloom, *All Our Children Learning*, p. 174.

45. Bloom, *All Our Children Learning*, pp. 167, 169, 170, 171.

46. Joseph P. Hannon, "The Chicago Plan: Mastery Learning in the Chicago Public Schools," *Educational Leadership* 37 (November 1979): 120, 121, 122.

47. Mastery Education Corporation, *Excerpts from Chicago Mastery Learning Reading* [Developed by the Board of Education, City of Chicago] (Watertown, Massachusetts: Mastery Education Corporation, 1980), p. 2. The Chicago mastery learning materials were developed by Michael Katims, Linda Adelman, and Beau Jones.

48. Mastery Education Corporation, *Excerpts*, pp. 17–22.

49. Mastery Education Corporation, *Excerpts*, p. 2.

50. Frank Smith, *To Think* (New York: Teachers College Press, Columbia University, 1990), pp. 95–97.

51. George N. Schmidt, "Chicago Mastery Reading: A Case Against a Skills-Based Reading Curriculum," *Learning* (November 1982): 38; Lynn Olson, "Chicago Scuttles Mastery-Reading Plan After $7.5 Million, 5-Year Commitment," *Education Week* (August 21, 1985): 1, 17.

52. Olson, "Chicago Scuttles Mastery Reading," p. 17.

53. Olson, "Chicago Scuttles Mastery Reading," p. 17.

54. Susan Lytle and Morton Botel, *PCRP 11: Reading, Writing and Talking Across The Curriculum* (Harrisburg, Pennsylvania: The Pennsylvania Department of Education, 1988), p. 17.

55. Lytle and Botel, *PCRP 11*, pp. 18–19.

56. John Dewey, *Democracy and Education: An Introduction to a Philosophy of Education* (New York: Macmillan Publishing Company, Free Press, 1966), pp. 5, 6, 8. [Originally published in 1916.]

57. Lee J. Cronbach, "Course Improvement Through Evaluation," in *Curriculum and Evaluation*, Arno A. Bellack and Herbert M. Kliebard, editors (Berkeley, California: McCutchan Publishing Corporation, 1977), pp. 319–33.

58. Derek Bok, "The Challenge to Schools of Education," *Harvard Magazine*, (May/June 1987): 52. Bok reports that many education journals are "filled with projects that are imperfectly designed, shoddily researched, and poorly reasoned." Bok clinches this indictment of the research establishment by saying that schools of education in research-oriented universities have demonstrated an inability to set a consistent course and that scholars have contributed little to educational practice despite the fact that "more than 100,000 articles are published each year."

59. Robert E. Slavin, "On Mastery Learning and Mastery Teaching," *Educational Leadership* 46 (April 1989): 78; and Ronald Brandt, "On Research and School Organization: A Conversation with Bob Slavin," *Educational Leadership* 46 (October 1988): 24. See also Robert E. Slavin, "Mastery Learning Reconsidered," *Review of Educational Research* 57 (1987): 175–213. Brandt's interview with Slavin incorporated replies by proponents of mastery learning, some of which I cite.

60. Brandt, "On Research and School Organization," p. 25.

61. Slavin, "On Mastery Learning," p. 78.

62. Brandt, "On Research and School Organization," p. 28.

63. Brandt, "On Research and School Organization," p. 24.

64. Noreen B. Garman and Helen M. Hazi, "Teachers Ask: Is There Life After Madeline Hunter?" *Phi Delta Kappan* 69 (May 1988): 670.

65. John Smyth and Noreen Garman, "Supervision-As-School Reform: A Critical Perspective," *Journal of Education Policy* 4 (1989): 343–61.

66. Barak Rosenshine and Robert Stevens, "Teaching Functions," in the *Handbook of Research on Teaching*, 3rd edition, Merlin C. Wittrock, ed. (New York: Macmillan Publishing Company, 1986) p. 379.

67. Rosenshine and Stevens, "Teaching Functions," p. 379.

68. Rosenshine and Stevens, "Teaching Functions," p. 379.

69. Rosenshine and Stevens, "Teaching Functions," p. 377.

70. Rosenshine and Stevens, "Teaching Functions," p. 377.

71. Rosenshine and Stevens, "Teaching Functions," p. 379.

72. Madeline Hunter, "Knowing, Teaching, and Supervising," in *Using What We Know About Teaching*, Philip L. Hosford, ed. (Alexandria, Virginia: Association for Supervision and Curriculum Development, 1984), pp. 175–76.

73. Hunter, "Knowing, Teaching, and Supervising," p. 169.

74. Madeline Hunter, "What's Wrong With M. Hunter?" *Educational Leadership* 42 (February 1985): 59.

75. Hunter, "Knowing, Teaching, and Supervising," p. 175.

76. Hunter, "What's Wrong with M. Hunter?", p. 60.

77. Ronald S. Brandt, "On Teaching and Supervising: A Conversation with Madeline Hunter," *Educational Leadership* 42 (February 1985): 61.

78. Brandt, "On Teaching and Supervising," p. 61; Madeline Hunter, *Mastery Teaching* (El Segundo, California: TIP Publications, 1982); and Madeline Hunter, "Appraising the Instructional Process," mimeographed, undated.

79. Madeline Hunter, *Teach More—Faster* (El Segundo, California: TIP Publications, 1969).

80. John Dewey, *The Sources of a Science of Education* (New York: Liveright, 1929).

81. Dewey, *Democracy and Education*. See Chapters 11–14 on thinking, for example.

82. Hunter, *Mastery Teaching* and Hunter, "Knowing, Teaching, and Supervising." Thinking, to select one important aim of education, is not an essential element in Hunter's approach to learning. One searches in vain for it in her written expositions on teaching.

83. Benjamin Bloom, *Taxonomy of Educational Objectives 1: Cognitive Domain* (New York: David McKay Company, 1956), p. 42.

84. Dewey, *Democracy and Education*, p. 170.

85. Kastle, "Madeline Hunter and the 'Science' of Education," course paper, University of Pennsylvania.

86. John Goodlad, *A Place Called School* (New York: McGraw-Hill Book Company, 1984); and Theodore Sizer, *Horace's Compromise* (Boston: Houghton Mifflin Company, 1984).

87. Jane Stallings, "For Whom and How Long is the Hunter-Based Model Appropriate? Response to Robbins and Wolfe," *Educational Leadership* 44 (February 1987): 64; and Robert E. Slavin, "The Napa Evaluation of Madeline Hunter's ITIP: Lessons Learned," *The Elementary School Journal* (November 1986): 167.

88. Rosenshine and Stevens, "Teaching Functions," p. 386.

89. My exposition and critique of the Hunter teaching method is based on a critical exchange between Madeline Hunter and me that was

published in *Educational Leadership* (1987). See Richard A. Gibboney, "A Critique of Madeline Hunter's Teaching Model from Dewey's Perspective," *Educational Leadership* 44 (February 1987): 46–50; M. Hunter, "Beyond Rereading Dewey: What's Next? A Response to Gibboney," *Educational Leadership* 44 (February 1987): 51–53; and Richard A. Gibboney, "The Vagaries of Turtle Research: Gibboney Replies," *Educational Leadership* 44 (February 1987): 54.

90. Thomas A. Romberg and Thomas P. Carpenter, "Research on Teaching and Learning Mathematics: Two Disciplines of Scientific Inquiry," in the *Handbook of Research on Teaching*, 3rd edition, Merlin G. Wittrock, ed. (New York: Macmillan Publishing Company, 1986), p. 865.

91. Goodlad, *A Place Called School*, pp. 112–13. When a supportive critic of the public schools—and a careful researcher—such as Goodlad writes that the classes he observed were passive and emotionally flat, that "exuberance, joy, laughter, abrasiveness, praise and . . . support of individual student performance . . ." were not part of the learning climate, it is difficult to see why Rosenshine and Stevens chose to ignore it.

92. Dewey, *Democracy and Education*, p. 42.

93. Richard F. Elmore and Milbrey Wallin McLaughlin, *Steady Work: Policy, Practice, and the Reform of American Education* (Santa Monica, California: The Rand Corporation, 1988), pp. 26–28.

94. Elmore and McLaughlin, *Steady Work*, p. 28.

CHAPTER 5

1. A. Leon Higginbotham, Jr., "An Open Letter to Justice Thomas," *The Philadelphia Inquirer*, 23 January 1992, p. A19.

2. Herbert J. Klausmeier and Wisconsin Associates, *The Wisconsin Center for Education Research: Twenty-Five Years of Knowledge Generation and Educational Improvement*, with a foreword by Fred Harvey Harrington (Madison, Wisconsin: Wisconsin Center for Education Research, University of Wisconsin, 1990), p. 37.

3. Herbert J. Klausmeier, Richard A. Rossmiller, and Mary Saily, *Individually Guided Elementary Education: Concepts and Practices* (New York: Academic Press, 1977) p. 16.

4. Thomas A. Romberg, ed., *Toward Effective Schooling: The IGE Experience* (Lanham, Maryland: University Press of America, Copyright Board of Regents of the University of Wisconsin System, 1985), p. 22.

5. Romberg, *Toward Effective Schooling*, p. 24.

6. Klausmeier, *The Wisconsin Center*, p. 216.

7. Klausmeier, *The Wisconsin Center*, pp. 30, 9.

8. Thomas S. Popkewitz, B. Robert Tabachnick, and Gary Wehlage, *The Myth of Educational Reform: A Study of School Responses to a Program of Change* (Madison, Wisconsin: The University of Wisconsin Press, 1982), pp. 46–47.

9. Popkewitz et al., *The Myth of Educational Reform*, p. 49.

10. Popkewitz et al., *The Myth of Educational Reform*, pp. 63–64.

11. Popkewitz et al., *The Myth of Educational Reform*, p. 65.

12. Popkewitz et al., *The Myth of Educational Reform*, pp. 42–43.

13. Popkewitz et al., *The Myth of Educational Reform*, p. 43.

14. Popkewitz et al., *The Myth of Educational Reform*, pp. 44–45.

15. Popkewitz et al., *The Myth of Educational Reform*, pp. 44–45.

16. Popkewitz et al., *The Myth of Educational Reform*, pp. 74–75.

17. Popkewitz et al., *The Myth of Educational Reform*, p. 75.

18. Popkewitz et al., *The Myth of Educational Reform*, p.75.

19. Popkewitz et al., *The Myth of Educational Reform*, pp. 77, 78.

20. Popkewitz et al., *The Myth of Educational Reform*, pp. 86–88.

21. Popkewitz et al., *The Myth of Educational Reform*, p. 89.

22. John Dewey, *Democracy and Education: An Introduction to the Philosophy of Education* (New York: Macmillan Publishing Company, Free Press, 1966), pp. 175–176. First published in 1916.

23. Popkewitz et al., *The Myth of Educational Reform*, p. 103.

24. Popkewitz et al., *The Myth of Educational Reform*, pp. 102–103.

25. Popkewitz et al., *The Myth of Educational Reform*, p. 103.

26. Popkewitz et al., *The Myth of Educational Reform*, pp. 103–104.

27. Popkewitz et al., *The Myth of Educational Reform*, p. 104.

28. Popkewitz et al., *The Myth of Educational Reform*, p. 97.

29. Popkewitz et al., *The Myth of Educational Reform*, p. 50.

30. Popkewitz et al., *The Myth of Educational Reform*, pp. 96–97, 111–12.

31. Popkewitz et al., *The Myth of Educational Reform*, p. 97.

32. Popkewitz et al., *The Myth of Educational Reform*, p. 99.

33. Popkewitz et al., *The Myth of Educational Reform*, p. 101.

34. Popkewitz et al., *The Myth of Educational Reform*, pp. 110–12.

35. Popkewitz et al., *The Myth of Educational Reform*, pp. 110–11.

36. Popkewitz et al., *The Myth of Educational Reform*, p. 97.

37. Jerome Bruner, *Acts of Meaning* (Cambridge, Massachusetts: Harvard University Press, 1990).

38. Popkewitz et al., *The Myth of Educational Reform*, p. 50.

39. Robert J. Bullough, Jr., Stanley L. Goldstein, and Ladd Holt, *Human Interests in the Curriculum: Teaching and Learning in a Technological Society* (New York: Teachers College Press, 1984), pp. 43, 47.

40. Bullough et al., *Human Interests*, p. 44.

41. Bullough et al., *Human Interests*, pp. 52, 53–54.

42. Bullough et al., *Human Interests*, pp. 52–53.

43. Bullough et al., *Human Interests*, p. 53.

44. John Goodlad, *A Place Called School* (New York: McGraw-Hill Book Company, 1984).

45. Bullough et al., *Human Interests*, pp. 55–56.

46. Bullough et al., *Human Interests*, p. 56.

47. Klausmeier et al., *Individually Guided Elementary Education*, p. 291.

48. Klausmeier et al., *Individually Guided Elementary Education*, pp. 293, 295–309.

49. I believe Michael Fullan's *The Meaning of Educational Change* (New York: Teachers College Press, Columbia University, 1982) is a commendable effort to make sense out of a wide range of empirical facts about the change process, derived from a huge and diverse body of research. It is accepted in the history and philosophy of science that social science (and by extension educational research) lacks the conceptual power to make scientific statements about the human condition. Without a coherent body of

theory, there can be no science of any kind (see note below). What passes for educational research today are atheoretical fact hunts into the jungle of the empirical world. And Fullan gives us a blizzard of facts about change. There is no end to the number of isolated facts that ambitious researchers can dredge up about change. Fullan tries to give us meaning, but he cannot—and neither can anyone else—given the body of disparate data he confronts. The research he cites springs from no acceptable theory in the scientific sense, and it feeds back into and modifies no theory in the scientific sense, because there is none. There can be, therefore, no cumulative growth in knowledge based on research about change or teaching or any other social phenomena as is true of the physical sciences. Most educators clothe research studies in the fancy dress of true science. I am sure that many of Fullan's readers believe they are getting "science" when they read his book.

I cannot begin a critique here of the omissions, contradictions, and the lack of intellectual coherence in this book—or recognize the data clusters in the book that I find helpful (but not scientific)—because a critique requires too many pages. But are little clumps of data on this or that about change going to help us to understand change, or enhance our practical power? I believe one paramount issue in reform is the question of a reform's educational worth. Fullan alludes to this issue, but he never systematically addresses it. I shall make some comments on pages 60–63 of his book merely to illustrate some of my concerns. I do not want to imply that I am as critical of all sections of the book. My frustration stems from the lack of some integrative structure within the book that might at least recognize (1) the problem of coherence, and (2) the excessive reliance on research studies whose technical adequacies are never assessed by Fullan.

1. Topic addressed: What kind of innovations get adopted? Fullan cites a number of studies that say that innovations with clear, detailed materials that meet the teacher's "practicality ethic" get used. He accepts the kinds of materials disseminated by the National Diffusion Network (p. 60). Comment: Are innovations with clear directions that meet the teacher's desire for how-to-do-it what we need? All of the technocratic and anti-intellectual curriculums I reviewed in chapter 4 share the characteristics of innovations that Fullan says get adopted. And none of them will make learning or teaching more humane or intellectually interesting. Fullan approves of the work done by the National Diffusion Network. I showed in my discussion of Chapter 1 remedial reading programs (chapter 4) that nineteen of twenty-five reading programs endorsed by the NDN in 1990 were mechanical drill-for-skill programs. These programs are terrible, a point I argue. I think education would be served if the NDN were abolished. Fullan lets these basic issues slip by in a blur of research citations whose quality criterion implicitly is "If they use it, it's good."

2. Topic addressed: Implementation and an innovation's quality. Fullan takes us on one of those wild rides through studies where implementation was studied and program quality was ignored (why in heaven's name separate the two?): the use of computers in schools, a comparison of the

quality of curriculum materials produced between 1962 and 1982, and a return to the question of how explicit and clear innovations should be if they are to be accepted (pp. 61–62). Comment: Fullan says that materials were better in 1982 in "some areas" (which he does not specify) than in 1962. This statement is too vague to be analyzed, but it gives the impression that "later" is better. My discussion in this book suggests that the 1980s valued mechanical approaches like mastery learning and defined teaching by using "research-validated techniques" for the most part. The 1980s, for example, offered nothing in curriculum that approached the conceptual quality of the new mathematics, science, and social studies courses of the 1960s, whatever other faults they might have had. Fullan's discussion of how explicit or general an innovation should be is disturbing. Again, research is cited on both sides of this superficial issue. The implicit assumption in this circular discussion is that teachers should use an innovation developed by someone else: by some agency that knows more than they do. Fullan never entertains and sustains a contrary assumption: if we help teachers and principals to approach learning and teaching and reform more *conceptually*, these fundamental ideas, coupled with the practitioners' practical knowledge and a knowledge of their school situation, will permit them to *develop their own innovations*. Research studies—even scientific ones—cannot resolve issues such as Fullan addresses. We have to move beyond the morass of empirical data to ideas linked to the common sense of practice. In the final paragraph Fullan, in a style typical of the book, waves his research wand in the direction of people, ideas and minds, quotes Seymour Sarason, and briskly moves on. He is often on all sides of an issue, a position that dependence on research studies leads to because they, too, are usually on all sides of an issue. But what is a thoughtful reader left with? Not much. Fullan's book ignores the power of ideas and values to order a messy issue like reform, to say here we stand, this is the direction we are moving toward, and, within this loose framework, this is what research says about it (if we must be so dependent on atheoretical studies). The book, despite the apparent soundness of its information in some sections—where "soundness" depends on one's theoretical orientation—slips, slides, and careens through an important subject that should have been treated from an explicit theoretical perspective. Doing so would at least make Fullan's good ideas more clear and firm, and it would, at the same time, give the reader notice to be on guard for possible weak points. Such a perspective would give the book more practical power because it would show that theory and ideas are basic to reform, and it would reduce dependence on the clutter and confusion introduced when raw empiricism is judged to be a source of knowledge in the absence of a unifying set of concepts. See Richard J. Bernstein, *The Restructuring of Social and Political Theory* (Philadelphia: University of Pennsylvania Press, 1976), pp. 3–54. Prominent social scientists such as Robert Merton and Neil Smelser are unable to come up with even approximations of explanatory theory. See also Richard A. Gibboney, "The Unscientific Character of Educational Research," *Phi Delta Kappan* 71 (November 1989): 225–27.

50. Romberg, *Toward Effective Schooling*, p. 222.

51. Romberg, *Toward Effective Schooling*, pp. 220–21.

52. Fullan, *Educational Change*, p. 61

53. Popkewitz et al., *The Myth of Educational Reform*, pp. 71–72.

CHAPTER 6

1. Wilford M. Aikin, *The Story of the Eight-Year Study* (New York: McGraw-Hill Book Company, 1942). Aikin's volume summarized the reform. Four other volumes in this series titled *Adventure in American Education* dealt with appraising student progress, student success in college, the curriculum of the experimental schools, and accounts by each of the thirty secondary schools of their work in this imaginative effort to reform secondary education five decades ago. It is a sad commentary on our neglect of history that most education students today have never heard of the Eight-Year Study, much less perused even one of its readable volumes.

2. Thomas P. Hughes, *American Genius: A Century of Invention and Technological Enthusiasm 1870–1970* (New York: Viking, 1989), p. 185.

3. Richard A. Gibboney, "Just Words: Talking Your Way Past Reform to Educational Renewal," *Journal of Curriculum and Supervision* 4 (Spring 1989): 232–33.

4. This dialogue is in the Owen J. Roberts School District, R.D.1, Pottstown, PA. The district serves a 100-square-mile rural-slipping-to-suburban area with 3500 students K–12. Terrance L. Furin, a reform-minded superintendent in the Deweyan-progressive tradition, supports the dialogue's read-think-talk-act approach to grassroots reform. This is the first time the dialogue has been tried in a total school district. The pace is deliberately slow and, we hope, solid within a five-to-eight-year time span. Approximately five years remain to be lived in this effort.

5. Harry B. Dissinger, "Implementing a Staff Development Project to Promote Active Learning and Increase Student Interest in Elementary School Social Studies" (Doctoral dissertation, University of Pennsylvania, 1988). This study in an urban school showed marked increases in student interest, teacher satisfaction, and active learning when veteran teachers rethought the way they taught social studies. The percentage of D and F grades given in social studies, for example, decreased from 40 to less than 5 percent. Students do not need remediation, educators do.

6. Kenneth D. Kastle in a conversation with the author March 1992.

7. Shelly K. Salaman, "An Evaluation of the Dialogue Approach to Staff Development in Effecting Change in a Comprehensive High School" (Doctoral dissertation, University of Pennsylvania, 1988) and Gary B. Campbell, "Staff Development through Dialogue: A Case Study in Educational Problem Solving" (Doctoral dissertation, University of Pennsylvania, 1989). I know that doctoral dissertations do not provide the strongest kind of research support for educational claims—particularly when the thing researched is a pet of the dissertation chair. I can say that we were aware of this bias and of the rosy claims too often made by advocates of a reform, and tried, therefore, to be as critical of our own work as we are of others' work. The only flat-out claim that I would make for informed conversation as a reform approach is that it has better content, process, and aims than any technological approach I know because it does not, in the spirit of Descartes' scientific materialism, remove the historical, social, and human influences from a reform effort.

8. Parts of this section on the structure of the dialogue are from Gibboney, "Just Words," pp. 233–36.

9. Denny G. Bolton, "The Documentation and Critique of the Dialogue Process in Two Schools" (Doctoral dissertation in progress, University of Pennsylvania).

10. Seymour B. Sarason, *The Predictable Failure of Educational Reform: Can We Change Course Before It's Too Late?* (San Francisco: Jossey-Bass Publishers, 1990), p. 11.

11. Sarason, *The Predictable Failure of Educational Reform*, pp. 11–12.

12. Gary Saul Morson, "Prosaics: An Approach to the Humanities," *The American Scholar* (Autumn 1988): 521.

APPENDIX A

1. These criteria are taken from a work in progress by Richard A. Gibboney and Clark Webb, *Teachers' Tales: Toward More Thoughtful Teaching* in cooperation with the Teacher Outreach Program of the Foxfire Fund, Inc., Rabun Gap, Georgia, Hilton Smith, Director.

APPENDIX B

1. George F. Will, "In This Land of Dolts . . . ," *The Philadelphia Inquirer*, 3 June 1991, p. 8A.

2. Jerome Bruner, *Acts of Meaning* (Cambridge, Massachusetts: Harvard University Press,1990), pp. 4–7.

3. Alan S. Brown, "Outcome-Based Education: A Success Story," *Educational Leadership* 46 (October 1988): 12.

4. William G. Spady, "Organizing for Results: The Basis of Authentic Restructuring and Reform," *Educational Leadership* 46 (October 1988): 5–6.

5. Brown, "Outcome-Based Education," p. 12.

6. Gary F. Bender, JeNell M. Padilla, and H. Mark Krank, "Assertive Discipline: A Critical Review and Analysis, "*Teachers College Record* 90 (Summer 1989): 609. This article is followed by a response from Lee Canter, the developer of Assertive Discipline, and a rejoinder by Bender et al., pp. 631–40.

7. Brown, "Outcome-Based Education," p. 12.

8. John W. Porter, "The Accountability Story in Michigan," *Phi Delta Kappan* 54 (October 1972): 98.

9. W. R. Nance, "How Fares Competency Development in Oregon?" *Educational Leadership* 35 (November 1977): 105.

10. Chris Pipho, "Competency Testing: A Response to Arthur Wise," *Educational Leadership* 36 (May 1979): 551–52.

11. Arthur Wise, "Why Minimum Competency Testing Will Not Improve Education," *Educational Leadership* 36 (May 1979): 548, 546.

12. Daniel Tanner and Laurel N. Tanner, *Curriculum Development: Theory into Practice*, 2nd ed., (New York: Macmillan Publishing Company, 1980), pp. 310–11.

13. George F. Will, "Few Adults Read Literature," *The Philadelphia Inquirer*, 7 June 1991, p. 16A.

14. Robert G. Scanlon, "Diagnostic-Prescriptive Teaching: Progress and Problems," paper presented at the annual meeting of the American Association of Colleges for Teacher Education, February 1978, p. 4.

15. Tanner and Tanner, *Curriculum Development*, pp. 310–11.

16. Scanlon, "Diagnostic-Prescriptive Teaching," pp. 6–7.

17. A. Sterl Artley, "Individual Differences and Reading Instruction," *The Elementary School Journal* 82 (November 1981): 148.

18. Bruce Joyce and Marsha Weil, *Models of Teaching*, 3rd ed., (Englewood Cliffs: New Jersey: Prentice Hall, Inc., 1986), pp. 321–22.

19. Richard A. Gibboney and Tamar Ariav, "The Locked Door: Cognitive Learning Theories as a Basis for Curriculum Development and Instruction," unpublished paper, March 1981, University of Pennsylvania, pp. 9–11.

20. Robert Glaser, "The Contributions of B.F. Skinner to Education and Some Counterinfluences," in *Impact of Research on Education: Some Case Studies*, Patrick Suppes, ed., (Washington, D.C.: National Academy of Education, 1978), pp. 217, 220.

21. Allan L. Thrush, "A Deweyan Analysis of the CoRT and Instrumental Enrichment Thinking Skills Programs" (Doctoral dissertation, University of Pennsylvania, 1987), pp. 133–70.

22. Thrush, "A Deweyan Analysis of the CoRT and Instrumental Enrichment Thinking Skills Programs," pp. 45–46, 70.

23. Thrush, "A Deweyan Analysis of the CoRT and Instrumental Enrichment Thinking Skills Programs," p. 48.

24. Thrush, "A Deweyan Analysis of the CoRT and Instrumental Enrichment Thinking Skills Programs," pp. 121–27.

25. Robert J. Sternberg and Kastoor Bhana, "Synthesis of Research on the Effectiveness of Intellectual Skills Programs: Snake-Oil Remedies or Miracle Cures?" *Educational Leadership* 44 (October 1987): 63.

26. Sternberg and Bhana, "Synthesis of Research," pp. 63–64.

Appendix C

1. Leon Lessinger, "Engineering Accountability for Results in Education," Myron Lieberman, guest editor, *Phi Delta Kappan* LII (December 1970): 219 and information item, 225.

2. Ellis B. Page, "How We All Failed at Performance Contracting," *Phi Delta Kappan* 54 (October 1972): 115–16.

3. Page, "How We All Failed," pp. 115–17.

4. Page, "How We All Failed," p. 117.

5. "The USOE and Research in Education," An Interview with Richard Loomis Bright, *Phi Delta Kappan* 48 (September 1966): 3, 4.

6. "The USOE and Research in Education," p. 3.

7. Wilbur B. Brookover, Laurence Beamer, Helen Efthim, Douglas Hathaway, Lawrence Lezotte, et al., *Creating Effective Schools: An Inservice Program for Enhancing School Learning Climate and Achievement* (Holmes Beach, Florida: Learning Publications, Inc., 1982), pp. 30, 31.

8. See Lawrence C. Stedman, "It's Time We Changed the Effective Schools Formula," and a response by Wilbur B. Brookover, "Distortion and Overgeneralization Are No Substitutes for Sound Research," *Phi Delta Kappan* 69 (November 1987): 215–17. Stedman has the final response in "The Effective Schools Formula Still Needs Changing: A Reply to Brookover," *Phi Delta Kappan* 69 (February 1988): 439–42.

9. Stedman, "The Effective Schools Formula Still Needs Changing," p. 442.

10. Lee Canter with Marlene Canter, *Assertive Discipline: A Take-Charge Approach for Today's Educator* (Santa Monica, California: Canter and Associates, Inc., 1976).

11. Gary F. Render, JeNell M. Padilla, and H. Mark Krank, "Assertive Discipline: A Critical Review and Analysis," *Teachers College Record* 90 (Summer 1989): 607.

12. Canter and Canter, *Assertive Discipline,* pp. 166–69.

Joy Girl. A happy student in the Milwaukee, Wisconsin, Public Schools. Photograph by Susan Lina Ruggles.

SELECTED BIBLIOGRAPHY

I have included books on ecology and the natural world because the primary source for the destruction of land, air, and water is the same source as that which destroys mind and feeling in schools: scientific-technical rationality in the service of a capitalism that shuns its social-democratic responsibilities. The entangling and pervasive economic, technological, and social effects of a high-tech society are still unseen by most intellectuals and policymakers. It takes a book like Howard Kunstler's *The Geography of Nowhere* to show, for example, how such seemingly unrelated things as automobiles, "free" super-highways, suburban housing tracts, and federal home subsidies are destroying our landscape, our sense of pride in civic spaces, and our sense of community as more places look alike with Burger Kings and Wal-Marts. The problem of reform in schools is related to and ultimately dependent on discarding a false faith in technology that uncritically views an increase in auto sales and 100,000 new housing starts as economic and social progress. John Dewey might say that we are unthoughtfully using science to serve outmoded technical ends; that what we must do is invent new and less destructive *social* ends in the service of which science and technology are humanized and tethered. Presently science-technology is a means to few significant social ends outside its own physically restricted limits.

Anderson, Lorin W. and Pellicer, Leonard O. "Synthesis of Research on Compensatory and Remedial Education." *Educational Leadership* 48 (1990):10–16.

Apple, Michael W. *Ideology and the Curriculum.* New York: Routledge, 1990.

Barrett, William. *Death of the Soul: From Descartes to the Computer.* New York: Doubleday, Anchor Books, 1986.

———. *The Illusion of Technique: A Search for Meaning in a Technological Civilization.* Garden City, New York: Doubleday & Co., 1979.

Barth, Roland S. *Improving Schools from Within: Teachers, Parents, and Principals Can Make the Difference.* San Francisco: Jossey-Bass Publishers, 1990.

———. *Open Education and the American School.* New York: Agathon Press, 1972.

Bloom, Benjamin S. *All Our Children Learning: A Primer for Parents, Teachers, and Other Educators.* New York: McGraw-Hill, 1981.

Borgmann, Albert. *Technology and the Character of Contemporary Life: A Philosophical Inquiry.* Chicago: The University of Chicago Press, 1984.

Bowers, C. A. *Education, Cultural Myths, and the Ecological Crisis.* Albany, New York: State University of New York Press, 1993.

Brown, Mary and Precious, Norman. *The Integrated Day in the Primary School.* New York: Agathon Press, 1969.

Callahan, Raymond E. *Education and the Cult of Efficiency: A Study of the Social Forces That Have Shaped the Administration of the Public Schools.* Chicago: The University of Chicago Press, 1962.

Campbell, Gary B. "Staff Development through Dialogue: A Case Study in Educational Problem Solving." Doctoral dissertation, University of Pennsylvania, 1989.

Clifford, Geraldine and Guthrie, James. *Ed School: A Brief for Professional Education.* Chicago: The University of Chicago Press, 1988.

Cremin, Lawrence A. *American Education: The Metropolitan Experience, 1877–1980.* New York: Harper & Row, 1988.

———. *The Transformation of the School: Progressivism in Education 1876–1957.* New York: Random House, Vintage Books, 1961.

Cuban, Larry. *How Teachers Taught: Constancy and Change in American Classrooms, 1890–1980.* New York: Longman, 1984.

Dewey, John *Experience and Education.* New York: Macmillan Publishing Co., 1938.

———. *The Quest for Certainty: A Study of the Relation of Knowledge and Action.* New York: G.P. Putnam's Sons, Capricorn Books, 1929.

———. *Human Nature and Conduct: An Introduction to Social Psychology.* New York: The Modern Library, Henry Holt & Co., 1922.

———. *Democracy and Education: An Introduction to the Philosophy of Education.* New York: Macmillan Publishing Co., Free Press, 1966; first published 1916.

Firestone, William A.; Fuhrman, Susan H.; and Kirst, Michael W. *The Progress of Reform: An Appraisal of State Education Initiatives.* New Brunswick, New Jersey: Center for Policy Research, Rutgers University, 1989.

Fiske, Edward R., with Reed, Sally and Sautter, R. Craig. *Smart Kids, Smart Schools: Why Do Some Schools Work?* New York: Simon & Schuster, A Touchstone Book, 1991.

Gibboney, Richard A. "Just Words: Talking Your Past Reform to Educational Renewal." *Journal of Curriculum and Supervision* 4 (1989):230–245.

———. "A Critique of Madeline Hunter's Teaching Model from Dewey's Perspective." *Educational Leadership* 44 (1987):46–50; Hunter, M. "Beyond Rereading Dewey: What's Next? A Response to Gibboney." *Educational Leadership* 44 (1987):51–53; and Gibboney, Richard A. "The Vagaries of Turtle Research: Gibboney Replies." *Educational Leadership* 44 (1987):54.

Girardet, Herbert. *The Gaia Atlas of Cities: New Directions for Sustainable Urban Living.* New York: Doubleday, Anchor Books, 1992.

Goodlad, John. *Teachers for Our Nation's Schools.* San Francisco: Jossey-Bass, 1990.

———, ed. *The Ecology of School Renewal.* Chicago: The University of Chicago Press, 1987. Eighty-sixth Yearbook of the National Society for the Study of Education.

———. *A Place Called School.* New York: McGraw-Hill, 1984.

Jacoby, Russell. *The Last Intellectuals in an Age of Academe.* New York: Basic Books, 1987.

Joncich, Geraldine M., ed. *Psychology and the Science of Education: Selected Writings of Edward L. Thorndike.* New York: Teachers College, Columbia University, 1962.

Kliebard, Herbert M. *The Struggle for the American School Curriculum.* Boston: Routledge & Kegan Paul, 1986.

Kohl, Herbert. *On Teaching.* New York: Schocken Books, 1976.

———. *The Open Classroom: A Practical Guide to a New Way of Teaching.* New York: Random House, Vintage Books, 1969.

Kunstler, Howard J. *The Geography of Nowhere: The Rise and Decline of America's Man-Made Landscape.* New York: Simon & Schuster, 1993.

Lieberman, Ann, ed. *Building a Professional Culture in Schools.* New York: Teachers College Press, 1988.

McKibben, Bill. *The End of Nature.* New York: Random House, 1989.

Meadows, Donna H.; Meadows, Dennis L.; and Randers, Jørgen. *Beyond the Limits: Confronting Global Collapse, Envisioning a Sustainable Future.* Post Mills, Vermont: Chelsea Green Publishing Co., 1992.

Mumford, Lewis. *The Myth of the Machine.* New York: Harcourt Brace Jovanovich, 1970.

Popkewitz, Thomas S.; Tabachnick, Robert T.; and Wehlage, Gary. *The Myth of Educational Reform: A Study of School Responses to a Program of Change.* Madison, Wisconsin: The University of Wisconsin Press, 1982.

Puckett, John L. *Foxfire Reconsidered: A Twenty-year Experiment in Progressive Education.* Urbana and Chicago: University of Illinois Press, 1989.

Ravitch, Diane. *The Troubled Crusade: American Education 1945–1980.* New York: Basic Books, 1983.

Reese, William J. *Power and the Promise of School Reform: Grassroots Movements During the Progressive Era.* Boston: Routledge & Kegan Paul, 1986.

Savage, David G. "Why Chapter 1 Hasn't Made a Difference." *Phi Delta Kappan* 68 (1987):464–647.

Schubert, William H. *Curriculum: Perspective, Paradigm, and Possibility.* New York: Macmillan Publishing Co., 1986.

Schweinhart, Lawrence J.; Weikart, David B.; and Larner, Mary B. *A Report on the High/Scope Preschool Curriculum Comparison Study: Consequences of Three Preschool Curriculum Models Through Age 15.* Ypsilanti, Michigan: High/Scope Educational Research Foundation, 1986.

Shor, Ira. *Empowering Education: Critical Thinking for Social Change.* Chicago: University of Chicago Press, 1992.

Silberman, Charles E. *Crisis in the Classroom: The Remaking of American Education.* New York: Random House, 1970.

Sizer, Theodore. *Horace's Compromise: The Dilemma of the American High School.* Boston: Houghton Mifflin Co., 1984.

Sleeper, Jim. *The Closest of Strangers: Liberalism and the Politics of Race in New York.* New York: W. W. Norton & Co., 1990.

Smith, Gregory A. *Education and the Environment: Learning to Live with Limits.* Albany, New York: State University of New York Press, 1992.

Smith, Page. *Killing the Spirit: Higher Education in America.* New York: Viking Press, 1990.

Stedman, Lawrence C. "It's Time We Changed the Effective Schools Formula." *Phi Delta Kappan* 69 (1987):215–224.

Tanner, Daniel and Tanner, Laurel N. *Curriculum Development: Theory into Practice.* New York: Macmillan Publishing Co., 1980.

Toulmin, Stephen. *Cosmopolis: The Hidden Agenda of Modernity.* New York: Macmillan Co., Free Press, 1990.

Trump, J. Lloyd and Baynham, Dorsey. *Guide to Better Schools: Focus on Change.* Chicago: Rand McNally & Co., 1961. (This book grew out of a study of secondary schools by The National Association of Secondary School Principals funded by the Ford Foundation.)

Weber, Lillian. *The English Infant School and Informal Education.* Englewood Cliffs, New Jersey: Prentice-Hall, 1971.

Weinberg, Steven. *Dreams of a Final Theory: The Search for the Fundamental Laws of Nature.* New York: Pantheon Books, 1992.

Westbrook, Robert B. *John Dewey and American Democracy.* Ithaca, New York: Cornell University Press, 1991.

Whitehead, Alfred North. *Science and the Modern World.* New York: Macmillan Publishing Co., 1925.

Wigginton, Eliot. *Sometimes a Shining Moment: The Foxfire Experience.* Garden City, New York: Doubleday & Co., Anchor Books, 1985.

Wilshire, Bruce. *The Moral Collapse of the University: Professionalism, Purity, and Alienation.* Albany, New York: State University of New York Press, 1990.

Wilson, William Julius. *The Truly Disadvantaged: The Inner City, the Underclass, and Public Policy.* Chicago: The University of Chicago Press, 1987.

Wood, George H. *Schools That Work: America's Most Innovative Public Education Programs.* New York: Dutton, 1992.

Wolcott, Harry F. *Teachers and Technocrats: An Educational Innovation in Anthropological Perspective.* Eugene, Oregon: University of Oregon, 1977.

Zilversmit, Arthur. *Changing Schools: Progressive Education Theory and Practice, 1930–1960.* Chicago: The University of Chicago Press, 1993.

INDEX

Note: To achieve greater internal coherence, each entry *within a major reform* is given in the order in which it is discussed in the text. This procedure reflects the logic of the text's exposition and critique. I have followed this procedure in indexing the following reforms: Coalition of essential schools, Competency-based education, M. Hunter's teaching model, Individually guided education, Mastery learning Chicago style, the new mathematics, the new science, nongraded schools and team teaching, open classrooms, Remedial programs in reading and arithmetic that are federally funded, and the Trump High School.